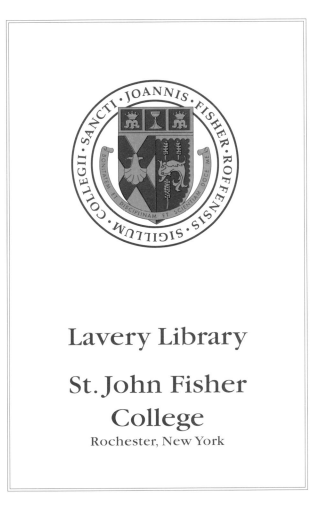

FAMILIES IN AGEING SOCIETIES

Families in Ageing Societies

A Multi-Disciplinary Approach

Edited by

SARAH HARPER

OXFORD
UNIVERSITY PRESS

OXFORD

UNIVERSITY PRESS

Great Clarendon Street, Oxford Ox2 6DP

Oxford University Press is a department of the University of Oxford.
It furthers the University's objective of excellence in research, scholarship,
and education by publishing worldwide in

Oxford New York

Auckland Bangkok Buenos Aires Cape Town Chennai
Dar es Salaam Delhi Hong Kong Istanbul Karachi Kolkata
Kuala Lumpur Madrid Melbourne Mexico City Mumbai Nairobi
São Paulo Shanghai Taipei Tokyo Toronto

Oxford is a registered trade mark of Oxford University Press
in the UK and in certain other countries

Published in the United States
by Oxford University Press Inc., New York

British Library Cataloguing in Publication Data

Data available

Library of Congress Cataloging in Publication Data

Data available

ISBN 0-19-925116-9

1 3 5 7 9 10 8 6 4 2

Typeset by Newgen Imaging Systems (P) Ltd., Chennai, India
Printed in Great Britain
on acid-free paper by
Biddles Ltd., King's Lynn, Norfolk

Foreword

The edited collection *Families in Ageing Societies* was compiled while I was developing the *Older People and their Families Research Programme* for the Nuffield Foundation. The Foundation wished to fund work that started from the perspectives, needs and interests of the older person and his or her family, and to support an international comparative perspective. The resultant Programme focuses on family solidarity and family obligations; caring responsibilities between generations and their implications for the labour market; legal and social obligations between kin; and the changing relaionships emerging within the family forms. *Families in Ageing Societies* reflects the Nuffield Foundation's broad and continued interest in these issues. I am grateful to the Foundation for their support in the compilation and editing of this collection, and for their commitment to research into and understanding of ageing and later life.

Sarah Harper
Oxford
May 2003

Contents

List of Contributors

W. Andrew Achenbaum is Dean of the College of Liberal Arts and Social Sciences at the University of Houston. A historian by background, he has written extensively on the history of ageing within the US, intergenerational relationships, work, and retirement.

Robert Anderson is co-ordinator of the Living Conditions research programme at the European Foundation for the Improvement of Living and Working Conditions, an EU agency based in Dublin.

Joanna Bornat is a Senior Lecturer in the School of Health and Social Welfare at the Open University. She has written extensively on ageing, reminiscence, and biography.

Brian Dimmock is a Senior Lecturer in the School of Health and Social Welfare at the Open University, researching the impact of family change on the lives of older people, with particular interest in stepfamilies.

Janet Finch is Vice-Chancellor of Keele University. A sociologist by background, her research expertise lies principally in studies of family relationships, especially relationships across generations.

Julien Forder is an economist at LSE Health and Social Care, at the London School of Economics and Political Science. He has research interests in industrial and organizational economics relating to health and social care systems.

Sarah Harper is Director of the Oxford Institute of Ageing, University of Oxford. She has written extensively on intergenerational relationships and ageing societies.

Mary Elizabeth Hughes is an Assistant Professor in Sociology at Duke University. She has particular interest in the relationship between community characteristics and the individual life course.

Richard W. Johnson is a Research Fellow at the Urban Institute, Washington, specializing in ageing and health care.

David Jones works in the School of Health and Social Welfare at the Open University, researching the impact of family change on the lives of older people.

Jeremy Kendall is a Research Fellow at the Personal Social Services Research Unit at the London School of Economics and Political Science. His research interests include the mixed economy of social care, the third (or voluntary) sector in comparative international perspective, and EU public policy and the third sector.

Martin Knapp is Professor of Social Policy at the London School of Economics, where he directs the Personal Social Services Research Unit, and co-Director of LSE Health and Social Care. He is also Professor of Health Economics at the Institute of Psychiatry, King's College, London, where he is Director of the Centre for the Economics of Mental Health.

Frieder R. Lang is an Assistant Professor in the Department of Education at Humboldt-Universität zu Berlin with research interests in the psychology of ageing.

Anthony T. Lo Sasso is a Research Associate Professor at the Institute for Health Services Research and Policy Studies, Northwestern University. He has particular interests in long-term care, ageing, and intergenerational impacts.

Mike Murphy is a Professor in the Department of Social Policy at the London School of Economics, specializing in the causes and consequences of population change in Britain and other western societies; intergenerational relations; and household and family formation methods.

Sheila Peace is a Senior Lecturer in the School of Health and Social Welfare at the Open University. She has particular research interests in environment and identity, and the impact of family change on older people's lives.

Linda Pickard is a Research Officer at the Personal Social Services Research Unit at the London School of Economics. She currently works on the PSSRU project concerned with demand for long-term care for older people over the next thirty years, with a particular interest in informal care.

Linda J. Waite is the Lucy Flower Professor in Urban Sociology at the University of Chicago, and the Director of the NIA Center on the Demography and Economics of Aging. Her current research interests include the family, especially working families, cohabitation, marriage and divorce, ageing, and the labour force.

Abbreviations

AARP	American Association for Retired People
BHPS	British Household Panel Survey
DfEE	Department for Education and Employment
EFIL WC	European Foundation for the Improvement of Living and Working Conditions
GHS	General Household Survey
HRCA	Hebrew Rehabilitation Center for the Aged
HRS	Health and Retirement Survey
ISSP	International Social Survey Program
LGMB	Local Government Management Board
MNL	multinomial logit
NBER	National Bureau of Economic Research
NCDS	National Child Development Study
NLTCS	National Long Term Care Survey
NSFH	National Survey of Families and Households
NVQ	National Vocational Qualification
OECD	Organization for Economic Co-operation and Development
ONS	Office for National Statistics
OPCS	Office of Population Censuses and Surveys
PSSRU	Personal Social Services Research Unit
RGN	Registered General Nurse
SIPP	Survey of Income and Program Participation
WHO	World Health Organization

Introduction

SARAH HARPER

The trends towards falling fertility and mortality, and increasing longevity, which have led to the demographic ageing of all western industrialized societies, have not occurred in isolation. They are part of wider social, economic, and political trends which have impacted upon all aspects of contemporary society. Both the factors *encouraging* these demographic trends and those *associated* with demographic ageing are directly influencing other areas of society, while demographic ageing *per se* is also influencing behaviour. Families have not been immune from the influence of such pressures for change.

This multi-disciplinary cross-cultural collection draws on scholars from sociology, economics, history, demography, psychology, anthropology, and policy studies to explore the processes and interactions between contemporary kinship and the demographic ageing of western industrialized societies. We can broadly identify three ways in which the issue of families and of ageing are reciprocally related, and this is reflected in the collection as a whole. Some authors discuss the impact of demographic change upon family structures, roles, and relationships. Others consider issues within those growing numbers of contemporary families who comprise a large proportion of older adults. Others focus on the particular kind of support and care required by dependent older and younger family members, and how this may be may be affected by both family and demographic change.

OUTLINE OF FAMILIES IN AGEING SOCIETIES

The collection begins with three chapters which provide an overview of some of the demographic and social forces affecting families within ageing societies. As Harper points out in Chapter 1, we need a broad analysis of the context, as the factors *associated* with demographic ageing (falling fertility and mortality and increased longevity) and those *contributing* to demographic ageing (increase in standard of living, education, public health, and medical advances) have also had a direct impact on society, while the *knowledge* of demographic ageing itself is influencing the social, economic, and political decisions and behaviours of both national and international institutions, and of individuals. Drawing on empirical evidence from Europe, North America, and Australasia,

Harper first considers changes in patterns of marital union. She then turns to explore the impact of these trends on contemporary families, discussing the structure and duration of family roles and relationships, the impact of divorce and cohabitation, and the various roles and relationships emerging within reconstituted families. While there are clearly multi-various definitions of the role of contemporary kinship, the chapter concludes by identifying three broad roles of importance within the context of ageing societies: families as mechanisms for intergenerational *support*; families as mechanisms for intergenerational *transfer*; and families as mechanisms for intergenerational *solidarity*.

In Chapter 2, Murphy uses information on kinship networks from the 1986 International Social Survey Programme set of co-ordinated surveys covering seven countries, to explore models of kinship in western industrialized countries. He analyses interaction between kin of various degrees of relationship by a number of demographic, socio-economic, and cultural factors in order to establish which of these play the major role in determining kin interaction. Variables used include age-group, sex, marital status, availability of kin, educational level, social class, country, and church attendance. Variation by country shows the most pronounced differences, with southern Europe revealing most contact, and the US and Australia the least. However, Murphy concludes that there is no evidence of distinct kinship systems, rather a gradient across the countries.

'While the European endeavours to forget his domestic troubles by agitating society, the American derives from his own home that love of order which he afterwards carries into public affairs' (de Tocqueville, i. 315). Thus Achenbaum begins his discussion of intergenerational solidarity and tension in Chapter 3, admitting that there was a modicum of exaggeration on both sides of the Atlantic. Using de Tocqueville's two-volume treatise as a text, Achenbaum considers the proposition that the structure and dynamics of family life have played a key factor in the development of US society. Unlike Europe, where 'stem' families and extended kin networks existed in specific settings during certain historical periods, nuclear families have always been the norm in America. Except during intervals of economic necessity married people lived together, apart from (though often in close proximity to) their relatives. Home ownership was an achievement or a goal for all, and children lived at home, or at least considered the family dwelling their primary residence, until they were capable of living independently. Since the late nineteenth century, however, long-term demographic changes have been slowly transforming this pattern. Alongside this, Achenbaum argues, age has increasingly become the major criteria for resource allocation, yet at a time when ageing itself (in terms of cumulative wisdom and ultimate demise) is being denied, leading to the paradoxical clash of cultural images with structural realities. Drawing these themes together, Achenbaum concludes that families provide sources of both tension and support, but that this is nothing new. Age differences are becoming more relevant—but then people of all ages are ageing, and therein lies the source of an intergenerational solidarity that outweighs age-specific tensions in contemporary America.

The following two chapters focus on specific roles and relationships that are emerging within contemporary families: the growing roles of extended kinship, and intergenerational relationships within step or reconstituted families. In Chapter 4, Lang addresses the issue of the specific functions and contributions of extended kin in later life. As he points out, while there is much empirical knowledge about the role of close family members in later life, the functions of more distant relatives are not well understood. Yet while these relatives may not have frequent contact, they belong to the 'latent kin network' (after Riley and Riley), typically sharing an historical and family biography, and may at times become close. Lang explores the availability and supportive functions of extended kin relationships in later life from two viewpoints. First, he asks how the structure and function of extended kin relationships differ from other social relationships in later life; second, he considers the perspective that kinship ties as resources in later life may be activated in response to personal loss experiences such as widowhood or death of siblings. Using data from the Berlin Ageing Study, Lang then explores ways in which older individuals activate extended kin relationships when nuclear family members are not available, identifying three compensatory mechanisms: a relation-specific, a function-specific, and an outcome-specific compensation. In Chapter 5, Dimmock and colleagues draw on an ethnographic study of UK stepfamilies to identify and discuss three broad areas of interest in the study of ageing and reconstituted families: the role of grandparenting following the divorce of parents; obligations to provide elder care within new family forms; and whether cohabiting induces the same intergenerational commitment as marriage. As Dimmock and colleagues discuss, one important contemporary change within British society is a more inclusive understanding of the diversity of British family forms and the recognition of divorce and recoupling/remarriage as normal rather than exceptional events.

The next three chapters turn to perhaps the most well researched of all the topics relating to ageing and families—that of care and support for older relatives. The specific themes selected within this area are, however, relatively novel: the reciprocal relationship between work and care from both the US and European perspective, and how changes in formal care are affecting informal family care, taking the UK as a case example. In Chapter 6, Anderson reviews the situation of the carers of dependent older people within the European Union, specifically with regard to those who combine eldercare with paid employment. Anderson highlights how the relationship between caring and working is addressed in the policies, programmes, and official documents of the EU institutions, as well as in member states. He then turns to look at the characteristics of, and problems faced by, working carers. As Anderson points out, while the debate on reconciliation of childcare and employment has moved forward supported by developments in public policies, collective bargaining, and workplace initiatives, corresponding action for eldercare appears to have been limited. The chapter concludes with a series of proposals to improve the opportunities for those wanting or needing to combine eldercare with employment.

Several of these themes are then taken up in Chapter 7 and explored in depth by Johnson and Lo Sasso with reference to the US situation. Using data from the Health and Retirement Study, they examine the relationship between labour supply, time given in help, and financial assistance to parents. As they argue, women's increasing participation in the labour force is likely to have important implications for eldercare, as women struggle to balance their traditional care-giving roles with their new responsibilities in the workplace. They found that women who helped their parents with personal care assistance worked significantly fewer hours than those who did not help their parents, while those who provided financial assistance worked significantly more hours. Although few persons at mid-life presently spend substantial amounts of time helping their elderly parents in any given year, for those who do the costs can be high. Anderson and Lo Sasso conclude that pressures on families are likely to mount in the near future as falling mortality and fertility rates continue to increase the proportion of the population that is very old and as women continue to play more important roles in the labour market.

As Knapp and colleagues highlight in Chapter 8, informal care by family, friends, and neighbours is the largest sector of social care for older people in the UK. In the course of two decades Britain has moved from a social care system for older people dominated by public sector provision, to one in which independent providers are more equally recognized. However, under both regimes, the contribution of family, friends, and neighbours has not been adequately recognized, despite the fact that informal carers outnumber their paid counterparts in formally organized public and non-public agencies by a factor of more than three to one. There is some evidence that the growth of the independent sector has had a profound impact on the care of older people by the family, while changes in families' willingness and ability to provide care has major ramifications for the scale of demands on formal providers. In this context the chapter describes independent sector providers of care for older people in the UK highlighting some of the implications for the family of this growth of independent sector provision, the policy environments in which they currently operate, and the policy and practice challenges for the years ahead.

Two topics which have not attracted so much attention, inheritance and the family's impact on the health of its members, complete the collection. In Chapter 9, Finch considers the reciprocal impact of inheritance on English intergenerational relationships. First, she discusses the impact of kinship on inheritance: how the handling of inheritance within families to whom this is a new experience is shaped by existing practices in intergenerational relationships; secondly, the impact of inheritance on kinship: how far, over time, this new experience might stimulate changes in those relationships. Finch concludes that English kinship is particularly individual, flexible, and adaptable, resulting

in open-ended legal and cultural expectations. This has allowed families to create their own sets of decisions, with the opportunity to adapt practices to individual circumstances. However, at the very time that many more families
within England are becoming owners of property, which enables them to leave
significant bequests to their children, they are facing increased healthcare
demands which encourage them to use such assets for personal late-life care.
Though Finch admits that current evidence is limited, she suggests that resistance to using up one's assets in this way to pay for long-term care is not so
much linked to a strong bequest motive among English families, but rather to
a feeling of entitlement to state-provided care.

The final discussion by Hughes and Waite in Chapter 10 considers the implications of new and diverse family forms for individual health and well-being.
The chapter sketches out a conceptual framework for understanding
the family as a context for well-being, focusing on the ways in which families
influence the health of individuals. Hughes and Waite argue that family plays
an important role in shaping health trajectories in the second half of life, point-
ing out that baby boomers will mature with markedly different and more heterogeneous family histories than those of previous generations. Furthermore,
this heterogeneity is increasingly cross-cut by race and ethnicity. The chapter
ends with a call for more research into this topic and the manner in which new
family forms are contributing to, as well as protecting against, ill-health.

1

The Challenge for Families of Demographic Ageing

SARAH HARPER

INTRODUCTION

There is considerable evidence from both Europe and the US that families still play an important role in the lives of their members (Finch, 1989; Waite, 2000), with the level of importance increasing with age (Waite, 2000). Because a greater proportion of people in western society are reaching old age or later life, families are increasingly an integral component of both social networking and reciprocal care. Yet, as Bengtson et al. (1990) have pointed out, individuals are growing older in families that are quantitatively and qualitatively different from those of their great grandparents, in terms both of the structure and duration of family roles and relationships.

This chapter draws on empirical evidence from Europe, North America, and Australasia to explore how the ageing of societies and other contemporaneous processes, are impacting upon families. While there are clearly multi-various definitions of the role of contemporary kinship, the chapter concludes by identifying three broad roles of importance within the context of ageing societies: families as mechanisms for intergenerational *support*; families as mechanisms for intergenerational *transfer*; and families as mechanisms for intergenerational *solidarity*.

FAMILY ROLES, RELATIONSHIPS, AND TRANSITIONS

Falling fertility and increased longevity have led to the demographic ageing of all western industrialized societies. At the same time, a combination of forces are resulting in the *delay of certain major life-transitions*, including first marriage, first childbirth, and even remarriage. These changes have significant implications for both family structure and kinship roles (Farkas and Hogan, 1995). First, the factors *contributing* to demographic ageing—increase in standard of living, education, public health, and medical advances—have also had a direct impact on other areas of society. The family mode of social organization, whereby kin groups pooled their resources and related to community as an intact unit, has altered as these ideological, economic, and social changes have shifted the locus of control away from the family towards the individual or other social institutions (Waite et al., 2000). Urbanization and technological change have produced new forms of communication, social intercourse, and entertainment, reducing the significance of that provided by the family (Burch and Matthews, 1987). In addition, the late twentieth century saw the mass emergence and consolidation of a variety of new kin structures within many industrialized societies—reconstituted or recombinant stepfamilies, ethnic-minority families, single-parent families, cohabiting couples.

Second, the factors *associated* with demographic ageing—falling fertility and mortality and increased longevity—have also impacted upon wider society. The shift to a low mortality/low fertility society results in an increase in the number of living generations, and a decrease in the number of living relatives within these generations. Increased longevity may increase the duration spent in certain kinship roles, such as spouse, parent of non-dependent child, and sibling. Marital unions, for example, have the potential to last far longer than historically has been the norm, and this has certainly placed strains on such relationships, contributing to marital break-up, divorce, and the formation of complex reconstituted families. A decrease in fertility may reduce the duration of other roles, such as parent of dependent child, or even the opportunity for some roles, such as sibling.

Third, the *knowledge* of demographic ageing is in itself impacting on social, economic, and political decisions and behaviours of both national and international institutions, and individuals themselves. So, for example, we are seeing the *ageing of some life-transitions*, with contemporary ageing societies displaying an increase of age at first marriage, at leaving the parental home, and at first childbirth. While public and legal institutions may be lowering the age threshold into full legal adulthood, individuals themselves are choosing to delay many of those transitions which demonstrate a commitment to full adulthood—full economic independence from parents, formal adult union through marriage or committed long-term cohabitation, and parenting. While the reduction in marriage and childbearing, and the rapid increase in divorce, are clearly related to the tremendous social changes of the last century, it can also be argued that, because infant mortality has fallen, and because early death through disease, war, famine, and, for women, reproduction, is no longer the common experience, individuals feel more comfortable about establishing marital unions later in life, bearing children later, and having fewer offspring. The ageing of family transitions in younger life leads to subsequent transition delay for both individual and other kin members. For example, the delayed birth of a first child may lead to long intergenerational spacings, and a transition to both parenthood and grandparenthood at a later age than has been the recent historical norm. Similarly, extended economic dependence on parents delays not only the individual's full transition to independent adulthood, but also the experience of the *empty-nest syndrome* for the parents themselves.

MARRIAGE, COHABITATION, AND DIVORCE

Changing trends in marriage have had a great impact upon turn-of-the-century families. Rates of cohabitation and divorce are increasing for adults of all ages. Individuals are marrying later, facing a greater possibility of divorce, and are increasingly less likely to remarry following marital dissolution. It is important to put this into perspective, though. On the whole, the length of many marriages is similar to those of earlier centuries. Historically, marriages ended because of the wife's early death, as a result of childbirth, or of related reproductive complications. In the twenty-first century, on the other hand, marriages are more likely to be cut short by divorce (Anderson, 1982). Those marriages that do not end in divorce will probably be longer than marriages at any other historical time, owing to lengthening life expectancy for both men and women (Bengston et al., 1990).

Marriage

Perhaps the major impact on turn-of-the-century families is rapidly changing trends in marriage. Cohabitation is increasing at all adult ages, with individuals marrying later, facing a greater possibility of divorce, and being increasingly less likely to remarry following divorce. Table 1.1 illustrates the

Table 1.1. *Trends in crude marriage rates in the European Union, 1960–2000*

	1960	1970	1980	1990	1995	2000
Austria	8.3	7.1	6.2	5.8	5.3	4.8
Belgium	7.1	7.6	6.7	6.5	5.1	4.4
Denmark	7.8	7.4	5.2	6.1	6.6	7.2
Finland	7.4	8.8	6.1	5.0	4.6	5.1
France	7.0	7.8	6.2	5.1	4.4	5.2
Germany	9.5	7.4	6.3	6.5	5.3	5.1
Greece	7.0	7.7	6.5	5.8	6.1	4.3
Ireland	5.5	7.0	6.4	5.1	4.3	5.1
Italy	7.7	7.3	5.7	5.6	5.1	4.6
Luxembourg	7.1	6.4	5.9	6.1	5.1	4.9
Netherlands	7.8	9.5	6.4	6.4	5.3	5.5
Portugal	7.8	9.4	7.4	7.2	6.6	6.3
Spain	7.1	7.3	5.9	5.7	5.1	5.3
Sweden	6.7	5.4	4.5	4.7	3.8	4.5
United Kingdom	7.5	8.5	7.4	6.5	5.5	5.1

Note: For Spain 1965 and the United Kingdom 1999.

Source: Council of Europe, 2001.

development in *crude marriage rates*[1] from 1960 to the year 2000 in the European Union. In terms of a *European pattern* in the development of marriage rates, the overall trend has been one of declining rates for most of the period with a modest upturn in some countries in the latter years, while the rest of the countries continue their decline in crude marriage rates. It is interesting to note that in 1960 Germany had the highest EU crude marriage rate standing at 9.5 per 1000, with Ireland having the lowest at 5.5 per 1000. By the end of the century, Denmark had the highest rate at 7.2 per 1000, with Greece having the lowest at 4.3 per 1000. By comparison, in the year 2000, Germany's rate had fallen to 5.1 per 1000, while Ireland's was almost back at its 1960 level. For those countries experiencing a modest upturn in rates at the end of the century, the rates levelled off in the mid-1990s for all countries except Denmark, where the lowest level had been in 1980. In the UK, crude marriage rates have been falling since the early 1970s and fell by 3–4 per cent per annum during this period (Murphy and Wang, 1999), with a fall from 330,000 first marriages in 1961, to 200,000 in 1997.

Crude marriage rates are, of course, strongly affected by the demographics of the population in question. A measure of marriage that avoids these problems is the so-called total first marriage rate, which expresses the probability of first marriage for a person if that person passes through his or her life conforming to the age-specific first marriage rates of a given year. The rate refers to a synthetic cohort and is the sum of the age-specific first marriage rates in a particular year (generally up to age 49), and can therefore exceed 1.0 in years of strong progression of the number of marriages, although it is excluded that a person can contract more than one marriage. Total female first marriage rates for the countries of the European Union for the period 1960–2000 are shown in Table 1.2.

It is interesting and reassuring to note that the trend over the period for the development in the total female first marriage rates is similar to that seen for the crude marriage rates in Table 1.1, with declining rates for all countries (with a little variation across countries in the onset of the decline) and with a modest upturn at the end of the century for some countries.

If we now consider the remarriage rates for males and females, the downward trend in the period is even more dramatic. The UK remarriage rates fell severely during the period in question, with the remarriage rate for divorced men falling by 75 per cent between 1971 and 1995 (Murphy and Wang, 1999). We should, however, note that, due to the increase in divorce (the vast majority of all remarriages during this period involved divorced people), there was an increase in the *number* of remarriages throughout the EU (Eurostat, 1998) with the number of remarriages in the UK rising from 50,000 in 1961 to 120,000 by 1997 (Family Policy Studies Centre, 2000). As illustrated in

---

[1] Crude marriage rate is the number of marriages per 1000 estimated mean population.

S. Harper

Table 1.2. *Total female first marriage rates in the European Union, 1960–2000*

	1960	1970	1980	1990	1995	2000
Austria	1.03	0.91	0.68	0.58	0.56	0.54
Belgium	1.05	0.98	0.77	0.72	0.57	0.52
Denmark	1.01	0.82	0.53	0.60	0.65	0.73
Finland	0.96	0.94	0.67	0.58	0.57	0.62
France	1.03	0.92	0.71	0.56	0.50	0.62
Germany	1.06	0.98	0.69	0.64	0.56	0.58
Greece	0.79	1.05	0.87	0.73	0.75	0.52
Ireland	0.93	1.10	0.84	0.70	0.59	0.59
Italy	0.98	1.01	0.78	0.69	0.63	0.62
Luxembourg	—	0.88	0.66	0.64	0.56	0.55
Netherlands	1.05	1.06	0.68	0.66	0.53	0.59
Portugal	0.94	1.21	0.89	0.88	0.77	0.73
Spain	0.99	1.01	0.76	0.69	0.60	0.61
Sweden	0.95	0.62	0.53	0.55	0.44	0.53
United Kingdom	1.04	1.04	0.76	0.63	0.54	0.53

Note: For Spain 1965, Ireland 1998, Italy 1999, and the United Kingdom 1999.
Source: Council of Europe, 2001.

Table 1.3, concurrent with the fall in crude marriage rates and total first marriage rates, there has been an *increase in the mean age of females at first marriage*, beginning for most countries of the Union around 1970. In 1960, Italy and Portugal had the highest female mean age at first marriage (24.8 years), while Belgium and Denmark had the lowest mean age (22.8 years). By the year 2000, Denmark had the second highest mean age at 29.5 years, with Sweden having the highest of all the EU countries (30.2 years) while Portugal (previously with the highest mean age) now has the lowest (25.2 years). The difference between the highest and lowest mean ages at first marriage for females has also increased, from just two years in 1960 to five years in 2000. As well as the cross-national differences pointed out above, there are also differences within countries. Those registered in lower socio-economic groups generally marry earlier than those in professional and managerial occupations.

One of the wider implications of these trends is a fall in teen marriages. The UK, for example, saw female teen marriages drop from one-third to 5 per cent between 1970 and 1995. Another is an increase in the proportion of single-never-married within a country (Office for National Statistics, 1997). Data from the US reveal that, in 1970, 16 per cent of US adults were single-never-married. This had risen to nearly one-quarter by 1996. Age at remarriage is also increasing. The age at which people remarry is dependent on the age at which they first marry, the length of that marriage, and the time interval between marriages. Australia provides a clear example of this. The length of marriage prior to

Table 1.3. *Mean age of females at first marriage in the European Union, 1960–2000*

	1960	1970	1980	1990	1995	2000
Austria	24.0	22.9	23.2	24.9	26.1	27.2
Belgium	22.8	22.4	22.2	24.2	25.4	26.1
Denmark	22.8	22.8	24.6	27.6	29.0	29.5
Finland	23.8	23.3	24.3	26.0	27.0	28.0
France	23.0	22.6	23.0	25.6	26.9	27.8
Germany	23.5	22.5	22.9	25.2	26.4	27.2
Greece	25.1	24.0	23.3	24.8	25.6	26.6
Ireland	26.9	24.8	24.6	26.6	27.9	—
Italy	24.8	23.9	23.8	25.5	26.6	—
Luxembourg	—	22.8	23.0	25.3	26.6	27.1
Netherlands	24.2	22.9	23.2	25.9	27.1	27.8
Portugal	24.8	24.2	23.2	23.9	24.7	25.2
Spain	—	—	23.4	25.3	26.8	27.7
Sweden	24.0	23.9	26.0	27.5	28.7	30.2
United Kingdom	23.3	22.4	23.0	25.1	26.4	27.3

Note: For Belgium 1999, France 1999, Germany 1999, Greece 1999, Spain 1965, Ireland 1998, Italy 1999, and the United Kingdom 1999.

Source: Council of Europe, 2001.

divorce and the length of time after divorce and prior to remarriage remained on average the same between 1977 and 1997. The increase in mean age at first marriage thus led to an increase in the mean age of remarriage, from 32 years for females and 36 years for males in 1977 to 38 years for females and 42 years for males by 1997 (Australian Social Trends, 1999). However, the largest factor to account for the ageing of remarriage in Australia appears to be the increase in cohabitation, particularly among previously married people; 78 per cent of all remarriages of partners who had both been divorced involve a period of prior cohabitation (Australian Bureau of Statistics, 1999).

These figures need, however, to be placed in the context of historical marriage patterns, and in relation to the various propositions which have arisen to explain these. It then becomes clear that the early marriage trends of the mid-twentieth century were themselves historically unusual following a longer felt pattern within western Europe for late marriage and low rates.[2] Hajnal (1965) maintained that there existed two dominant marriage patterns within

---

[2] The dominant thesis concerning the Western European Marriage Pattern was expounded by Hajnal in 1965 and, while subject in later years to a critical reassessment (Lundh, 1999) and an acknowledgement of regional and sub-group variation (Devos and Kennedy, 1999), the basic descriptives remain sound.

Europe—in western Europe marital age was high and rates of marriage low, and had been thus since at least the sixteenth century. Following the ideas of Malthus, whereby delays in marital union performed a check on unbridled reproduction and overpopulation, Hanjal argued that the nuclear family system required the delay of marriage until a man could establish an independent livelihood adequate to support a family. Alternatively, in societies with extended or joint families, newly married couples could be incorporated into the existing economic unit. In addition, there is evidence from throughout Europe that other economic and demographic constraints, such as gender imbalances and differential labour participation, also restricted partner availability at certain times. By the early twentieth century in western Europe nuptiality started to increase and both men and women to marry earlier (Engelen, 1999). Explanations for this include growing economic prosperity and the introduction of contraceptive practice within marriage. These trends were encouraged throughout western Europe after the Second World War, due to the post-war marriage boom. However, by the 1960s, 95 per cent of people in western Europe were or had been married in what was, perhaps, the *heyday* of marital life. By the 1970s, the rates had fallen to those of 1900 and, as we saw, have declined ever since. As Engelen (1991; 1994; 1997) has argued, new behaviour has to be both culturally and socially acceptable as well as economically advantageous and, thus, ideas based on increased productivity or intergenerational wealth transference, must also be placed in a social context. As the economic constraints to marriage were dismantled in the nineteenth century, so it became socially and culturally acceptable to reject the concept of a period of celibacy and to take up marital partners in early adulthood. By the 1970s, at least in western Europe, the social and cultural constraints on sexual relations outside marriage had also been removed and so cohabitation began to supplement and then replace marriage. The fall of the final barrier, that of childbirth outside wedlock, has led to the recent dramatic falls in marital union, particularly in the Scandinavian countries.

While for some time it was argued that within the colonial US, strong economic opportunities for young men allowed marriage at early ages (Landale, 1989), a recent reanalysis (Fitch and Ruggles, 2000) of the limited data suggests a broad similarity between the US and western Europe during this time. Though there were some regional variations, by 1890, marriage ages had reached a peak of 22 for women and 26 for men. Explanations for this include the low availability of men following the losses of the Civil War (Fitch and Ruggles, 2000) and the declining availability of land at this time (Easterlin, 1976; Landale, 1989). The rapid growth of well-paid wage labour stimulated by urban industrial growth was probably associated with the fall in first marriage rates, for white men at least, in the late nineteenth and early decades of the twentieth centuries, with another economic boost to lower rates occurring again in the 1960s, when median marriage rates hit 22 for white men and 20 for white women. As we saw, these have been rising ever since, at around one year per decade, and by 1999 the marriage age had returned to overtake that of a century before.

While economic theories have dominated the explanations for these changing marriage rates, there seems far less understanding of the sudden rise in marriage age in the western world in the last decades of the twentieth century. Fitch and Ruggles (2000) suggest that for the US a growth in low-income employment for young white males after 1970, leading to an overall reduction in wages for this group, may have encouraged a delay in marriage. It seems, however, that these income-related arguments may need to be revisited in the light of changing late twentieth-century social norms and employment patterns. In particular, as Hughes and Waite point out in Chapter 10, for the US, we need to include the gender dimension as a dynamic variable in the equation. Drawing on the independence theory of marriage, which postulates that women will delay marriage if other more attractive alternatives are present, Waite et al. (2000) suggest that the growth of female occupational structure had a significant influence on marriage ages and rates. The growth of female educational and employment opportunities since 1970 have substantially decreased women's economic dependence on a spouse, allowing women the possibilities of delaying marriage. We may also turn around the relationship between fertility and marriage and postulate that, for women in particular, ever lengthening lifespans have also allowed them the liberty to delay childbirth, and the strong association between marriage and childbearing, which still remains in most western societies, is also contributing to an increased age for, or delay in, marriage.

Cohabitation

As indicated, both falling marriage rates and increasing age at marriage is partly accounted for by a growth in pre-marriage cohabitation by both never-married and formerly married couples (Ermisch and Francesconi, 1996; 1998) (Table 1.4). At the turn of the twentieth century, around 10 per cent of all couples living in the European Union were cohabiting, despite cultural and cohort/age differences. This percentage has changed significantly over the past hundred years. Couples of all ages and from all countries now undertake a period of cohabitation before, between, or after legal marriage (Kiernan, 2000). Percentages reflecting this trend vary across Europe, from 25 per cent of people in Denmark to less than 3 per cent in southern Europe and Ireland. Nearly one-third of all European couples under 30 engage in such behaviour, as opposed to approximately 3 per cent of couples involving people over 45.

Data from the UK can help elucidate the phenomenon of cohabitation before marriage. Though accurate longitudinal data on cohabitation are limited (Haskey, 1999), some indication of general trends can be gained from

Table 1.4. *The percentage of couples living in a consensual union by age group in the European Union, 1994*

	Total 16+	16–29	30–44	45–64	65+
Belgium	10	27	11	6	3
Denmark	25	72	28	8	6
France	14	46	14	4	3
Germany	9	30	8	4	4
Greece	2	9	1	1	1
Ireland	3	11	2	1	0
Italy	2	6	2	1	1
Luxembourg	10	28	10	5	2
Netherlands	13	54	15	4	3
Portugal	3	10	2	1	2
Spain	3	14	4	1	1
United Kingdom	11	38	12	3	1

Source: Eurostat, 1998.

analysis of the UK General Household Survey (GHS) and the British Household Panel Survey (BHPS). The GHS, for example, estimates a fivefold increase in cohabitation between the years 1979 to 1995 (Haskey, 1999). This is further supported by data from the BHPS suggesting that by the turn of the twenty-first century 70 per cent of all newly formed, couple relationships were cohabitations (Buck and Scott, 1994). While cohabitation is generally seen as a transient state, the average length of cohabitation is increasing. Data from the GHS suggest that average length of cohabitation rose by 70 per cent in the 1980s and 1990s, reaching an average of 34 months by 1995 (Murphy, 1999). A similar trend has been noted in the United States; between 1960 and 1993, there was a sixfold rise in cohabitating couples (Farley, 1996). Only 7 per cent of those women born in the United States in the late 1940s cohabited before age 25, at which point nearly three-quarters of women had already married. Of those women born in the 1960s, on the other hand, nearly 55 per cent cohabited before turning 25 (Raley, 2000). Australia and New Zealand show similar tends. Approximately a quarter of men and women aged 15–44 are in cohabiting partnerships in New Zealand. Around two-thirds of those in their early twenties are in such relationships. According to the Australian Bureau of Statistics, 67 per cent of marriages in 1998 were preceded by a period of cohabitation.

Divorce

In most western countries, *divorce rates* have risen steadily since the early 1970s (Table 1.5). The factors effecting divorce rates are complex—including

Table 1.5. *Crude divorce rates in the European Union, 1960–2000*

	1960	1970	1980	1990	1995	2000
Austria	1.2	1.4	1.8	2.1	2.3	2.4
Belgium	0.5	0.7	1.5	2.0	3.5	2.6
Denmark	1.5	1.9	2.7	2.7	2.5	2.7
Finland	0.8	1.3	2.0	2.6	2.7	2.7
France	0.7	0.8	1.5	1.9	2.1	2.0
Germany	1.0	1.3	1.8	1.9	2.1	2.3
Greece	0.3	0.4	0.7	0.6	1.1	0.9
Ireland	—	—	—	—	—	—
Italy	—	0.2	0.2	0.5	0.5	0.6
Luxembourg	0.5	0.6	1.6	2.0	1.8	2.3
Netherlands	0.5	0.8	1.8	1.9	2.2	2.2
Portugal	0.1	0.1	0.6	0.9	1.2	1.9
Spain	—	—	0.5	0.6	0.8	0.9
Sweden	1.2	1.6	2.4	2.3	2.6	2.4
United Kingdom	0.5	1.1	2.8	2.9	2.9	2.6

Note: For France 1999, Germany 1999, Italy 1975 and Spain 1985/1999. No data for Ireland.
Source: Council of Europe, 2001.

both demographic and social trends. Divorce appears more likely in marriages involving no children (Lilliard and Waite, 1995); those preceded by more than one cohabitation (Kiernan and Mueller, 1999; Lilliard et al., 1995); those established when at least one partner was very young (Murphy, 1985); and those containing at least one previously divorced partner (Australia Bureau of Statistics, 1995; Haskey, 1998; Kiernan and Mueller, 1999; Martin and Bumpass, 1989). All of these have increased over the past thirty years.

More detailed analysis, however, indicates that there was a sharp increase in rates throughout the 1970s, which plateaued out during the early to mid-1980s. The plateau has persisted, with the 1990s producing steady divorce rates across the decade. Part of this deceleration in rates may be accounted for by the increasing age at first marriage, younger people—especially teenagers—being especially vulnerable to marital break up, and social and legal factors; for example, many countries initiated a relaxation of divorce laws in the 1970s, allowing a backlog of divorces to travel through the system, creating a temporary upsurge.

Again it is difficult to talk of a *European pattern of* divorce in as much as individual countries varied significantly in their propensity to divorce in the period covered, and this variation has in some ways increased by the end of the century. In 1960, there was a clear north–south divide in relation to divorce, with the northern countries of Sweden and Denmark having dramatically higher crude divorce rates than the southern countries (0.1 per 1000 population in Portugal and 1.5 in Denmark). By the year 2000, there is still a north–south divide but the majority of countries in the Union have crude divorce rates of 2 or more per 1000 population, while only Greece, Italy, and Spain continue with rates below 1 per 1000. While acknowledging this north–south divide (which probably includes Ireland in the southern European group), it should be noted that all countries of the European Union have experienced significant increases in the crude divorce rates in the period 1960–2000, with most countries experiencing between two- and five-fold increases. At current rates, just under 50 per cent of all US marriages will end in divorce (Cherlin, 1992), compared with around 30 per cent of all EU marriages, ranging from less than 10 per cent of Italian marriages, to 40 per cent of marriages in the UK. The annual number of divorces in the UK, for example, rose from 74,000 in 1961, to 145,000 in 1997 (Family Policy Studies Centre, 2000), resulting in the current dissolution of around 40 per cent of marriages in the UK.

However, while families in all industrialized nations have faced an increase in marital divorce over the past century, they have also faced a reduction in marital disruption due to death. If the figures for marital dissolution are taken as a whole, combining the numbers of dissolved marriages due to both death and divorce, the dissolution level at the end of the twentieth century is remarkably similar to that of the nineteenth. Both indicate that one-third of marriages broke down after twenty years (Anderson, 1982).

AGEING OF LIFE TRANSITIONS

Clearly then, there are a range of complex interacting factors that encourage such demographic trends. For example, both current delayed marriage and remarriage are clearly associated with the growth in cohabitation, and thus it may be argued that they only represent a shift from one form of adult union to another. However, other life-transitions are also being delayed, in particular age at first childbirth and age at leaving the parental home, and thus the contextual drive of the late twentieth century may well also include the trend towards delaying various adult transitions in general.

Despite an increase in out-of-wedlock births (Kiernan and Mueller, 1999), delayed marriage is still associated with *delayed first childbirth*, with both the average age at birth of first child and median age for childbearing rising throughout the western industrialized world. Average age at birth of first child thus rose from 24 in 1970 to 26 by 1995 for European Union women, while median age of childbearing had reached 28.4 for women in England and Wales and 29 in Australia and New Zealand by 1995 (Armitage and Babb, 1996). The delaying of this first childbirth impacts upon subsequent family structure, particularly on the age at which subsequent life-transitions occur. These include, for example, grandparenthood and the 'empty-nest syndrome', or the extended post-parental period following the departure from the family home of the child/children.

Another example is a rapid recent *increase in the age at which young people leave the parental home* (Grundy, 1999a). There needs to be careful examination of this trend. While there appears to have been an increase in young single households (25–29), there has been an increase in those in their twenties remaining in the parental home.[3] This may be an artefact of measurement, but it may also indicate a growing trend to delay the commitment to full independent adult living, as opposed to an extended form of independent adolescent living. Within Europe, for example, every EU member state, with the exception of Denmark and the Netherlands, saw an increase between 1987 and 1996 in those aged 20–29 remaining within the parental home. A similar picture emerges in the US. A range of factors are associated with this ageing of flying the nest, including remaining in education, financial uncertainty, and peer example. This additional increase in age of leaving home also increases the age at which parents experience the *empty-nest syndrome.*

If we wish to gain any understanding of the roles and relationships within families, and how these may change, we need to have some prediction of the trends in family formation and dissolution over the next few decades. Murphy and Wang's (1999) recent modelling of 1 per cent SAR from the 1991 Census gives us some indication of such trends. Basing their models on the broad premise that British divorce rates will remain more or less constant at around 40 per cent, that remarriage after divorce will continue to be lower than after widowhood, that fertility will become increasingly disassociated from partnership behaviour, and that the trend toward independent living will continue, they discuss the most probable scenarios: first, that marriage rates will decline by 3 per cent and entry into cohabitation rise by 0.5 per cent; second, that marriage rates will decline by 2 per cent and entry into cohabitation rise by 2 per cent. The resulting forecasts predict that by 2016 there will be more entries into cohabitation than into marriage, which would result in an increase in unwed births to reach up to 50 per cent of all births. There would be a decrease in the number of married persons, from 24.2 to 22.3 million, and an increase in the number of adults not living in a family situation, from 7.9 to 9.2 million.

Within the British context then, the current cohort of older adults, aged 60 to 90, were thus establishing their family lives at a time of low marital dissolution, relatively early age of marriage and birth of first child. The current cohort of young and mid-life adults is experiencing relatively high levels of divorce, late age of marriage and first childbirth, and periods of extended cohabitation and possibly a range of reconstituted families. Future cohorts, if we are to believe Murphy, will experience high levels of divorce and ever-extended periods of cohabitation, before and between martial union, or replacing it completely. Whether these patterns of family formation and dissolution impact upon later life experience, and in particular upon the experience of reciprocal

---

[3] Eurostat, 1998: it is currently unclear how these are measured.

care, is currently a matter of debate. The impact of divorce and reconstituted or stepfamilies, and the wider family relationships that are incurred and potentially supported by cohabiting couples, are also of particular concern.

The ageing of western societies is currently accompanied by a variety of trends, some inspired demographically, some socially; some directly related to the ageing of societies; some clearly associated with lengthening life. Marital unions, for example, have the potential to last far longer than historically has been the norm, and this has certainly placed strains on such relationships, resulting in marital break-up and reconstituted families. Similarly, it can be argued that individuals are delaying life-transitions in the light of ever lengthening lifespans, women in particular being able psychologically to justify delaying marriage and child-rearing as rates of both infant and maternal mortality have declined so rapidly over the past couple of centuries. However, the reduction in marriage and childbearing, and the rapid increase in divorce, have also been influenced by the tremendous social and economic developments of the last century. It is thus necessary to differentiate between the implications of declining fertility and mortality, and those associated with the ageing of family life transitions. The former trends are likely to broadly continue, in particular the tremendous advances made in longevity; the latter are equally likely to change or even reverse should social norms and economic circumstances dramatically alter. The demographic ageing of societies is *currently* associated with the ageing of family life transitions, but not *necessarily* so. Contemporary trends reflect historical developments.

STRUCTURE AND DURATION OF ROLES AND RELATIONSHIPS

Let us now consider the impact of these trends on contemporary families, considering the structure and duration of family roles and relationships, the impact of divorce and cohabitation, and the various roles and relationships emerging within reconstituted families.

The Verticalization of Family Structure

For the past twenty years it has been generally accepted that many people alive today in western industrialized nations will spend some time as part of a four-generation family. These however, will have increasingly fewer members, and longer gaps between the generations (Farkas and Hogan, 1995; Shanas, 1980), and family members will spend longer occupying intergenerational family roles than before. Data from the US indicates that a fifth of all women who die after 80 spend some time in a five-generation family as great-great-grandmothers (Hagestad, 1990). The *beanpole family*, or the *verticalization* of family structure, has been well recognized, in the US in particular (Bengtson et al., 1990; Goldman, 1986). In two recent national surveys, the Health and

Retirement Survey and the AARP intergenerational linkages survey, more than half the respondents reported membership in four-generation families (Bengtson, 1995; Bengtson and Hayrootyan, 1994).

Similarly, work in the UK confirms that as mortality rates continue to decline, more children will have surviving grandparents (Grundy, 1999*b*) and more people in late middle age and early old age will have both upward and downward generational ties (Grundy, 1999*a*). In a recent British survey by Dench, three-quarters of respondents were part of a three-, four-, or even five-generation family group (Dench et al., 1999). This suggests that recent mortality and fertility trends within Britain have also resulted in the reduction of horizontal ties or *intergenerational contraction*, that is, a decrease in the number of members within each generation, an increase in vertical ties or *intergenerational extension*, and a rise in the number of living generations (Bengtson et al., 1990). However, while the number of living generations will increase, the absolute number of living relatives will decrease (Crimmins, 1986).

More recently, however, the full extent of this verticalization has been questioned (Farkas and Hogan, 1995). Analysis of cross-sectional data from the International Social Survey Program (ISSP) covering the US, Australia, and five European countries (Austria, West Germany, Great Britain, Hungary, and Italy) (Table 1.6) revealed, that at least at the end of the 1980s, a very small percentage of individuals living in a complex multigenerational family. Just under half of the 10,000 respondents lived in a two-generation family, 43 per cent had three living generations, but fewer than 3 per cent were part of a four-generation family. There was also considerable difference between the countries, particularly with respect to the US and Europe, with an individual's chances of being a member of a particular type of multi- or single-generation family, and the position within this, varying significantly. An individual in the US was more likely to have both a surviving child and surviving parent, than in any of the European countries. This has recently been exemplified by

Table 1.6. *Multigenerational families (%)*

Generational structure	18–24	25–44	45–64	65+	Total
One generation	0.6	5.6	9.3	15.9	7.4
Two generation—youngest	27.4	52.1	8.3	1.2	29.1
Two generation—oldest	0.1	2.6	41.9	31.7	17.4
Three generation—youngest	69.7	28.5	0.3	0.1	22.3
Three generation—middle	0.6	9.4	29.1	1.9	12.7
Three generation—oldest	0.0	0.1	7.3	46.8	8.7
Four generation	1.6	1.8	3.7	2.4	2.4
Number: 10,131	100.0	100.0	100.0	100.0	100.0

Source: International Social Survey Program (ISSP) covering the US, Australia, Austria, West Germany, Great Britain, Hungary, and Italy; adapted from Farkas and Hogan, 1995.

Grundy (1999a) who found that only 19 per cent of middle-aged UK women (aged 55–63) had both a surviving child and parent, compared to the US's 35 per cent. Such cross-sectional data has its limitations in that it cannot comment on the process of change within these families. However, such findings put the verticalization debate in perspective. While it is likely that during an individual's lifetime, he or she will experience a period of complex, possibly four- or even five-generational living, even if for only a short portion of the life-course, at any one time the percentage of such long chain multigenerational families within a society is still low. Clearly we do not as yet have sufficient longitudinal data to claim the beanpole or vertical family as the common norm in western industrialized societies.

Long Intergenerational Spacings

The increasing delay of first childbirths, highlighted above, has the potential to create a family structure with long intergenerational spacing. Recent work by Grundy (1999a) exemplifies this for Britain. Drawing on data from the 1992 Second Wave of the BHPS, she highlights the relationship between parity, age at birth, and age at children's departure from the parental home. Parents of large families generally commenced childbearing earlier and finished later than parents of small families. Parents with four or more children had a median age of departure of the first child some seven years younger than that of parents with only one child, and a median age at departure of the last child some eight years older than parents of only one child. While British research supports the extensive findings in the US that co-residency in not a requirement for late-life kin support, it clearly does impact upon broader kin and intergenerational relationships. In particular there is evidence that falling fertility leading to earlier completion of childbearing is a key determinant of parental passage to the empty nest (Murphy and Grundy, 1996). Bengtson et al. (1990) in the US have also argued that the longer age spacing may well create difficulties in the development of bonds across the life course, especially as this may result in simultaneous demands from adolescent children and ageing parents, the sandwich generation, or women-in-the-middle phenomenon (Rossi, 1987).

The Extended Duration of Family Roles and Relationships

Directly related to longer life expectancy, the average length of marriages has increased, with WHO data suggesting that by the turn of the century the great majority of those marriages not terminated by divorce would exceed forty years (Myers, 1990). This is in contrast to figures that reveal that the common experience of marriage at the beginning of the twentieth century was likely to be under twenty-five years (Gillis, 1985). Bengtson et al. (1990) report from the US that for these long-lived marriages, marital satisfaction tends to rise in later life to levels expressed by younger married people, after a typical dip in mid-life. There is of course a survivor effect here, with many of the dissatisfied mid-life marriages ending in dissolution. In addition the dimensions which make early-and late-life marriage happy and successful differ, with elements such as physical attraction and passion being replaced by familiarity and loyalty (Brehm, 1992).

Second, as populations age, so the child–parent dyad shifts from one of dependency to one primarily experienced as an adult relationship. Grundy's recent analysis of US/UK data supports earlier predictions by Riley (1983) that many parents and children would soon experience sixty years of joint life, of which under one-third would be spent in the traditional parent/dependent-child relationship. Around a quarter of UK women and nearly 40 per cent of US women aged 55–63 still have a surviving parent. These women have thus spent around sixty years as a child, some forty of them in an adult relationship with a living parent. However, not only will parents and children spend longer in non-dependent relationships, but the time spent as a child with dependent parents is also increasing. There is evidence, for US women at least, that the time spent as the daughter of a parent over 65 now exceeds the time spent as the parent of a child under 18. This must, however, include the caveat that, while for much of the last two centuries, a high proportion of those over 65 would be in varying degrees of dependency on others for some aspect of their daily living, this is now no longer the case. Indeed, given that it is now not until after age 80 that the crucial stage for relying on children for assistance is reached (Uhlenburg, 1995) we should perhaps be comparing age over 80 with under 18. What is then apparent is that adult US women now spend more time *without* a dependent—be it a dependent child or potentially dependent parent—than with one.

Both these lengthening relationships—that of husband–wife and child–parent—share similar features. As the common experience of parenthood moves to more than fifty years of shared life, parents and children are adjusting to spending most of their relationship as independent adults. Similarly husbands and wives are spending fewer years of their joint lives as parents of young children. Clearly the association between marital and parental roles will loosen. Relationships which have been historically based on a hierarchy which existed in part to support successful reproduction must move to greater equality, both child–parent and husband–wife, as traditional roles based on parenthood give way to companionate relationships.

COHABITATION AND DIVORCE

The Impact of Cohabitation

As we earlier described, many couples currently cohabit for a period of time before marriage, yet we still know little about the impact of a period of cohabitation on later life or on wider family relationships (Haskey, 1992). There is some evidence, however, from both the US (DeMaris and Rao, 1992) and UK (Popenoe, 1993), that people who cohabit prior to marriage have a higher propensity to divorce, regardless of whether they marry their initial cohabiting partner, though this may not apply to cohabitations when both partners are never-married (Kiernan and Mueller, 1999). Furthermore, evidence from both the UK (Kiernan and Mueller, 1999) and Scandinavia (Prinz, 1995) suggest that we are probably seeing two forms of cohabitation—those who are about to enter a long-term, probably marital commitment, and those who form a series of frequently dissolved temporary unions. For example, Kiernan (2000) has recently drawn on NCDS data to argue that it is partnership turnover, whether within a marital or cohabiting union, which has the propensity to lead to subsequent break-up and turnover. If this is the case, given the large percentages of cohabitations that lead on to marriage between the two individuals formerly cohabiting, then subsequent marital break-up is not as likely as earlier predicted. Thus many of the existing and future consensual unions may well support the long-term vertical and lateral kin relationships developed through marriage. Alternatively, those who cohabit may exhibit specific characteristics which not only lead to the selection of cohabitation over marriage, but to multiple partnering. If these characteristics are becoming more widespread, then one would expect to see an increase in both multiple cohabitations and divorce.

Yet existing studies comparing the wider cohabiting and marital relationships (Leridon and Villeneuve-Gokalp, 1989; Lesthaeghe, 1992; Lewin, 1982) rarely distinguish between these two forms of cohabitation. Similarly their analysis of wider kin relationships is limited. However, given current work which suggests that children whose parents divorce have a preference for cohabitation (Kiernan, 2000), we are likely, given the current increase in divorce rates, to see a continuation in the rate of growth in cohabitations.

Perhaps the biggest potential impact, however, is the growth of cohabitations in later life, particularly following divorce, as these are less likely to end in marriage. Given that it is generally acknowledged that cohabitation has a higher likelihood of separation than legal marriage (McRea, 1993; Nock, 1995; Popenoe, 1993), it may be argued that such late-life alliances do not provide the stability for the extensive cross-kin interactions and relationships supported within marriage-based families or stepfamilies. Increased cohabitation among those in later life may have neutral or negative effects on future social networks. Australian data from 1998 show that around 15 per cent of all cohabitations involved people aged 40 to 59 (Australian Bureau of Statistics, 1998). Given that cohabitation has a higher likelihood of ending in separation as opposed to legal marriage (McRae, 1993; Nock, 1995; Popenoe, 1993), it may be argued that late-life alliances cannot provide the same stability or cross-kin interactions and relationships as those supported or created by marriage-based families or stepfamilies. This may have consequences in later life with regard to reciprocal care. Family or kin tends to take responsibility for their ageing or ailing relatives. If networks of these people do not exist, the question is to whom a person will turn in later life for assistance. It is important to keep in mind, though, that the assertion that cohabiting relationships are less stable is based primarily on evidence gathered from younger couples. As older adults move to this living situation in their middle and late life, the picture may be very different.

Divorce

There is a range of cross-cultural evidence that indicates that, in comparison with the non-married, married people have an advantage that may be measured across both health and socio-economic variables (Gove et al., 1970; Waite, 1995). The marital status of a person is a dimension of family structure that deeply affects their living arrangements, support systems, and individual well-being (Myers, 1990). As Waite and Hughes argue in Chapter 10, intact husband–wife families provide a multiple support system for each spouse in terms of emotional, financial, and social exchanges, and married people tend to enjoy higher levels of health and survival, social participation, and life satisfaction than persons who are not married. There is limited British evidence, however, on the impact of divorce in later life, and how this contrasts with widowhood. Again we need to turn to the US for some indication.

Most studies exploring the impact of divorce on *economic well-being* and standard of living have indicated that immediately after divorce younger cohorts appear to experience a general improvement in the economic situation for men and a significant decline for women (Waite, 2000). However, the interruption of savings and destruction of assets associated with divorce are likely to depress the economic well-being of both men and women divorced in later life. Indeed, the rather limited empirical evidence we have suggests that divorce is associated with lower economic well-being among all elderly people. Thus US data (Waite, 2000) on both income and wealth indicate that older persons who are married enjoy much higher standards of living than non-married persons, with the highest rates of poverty being experienced by those who are divorced; as much as three or four times the married rate. Uhlenberg's work on older divorced women, for example, which controlled for both race and educational attainment, found that these women were more likely to continue to work in later life and to reduce living expenses by sharing their homes. In addition, compared with those who were married, never-married, widowed, and divorced men and women both reported highest levels of dissatisfaction with their economic condition.

It has long been recognized in the US that married people have an advantage in terms of both *health and longevity* (Gove et al., 1990), with these figures being substantiated outside the US in a cross-national study of sixteen countries. Among the non-married category at all ages, most studies find the divorced have the highest mortality rate, followed by the widowed and then the never-married. This pattern also seems to pertain to the elderly, with both cross-sectional and longitudinal evidence from the US and Europe indicating that the divorced tend to have the highest death rates of any marital status category, with the disadvantage being greater for men than for women (Gove et al., 1990; Uhlenberg, 1995). Waite and Hughes explore these ideas in some detail in Chapter 10, arguing that social support is beneficial to health. The various studies considering cause of death among married and non-married people tend to suggest that not having a spouse is one of the critical factors. In particular, marital dissolution in later life can lead to loneliness, lack of support and care, and loss of roles.

This is particularly the case for men. Divorced men are at an extra disadvantage over widowed men, however, in that they frequently also lose social support networks, which appear more likely to be retained by both widowed men, and widowed and divorced women. Given that women generally have stronger and more multi-faceted networks than men, they are able to retain stronger social support following divorce.

However, marital dissolution clearly also has implications beyond those for the couple themselves. Dissolution in younger life often leads to remarriage or cohabitation by one or both partners, introducing a variety of complex reconstituted family structures, which impact upon both reciprocal family care, and intergenerational transmission. Yet there is limited research evidence on the impact of divorce on late-life intergenerational relations owing to the still relatively low numbers of divorced elderly. It does seem, however, that mother–child relations for older divorced women remain quite similar to those of women who do not divorce. In fact, there may be some intensification of mother–child relationships among divorced women. Data from the end of the century suggest that, in both the UK and US, 80–90 per cent of all children live with their mothers after divorce (Bornat et al., 1998a; Cherlin, 1981), and there is evidence that maternal attachment by children increases after divorce, and that women intensify their kin relationships generally after divorce (Hagestad, 1986). Most of these surveys, however, also report that interaction between fathers and their children tends to decline significantly following divorce (Furstenburg, 1987). While older divorced women are as likely as widowed women to co-reside with a child, and supportive intergenerational relationships are likely to continue for widowed, divorced, and married older women, data from the US National Survey of Families and Households suggests a contrasting picture for men. Among nationally representative divorced men aged 50–79 only half of the fathers saw or communicated with at least one child weekly, only 11 per cent maintained contact with more than one child, and one-third had no contact at all with their children. This suggests that these men are less likely to have adult children available for them in time of need. In summary, while older divorced men and women both experience the highest poverty rates of any unmarried group,[4] divorced men experience the

---

[4] This is in contrast with research on younger age groups that indicates that younger men actually improve their standard of living following divorce, while younger women see a decline (Fethke, 1989).

highest mortality rates, have weaker social support networks, and have less contact with their children (Fox and Kelly, 1995; Waite, 1995).

Divorce versus Widowhood

A comparative analysis of the impact of divorce and widowhood is complex, in part because widowhood is predominantly a late-life experience, while divorce has been a young and mid-life phenomenon, though increasingly a growing late-life experience. While the personal implications of the two processes—death and divorce—clearly differ in experience, their structural effects remain similar,[5] leading to reconstituted families, and the loss of some of the former extended ties and relationships. Yet while both death and divorce have their impact on the wider family structure, and may lead to varied constituted family forms, there are significant gender differences in the experience of the two. US research looking at the differing impacts of divorce and widowhood on family and intergenerational relationships has suggested that while there is not much difference for women, there is considerable difference for men. Women thus face economic decline through both widowhood and divorce, but are able to maintain strong family and other relationships; men, however, are cut off from personal relationships through divorce to a far greater degree than through widowhood (Hughes and Waite, 2000).

In summary, the last century saw a shift in the cause of marital dissolution from death to divorce (Anderson, 1982). Historically, men and women have both experienced high levels of widowhood, including multiple widowhood. Now men and women in early late-life are more likely to be divorced than widowed. With a rising incidence of divorce and declining propensity to remarry, it is likely that a greater number of older people will live alone in future than before. The rise will be greatest for men, who formerly have escaped being alone in old age due to their greater likelihood of dying before their spouse. Now, the rising incidence of divorce for all ages means that men will be more likely to find themselves living alone. In addition, under a regime of low fertility, both men and women will have less children—and in all western industrialized countries, geographical mobility results in separation from children. Given that, as we discussed earlier, children currently have a higher propensity to remain with the mother after a marital divorce or cohabitation split, an increasing number of men may find themselves without child support in later life. However, in the future, many of these older men may well have experienced periods of independent living throughout their lives, and thus be better adapted to cope with this.

In addition, the recombinations of new kin relationships following divorce are far more complex than those formed through death. In the latter, while

---

[5] Though in the UK at least, remarriage rates after widowhood are falling less sharply than after divorce.

new combinations are formed, and this has historically been the case, there is but one family line to follow. The deceased spouse does not form his or her own descendent kin line, bringing second, third, or even multiple stepfamilies into the kinship network. While marriages cut short by death have only to integrate biographies from the past on remarriage, those divided by divorce have also to include the new kin narratives which develop parallel to their own new family lines.

RECONSTITUTED FAMILIES

There has been limited research on the role of reconstituted or stepfamilies in caring for older adults (Allan, Crow, and Hawker, 1999; Bornat et al., 1999; Finch and Wallis, 1994). As Simpson's (1998) ethnographic account of divorce demonstrates, second marriages and subsequent-birth children often have to be assimilated into the ongoing relationship between a former husband and wife, in addition to the assimilation of a former spouse's latest offspring, and the inclusion of step and half-siblings from current and previous marriages. What is unclear, however, is the point at which affinity ends within modern kin relationships. Nor do we understand the process by which family members set about rewriting their new roles and relationships, becoming in essence new kin to each other. In particular, few have explored this question in relation to antecedent generations. One family today may well have several lateral tiers of grandparents each with a biological link to one or more children of a reconstituted family. Dimmock et al. in Chapter 5 explore how modern families incorporate grandparents, step-grandparents, and grandparents-in-law into the complex network of modern western kinship asking whether there are normative rules for such incorporation.

The broad conclusions from all these studies are that the complexities of the ensuing relationships do not lend themselves to any particular pattern or structure of care. However, the dominant care relationship of blood-related daughter for mother, found within non-reconstituted families, seems to remain central. As Dimmock et al.'s study concludes, whilst there is a growing awareness of the possibilities of looser-knit, divorce-extended families, the availability of care will usually depend on access to close 'blood ties'. While there is some US evidence (Soldo, 1998) that this is the case in relation to the bequest motive, we clearly need more research in this area to quantify this assertion.

AGEING AND THE FAMILY

Two of the twentieth century's key hypotheses on the nuclear family have been questioned in recent years. The first main theory was that of the emergence of the nuclear family following the Industrial Revolution, when, it was argued, families moved from an extended structure, a social institution supported by law and custom, to a nuclear structure based on sentiment and companionship.

As the work of the Cambridge Population Group revealed in the 1960s and 1970s, the pre-industrial extended family was a myth (Laslett and Wall, 1972). Rather than the household comprising extended kin generations, more typical was a small nuclear family group, living alongside non-kin. The second hypothesis concerns the decline of the family. As the nuclear family structure becomes increasingly replaced by alternative structures, proponents of the theory argue that the social institution of the family as an agent of socialization for younger members and a source of nurture and companionship for all is also being destroyed (Popenoe, 1993; 1996). This has been questioned by both feminist and post-modern writers and family sociologists, who point out that the traditional nuclear family is ill-suited for a post-modern society, and alternative forms are emerging which include both members not formerly defined as kin, and an increase in multigenerational relationships (Bengtson, 2001). Furthermore, as Waite (2000) has recently pointed out, despite considerable structural changes, the family still retains responsibility for reproduction, socialization, co-residence, and transmission of property across the generations. It is also a major unit of consumption, and still provides the majority of support and care to older adults (Logan and Spitze, 1996), and almost all the financial, emotional, and instrumental support to children. Let us conclude by highlighting three roles that the contemporary family can play in the context of ageing societies.

Families as Mechanisms for Intergenerational Support

Despite the growth in modern dispersed living arrangements (Grundy, 1987; Grundy and Harrop, 1992; Roberts and McGlone, 1996) and individualistic values (Scott, 1999), individuals remain committed to the reciprocal care and support of kin. As is evident in many of the chapters of this book, in particular Chapters 4, 5, 6, 7, and 8, families, nuclear and extended, step- and reconstituted, still provide the locus of reciprocal care, particularly when there are older adults among the kin network. With the increasing number and proportion of older adults within developed countries, this will increase in significance over the next few decades.

Intergenerational transfer of care and services are age-related. While they generally flow from older to younger generations, these decline during the life course, and those from younger to older generations increase. From a peak of parent-to-child transfers when the parents are in their early sixties and/or the children are young adults, this declines rapidly so that as the parent reaches the mid-seventies, child-to-parent transfers begin to dominate, though this scenario questions whether there is sufficient recognition of the full extent of services provided by parents to their children, even in extreme old age. These reciprocal relationships are also dependent on the health and economic resources, commitments, and life stage of the individuals, and increasingly on changing family structures and networks. Two broad elements of such reciprocal care comprise care for older adults by other older or younger adults, and care for children by younger adults (typically parents) and older adults (typically grandparents).

There has been considerable research into care for older people by kin (see Binstock and George, 2001, for a full review). While within most western societies there are no formal mechanisms to ensure family care in late life, it is possible to identify a series of determinants of support criteria used by individuals to select kin caregivers. In most cases, those defined as closest to the care recipient are most likely to provide maximum support. This is typically the spouse or child, in the latter case most likely the daughter.

Despite the fact that grandparents occupy an 'expanding' position within the family (Roberto and Stroes, 1995), the care and support to dependent children by older adults has not been as well developed. Various estimates suggest that just under a third of both the US's and UK's population are grandparents (Tunaley, 1998). Currently 60 million American adults are grandparents, forecast to reach 80 million by the end of the decade—a role which may last up to forty years (Kornhaber, 1996), though twenty-five years appears to be the average. In addition, there is the apparently growing phenomenon of grandparents assuming primary responsibility for raising grandchildren (Fuller-Thompson, Minkler, and Driver, 1997), with some 5.4 million children being cared for full-time by their grandparents.

What is clear from several of the following chapters is that at the very time in which the family may be called upon to provide reciprocal care, both upwards and downwards through the generations, societal and familial-based tensions are also challenging the available kin nexus of care. The emergence of these new family forms has thus ignited considerable interest into the question whether the new and complex myriad of family forms will be able to sustain the care and support required for the demographically ageing population in the twenty-first century. While Silverstein and Long (1998) have argued that new multigenerational relationships are emerging which provide a latent network of kin (after Riley and Riley, 1993) that can be activated in time of need, we still clearly need more cross-cultural research into this question.

Families as Mechanisms for Intergenerational Solidarity

An equally important question is whether contemporary families are able both to support the close micro level intergenerational interaction needed for societies to successfully age, and to understand the importance of intergenerational relations and the family as a means of providing a vital link between the macro and micro experience of change within ageing societies. The concern in the mid-1980s, particularly in the US, that demographic ageing, necessitating a considerable shift in resource allocation towards older people, would result in intergenerational age wars has not yet been justified. As Foner (2000) points out, younger cohorts have not risen up to protest against policies which benefit older adults; policies which may seem to operate against the interests of younger and mid-life people. First, younger people have a stake in protecting public programmes for older adults because these programmes relieve them of financial responsibility for the elderly people in their own families. Second, as Achenbaum argues in Chapter 2, younger adults wish to protect these programmes for their own old age. What may be of more significance, however, is the relationship between the macro and micro experience of social relations. For while these public programmes operate at the national level, most people actually experience them at the individual, family, or community level. First-hand knowledge of people of other ages typically comes from local and family settings. Younger people thus do not experience older people as the 'other'—an unknown group of strangers—but as their own kin: parents and step-parents, grandparents and step-grandparents, etc. In other words, within the family there is *contact between and knowledge of* those of other generations. In addition, most younger people see older members of their own families benefiting from macro-level policies even if they personally do not. Such *affective intergenerational ties* form important bondings between generations. Furthermore, younger people may receive direct or indirect benefits via their links into families, and there is some element of *intergenerational transmission* within these macro programmes. However, Harper (2003) argues that ageing societies benefit from strong kin interaction at the very time that intimate kin interactions are changing due to the pressures emanating from and associated with demographic ageing. While there has been interest from US researchers in the question of ageing, intergenerational solidarity, and intergenerational ambivalence, most recently by the historian Achenbaum (Chapter 2), and sociologists Bengston (2001) and Luscher, this has tended to concentrate on the dynamics within the family *per se*. In particular, this work has focused on whether multigenerational families can replace socialization, nurturance, and support roles formerly carried out by nuclear families as marital instability and divorce weakens the ability of traditional nuclear families to provide these, a question which is also taken up in some detail by Lang in Chapter 4. Harper (2003) argues that we should also consider these new dynamics in relation to the macro/micro experience of intergenerational relations.

Families as Mechanisms for Intergenerational Transfers

The study of intergenerational transfers has broadly fallen into two categories—the transmission of goods (and services) through, for example, bequests (Hurd, 1987), and of values. We have already considered transfers of support and services. Here we shall focus on the movement of goods and values down through the generations. Economists have suggested that bequests are either altruistic (Becker, 1981) or strategic (Bernheim et al., 1985) to induce desired behaviour from descendants through the promise of bequests. However, there is evidence from HRS that the bequest motive is stronger through the blood line than through the step-line, which clearly has implications for the new family forms which are emerging. Bourdeu's concept of intergenerational transmissions and cultural capital argues that the family is institutionalized through a variety of ritual and technical mechanisms aimed at creating a shared vision of family goals. During this process, kin-based value systems are shared and transmitted from one generation to another. Again we need to know more about how this varies between different generational patterns. Finch touches upon both these issues— bequests and values—among the English kinship system in Chapter 9.

IN CONCLUSION

Early work on ageing and the family focused on the implications of demographic predictions; in other words, increasing longevity equalled increasing numbers of older people requiring care. At the same time, declining fertility was perceived as shrinking the reservoir of family care for the old, and placing increasing pressures on the middle-aged to cope both with dependent children and ageing parents. The complexity of the equation is now apparent, as well as the recognition that the environments which were producing ageing societies were also producing new family situations, and that the demise or shrinking of the family was too general a concept. Rather, more heterogeneous family forms are emerging, developing their own sets of roles and relationships. Family roles and relationships are being influenced by demography but this must also be placed in the context of wider social and cultural change. As historians Hareven (1996*b*) and Achenbaum, in the following chapter, remind us, there has always been considerable diversity in cultural obligations to family members, even within the same society, and these family obligations continually evolve and change over time.

2

Models of Kinship from the Developed World

MIKE MURPHY

INTRODUCTION

Over time, the focus of interest in empirical social research has expanded from consideration of individuals' behaviour to that of the groups in which people live together; families and households. The family is defined in statistical publications as a co-resident unit; a couple with or without never-married children or a lone parent with never-married children (United Nations Statistical Commission and Economic Commission for Europe Conference of European Statisticians, 1987). The definition reflects the western focus on the nuclear or conjugal family unit, rather than the extended family, either 'traditional' (a co-resident group containing two or more such family units) or 'modified' (a loose set of kin relations in which geographically dispersed nuclear families retain links). Since most households consist of one family only, the family definition is largely synonymous with the household in practice. 'Kin' clearly includes relatives by blood or marriage, whether or not they co-reside, and possibly non-affined fictive kin as well. As statistical data on households have become more comprehensive from sources such as the European Community Labour Force and Household Panel Surveys, more emphasis has been given to the family as a nuclear co-resident unit. In historical analysis, the concentration on co-resident groups may have been a factor in the establishment of the myth of the 'isolated nuclear family' (Hareven, 1978: 152). However, modern trends make the

Thanks are due to the Economic and Social Research Council who funded this work as part of a project *Evolving trends in British kin distributions and family life experience Ref. R000237076*; to the Zentralarchiv für Empirische Socialforschung an der Universität zu Köln for making the International Social Survey Programme data available; to The Data Archive for access to the 1995 British Social Attitudes Survey; and to the Office for National Statistics who collected the Kin Module data in the 1999 Omnibus Survey, funded by Economic and Social Research Council grants reference numbers R000237776 and R000237076 and to Dr Emily Grundy (London School of Hygiene and Tropical Medicine) and Olwen Rowlands (ONS) in preparing the questions used. The original collectors, the Zentralarchiv, and The Data Archive bear no responsibility for the analyses or interpretation presented here.

existence of wider kin networks potentially much more important than hith-
erto. As discussed in Chapter 1, there are now over four million divorced
people in Britain, the great majority of whom have a former partner alive. In
1991 there were three million dependent children living apart from one or both
natural parents, one million living in stepfamilies (Haskey, 1994; Shaw and
Haskey, 1999). These children have complex networks of relations and differing degrees of contact with both natural and stepparents, and other kin such as
grandparents (Bumpass, Martin et al., 1991; Cherlin and Furstenberg, 1994),
which we shall explore in later Chapters 4 and 5. At the other end of the age
range, there were three million people aged 65 and over living alone in Britain
in 1991, the majority of whom have living kin who form a major resource for
social contact and support, but do not live with their elderly relatives as would
have been common in the past (Wall, Robin, and Laslett, 1983).

From a lifecourse perspective, an individual will move through a variety of
household and family states and many of the relationships made will remain
important long after they were formed. Relatives such as grandparents, aunts,
and uncles with whom an individual never lived may also be important figures.
The boundary between the co-resident group and the rest of the world is not as
impermeable as many studies assume. Although the importance of wider networks is recognized, data on them have frequently been lacking. Key data
sources such as censuses and surveys usually collect information only on individuals and households, and information on kin and social networks has perhaps been assumed to be of 'academic' rather than 'practical' or policy interest.

Having kin is a necessary, but not a sufficient, condition for receiving and
giving kin contact and support. Over recent generations, the nature of kinship
universes has altered as changing levels of fertility and mortality and, more
recently, patterns of family formation and dissolution have altered the numbers and types of kin (Smith, 1987; Wachter, 1997). Thus it is also necessary
to relate kinship interactions to the number and types of kin that exist. This
chapter considers the levels and patterns of kin interaction by a variety of
demographic, socio-economic, and cultural factors in order to establish which
of these have the major role in determining 'day-to-day' social contact between
kin rather than the determinants of the provision of care. Since many of the
basic parameters of kin interaction have not been comprehensively documented, especially at the cross-national level, a key objective is to establish the
main patterns of interaction.

PREVIOUS WORK

As Harper discussed in Chapter 1, surprisingly little work has been done in
developed countries on the topic of kin interactions using large nationally
representative data sources. This may be because the major funders such as
governments have often given it low priority, except perhaps in the special case
of older people, and because the disciplines which have traditionally been

interested in this area, anthropology and sociology, have often preferred to use locally-based research designs. The classic examples in Britain include Young and Willmott's (1957) study of family and kinship in Bethnal Green, at that time a traditional working-class community in the East End of London, although one where the social composition has changed substantially in recent decades, and smaller studies such as Firth (1956) of about 75 people living in a South London housing estate and 50 Italians living in London, Bott (1957) of 20 middle-class families, and Rosser and Harris's (1965) survey of 2,000 people in Swansea. Local studies, whose strength is their sensitivity to the specific nature of local communities, provide little usable information on national-level patterns or on broader trends through time, but by default have frequently had to take on these roles. For example, Hunt (1973) found that the proportion of married women with dependent children who saw their living mother less than once a week was over twice as high in an outer London borough as in a Welsh county in 1970; 55 per cent compared with 25 per cent. These local studies were rarely analysed using statistical methods, and indeed their designs were such that generalization to wider populations was not possible, which may account for the lack of reproducibility of early studies. While overall national figures may conceal substantial local variations, they are indispensable for putting local studies into context, and for making comparisons between countries and across time.

Moreover, Parsons' (1949; 1964) influential theoretical functionalist arguments had been interpreted—possibly simplistically—as suggesting that kinship ties should be becoming increasingly weak in industrialized societies. Adams (1970: 575) referred to the implicit assumption in the 1940s that 'kin are relatively unimportant to the functioning of modern society and the nuclear family is comparatively isolated from its kin'. As a consequence, a considerable body of work in the 1960s and 1970s was devoted to the analysis of this issue. Topics such as the relationship between social mobility and kinship interaction that were thought to be particularly relevant to this debate received considerable attention. Indeed studies devoted to the investigation of social mobility have been major source of data on kinship interactions, but their limitations for investigating more general aspects of kinship than for their originally intended purpose must be recognized. Goldthorpe and Llewellyn's (1987) analysis concentrated on social class differences in the British 1974 Social Mobility Survey. They concluded that there were substantial differences in the frequency of contact with close kin, with considerably lower proportions of intergenerationally stable professional workers than manual workers meeting close kin at least weekly, 45 per cent compared with 81 per cent. However, these proportions were much closer both when the reference period was one month, 87 per cent compared with the 92 per cent, and when analysis was confined to weekly contact with kin living within about 10 minutes walking distance. They attributed the large overall differences to the greater geographical mobility of higher social class groups, which inhibited frequent contact.

Fischer (1982) surveyed about 1,000 adults living in northern California in 1977. His particular focus was on patterns of kin contact in relation to educational level and geographic mobility, and he found an inverse relationship with both variables. He concluded that educational differences in kin contact were eliminated when distance between kin was taken into account and, indeed, distance was the only useful explanatory variable. However, other forms of contact, such as by telephone, are much less affected by distance.

While the particular importance of face-to-face contact should not be dismissed, much of it is of short duration and involves 'just keeping in touch' (Aiken and Goldberg, 1969), and other forms of contact may substitute for such casual contact. It is, moreover, possible for levels of giving and receiving kin support and assistance to decline while overall kin 'social' contact increases, or for face-to-face contact to fall while other forms of contact rise. Moreover, the relative levels of kin contact by population sub-groups, such as social class groups, may depend on whether 'contact' is defined in a broad or a narrow sense. Thus existing data sources provide a fragile base for making generalizations about the decline or otherwise of kinship ties in industrialized societies. Type of contact and proximity will be considered in more detail in later sections.

Parsons' theory received some empirical support, but a series of studies including those by Bott, Firth, Young, and Willmott (1973), and a number summarized in Sussman and Burchinal (1962) showed that wider kin ties remained important, at least until around 1960. Litwak (1960) designated the kinship system as a modified extended family one. Litwak and Szelenyi's (1969) influential comparison of USA and Hungary led them to argue that the most industrialized societies place more emphasis on nuclear family relations; that urbanization shifts the balance from kin to non-kin networks; and that countries with high mobility have weaker kin links. However, they found that the primary kin group remained important especially for emergencies and that some residues of historical family structure remain. During the 1970s, interest in kinship analysis appeared to decline (Lee, 1980). Another important source of kinship data has been studies of kin interaction of elderly people, often arising from policy concerns and usually embedded within a framework concerned with more general social networks and social support, including friends and neighbours as well as relatives (Shanas et al., 1968; Hunt, 1978; Grundy et al., 1996).

The policy process is interested in how many elderly people receive assistance from informal sources such as friends and/or relatives, but less so in who provides the help, and even less in those kin who do not do so. Such studies tend to be concerned with the patterns of contact, and more especially with the provision of care, rather than with the existence of kin *per se*, such as the series of modules about elderly people contained in the General Household Survey in 1980, 1985, 1991, and 1994 (see e.g. Office of Population Censuses and Surveys, 1996). While questions about assistance received from children may be included, questions about whether the respondent has any children are rarer. With the pressure on the number of questions in surveys, sponsors may prefer to include more questions on types of help received rather than questions on numbers of kin, but as a consequence, important variables such as the proportion of relatives who provide assistance cannot be calculated. The main focus in such studies has tended to be on kin support rather than on kin availability or kin social networks. However, this narrow focus may be too restrictive even for policy purposes. In recent years the key role of kin and other social networks in maintaining health and in promoting recovery have come to be recognized. For example, House, Landis, and Umberson (1988) commented that the appreciation of the importance of social networks for health at that time was at a similar level to that of smoking as a risk factor for mortality and morbidity in the mid-1960s. More recently, the increasing importance of extra-household kin relationships arising from emerging family forms due to increased union breakdown, the ageing of developed society populations, and the recognition of the importance of social networks have led to renewed interest, and therefore patterns of contact forms the subject of this chapter. Among other disciplines, historians have tended to emphasize demographic influences on kinship (Wellman and Wetherell, 1996) and formal modelling of kinship universes remains an active, if relatively specialized, area of demographic research (Wachter et al., 1978; Smith, 1987; Wolf, 1994; Zhao, 1996).

DATA AND METHODS

The rest of this chapter considers the types and frequency of contact with kin of various degrees of relationship. The data are drawn from the 1986 set of the co-ordinated surveys referred to in Chapter 1 which were undertaken as part of the International Social Survey Programme (ISSP), which included seven countries; Australia, Austria, the former Federal Republic of Germany, Great Britain, Hungary, Italy and the United States. Sample sizes were around 1,000 to 2,000 adults in each country (see Table 2.1). These data were collected in a co-ordinated way and therefore they permit more comparable analysis than would otherwise be the case.[1]

Two analyses using the cross-nationally representative data on kin and social networks used in this chapter have been undertaken, although with rather different emphases. Finch (1989) was principally concerned with contact and support, gender relations, and the respective roles of families and friends, but she also drew attention to the large differences in kin contact between countries. Höllinger and Haller's (1990) interest was in the thesis that more modern societies had looser kin ties than more traditional ones: they

---

[1] Because of the sample designs, it is necessary to weight some of the country surveys in order to make the results representative of the country and therefore to be comparable between countries and other groups. For example, the British survey was based on a random sample of households in which one adult was interviewed. Therefore those in households with n adults have only $1/n$ of the overall chance of being included as those living alone. All results here have been appropriately weighted.

M. Murphy

Table 2.1. *Sample sizes by age (weighted), ISSP kinship module 1986*

Age group	Australia (Oz)	Austria (Aus)	Federal Republic of Germany (FRG)	Great Britain (GB)	Hungary (Hun)	Italy (Ita)	United States (USA)
16–24	173	185	426	186	120	156	143
25–34	316	176	485	260	200	195	379
35–44	256	160	441	285	177	194	301
45–54	179	163	515	217	152	193	188
55–64	176	136	441	220	128	151	174
65+	150	180	568	219	135	111	285
Total	1250	1000	2876	1387	912	1000	1470

Note: Mnemonics for countries used in later tables are given in parentheses.

concluded that Americans and Australians had weaker links than Britons, Germans, and Austrians, and that Italians and Hungarians maintained the highest levels. While socio-economic influences were found to exist, they argued that cultural factors, dating back to pre-industrial times, were also important in understanding these differences.

Although information was collected on a wide range of living adult kin types including father and mother, brothers and sisters, sons and daughters, aunts and uncles, in-laws, grandparents, and grandchildren of all ages, attention will be concentrated on the three primary kin types of parents, sibs, and adult children. The information collected on these kin groups included whether they were co-resident with the respondent, and the frequency and types of contact. The indicators of kin contact used subsequently for each of these three kin types are as given in Box 2.1. Questions 3 and 4 refer to the relative of the particular type with whom the respondent has the most contact, and 5 to the one who lives closest. Questions were asked about male and female kin separately, the response showing the greater interaction which has been taken.

Box 2.1. *Indicators of kin contact*

1. Does the respondent have any such living relative?
2. If there are living kin, does the respondent live with at least one of them?
3. If there are only non co-resident kin, does the respondent meet or visit at least one of them once a week or more often?
4. As question 3, but based on all forms of contact including writing, phoning, etc. at least once a week.
5. For those with only non co-resident kin, whether any live within 30 minutes journey time from the respondent.

Box 2.2. *Main variables in the analysis*

1. Age-group, sex, marital status, and availability of kin as demographic factors.
2. Educational level and social class as socio-economic factors.
3. Country and religious participation as reflecting cultural factors.

The main variables used in the analysis are as given in Box 2.2. While such a typology is simplified, it serves to indicate which of these broad domains are likely to provide the best explanations of differentials in patterns of kin inter-action. In addition to age, sex, and marital status, the number of the relevant kin type is used as a demographic variable, since how kin interaction varies with the number of kin is not obvious. For example, if visiting parents is con-sidered to be a chore to be shared among sibs, then the more sibs, the less expected interaction per sib. However, if large families have more overall con-tact, then seeing parents may be more frequent among those with more sibs. There could also be 'competition' from other types of kin, for example, those with older children may reduce contact with their own parents.

Educational level is used as the main example of a socio-economic variable for a number of reasons. It is available for all countries; there are very few missing variables compared with occupationally derived measures such as social class; it is a variable that is largely fixed across a person's adulthood; and it is highly associated with other indicators of social status such as social class and income, and correlated with proximity (Fischer, 1982). Because num-ber of years of schooling varies substantially between age groups and coun-tries, the same number of years of schooling could indicate a highly educated older person, but a poorly educated young person, since the overall level has increased over time. Therefore within each country, sex, and age group, the quantiles of years spent in education are calculated and the educational level variable divided into three groups of approximately equal size, the bottom third, the middle third, and the top third. Thus it measures the value relative to comparable groups rather than the absolute level. This method of con-struction has the added advantage of ensuring that education is uncorrelated with age and country of residence.

Some analyses by self-reported social class are also presented since this has been extensively analysed but analyses of social class differentials compared with less widely discussed variables are rare. Because the question was worded differently in different countries, the variable has had to be categorized into two groups only; middle-class and working/lower-class, for making cross-national comparisons. These data were not collected in Hungary, and much higher pro-portions in the Anglophone countries reported themselves as working class than in the other countries, so lower emphasis is given to this variable.

Country is used as the principal indicator of 'culture' in this analysis. Space precludes discussion of the definition of this term (see Hammel (1990) for an extended discussion). Firth (1956) and Litwak (1965) noted that the kinship systems in southern and eastern Europe gave more emphasis to extra-nuclear kin than the western European model. Other variables that might be expected to reflect aspects of 'culture' were also examined. For example religion has been shown to be associated with different patterns of kin interaction (Winch et al., 1967). Religious denomination is highly correlated with country, and may in part reflect ascribed and passive, rather than achieved or active status. Therefore the frequency of church attendance as an additional cultural variable is used.

While not comprehensive, this set of variables includes a number that previous studies have identified as potentially important in the discussion of kinship differentials.

RESULTS OF THE ANALYSIS

Availability of Kin by Age

Figure 2.1 shows the proportions of respondents with living kin of various types averaged over the seven contemporary developed countries: these data have been smoothed to reduce sampling fluctuations. Whether one's parent(s) are alive depends on parental age at the child's birth and their experience of older age mortality (Coale, 1965). Virtually all of those in their early twenties have both parents alive, though of course, some may have lost contact with one or both natural parents for various reasons. The crossover point—the age at which half of the sample has a parent alive and half has not—is about 40 years for father alive and 50 for mother alive. However, the variability is also of interest: the interquartile range for deaths of fathers and of mothers is about 20 years: this period is when half of these events occur, and it is a substantial period of time that leads to consequent variation in people's life experiences (Figs. 2.1a and 2.1d). The median age for losing the first parent is 38, and for both parents it is 51. People who have only one parent alive may have a different relationship with the remaining parent than before. Older respondents are much more likely to have a surviving mother than a surviving father since fathers on average are older than mothers at the birth of their children and they suffer higher mortality. Although some differentials do exist by variables such as country and educational level, these are small compared with the age effect.

There are fewer adult living sibs at the youngest and oldest ages because some sibs of young respondents will be below age 18, and some sibs of the oldest group will have died. However, having living sibs is a much more enduring phenomenon than having living parents or adult children. Over 80 per cent of people have a brother or sister alive for the great majority of their adulthood. While the chance of having a sister remains high, at around two-thirds, the proportion with a brother starts to decline from about age 50 as higher mortality among older age males sets in.

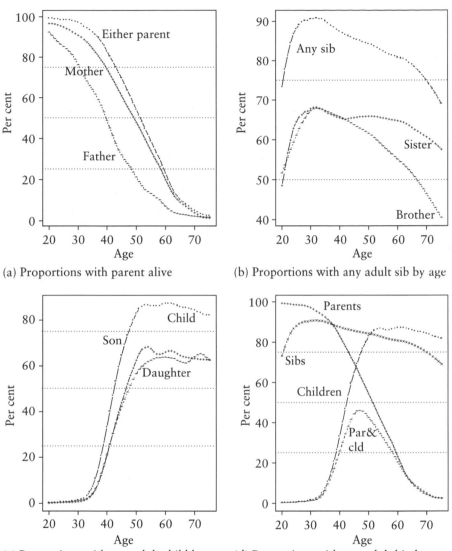

(a) Proportions with parent alive (b) Proportions with any adult sib by age

(c) Proportions with any adult child by age (d) Proportions with any adult kin by age

Fig. 2.1. Availability of kin by age (Source: ISSP, 1986)

The proportions with adult children rise from a low level among young adults whose children are unlikely to be over age 18, but remains at about 80 per cent from age 45 when the proportion with at least one son is around 60 per cent, and the same proportion have at least one daughter.

Figure 2.1*d* shows that the proportions with both adult children and parents has been small, never reaching 50 per cent for any age group and being above

25 per cent only for those between ages 40 and 60. Thus while the existence of ascendant and descendent kin may lead to particular demands, in quantitative terms, the proportions in this situation are relatively small.

Interactions with Primary Kin by Age and Sex

Having considered the existence of primary kin, we shall now discuss levels and types of kin contact, using graphical presentations to draw out some of the main features of kin interaction.[2]

Age and sex differentials are important: older people are more likely to live with their children than those of late middle age, and mothers and married daughters are likely to have particularly cohesive bonds. Figure 2.2 shows patterns of kin interaction by sex and age group by those with kin of the particular type. Thus overall levels of contact with a parent, for example, will be the product of the proportion with a parent alive shown in Fig. 2.1 and the proportion of these that maintain contact with their living parent shown in Fig. 2.2. Since there are broadly similar numbers of men and women in each age group, except at older ages where there are relatively more women, the overall trend with age is effectively the simple average of the male and female values.

A particularly intense form of contact exists when the child lives with his or her parent(s). As would be expected, co-residence with adult kin apart from a spouse is relatively rare once the children of the family depart, showing only some tendency to increase among older groups. Young adults, especially men, are likely to be living with their parents, but having left the parental home, daughters have more contact with their parents than do sons, and mothers have more contact with their daughters than do fathers in almost every age group and for every type of contact, as expected given the evidence from earlier studies of the importance of contact between mothers and daughters (Young and Willmott, 1957; Komarovsky, 1964; Sweetser, 1964). These differentials are most pronounced for the variable measuring all types of contact, indicating that women take a disproportionate role in maintaining links through non face-to-face contact, such as by telephoning, writing, etc. Overall, women have about 50 per cent more contact with parents and about 25 per cent more contact with adult children than men do. However, the pattern of more contact by women than men with their sibs is seen only at older age groups. There is some evidence that changing to a more nuclear family model involves a shift from the dominance of male instrumental to female expressive kin contacts. However, more recently, Willmott (1987) found that the results of his early studies in both working-class and middle-class areas, which showed very strong

---

[2] Graphical presentation is used since it conveys more information than tables, and the relatively small sample sizes would require sophisticated statistical models that may be inaccessible to many. Small sample size groups have been excluded from the panels, and the main emphasis is on the overall patterns shown. For a discussion of the ways in which the maximum amount of information may be obtained from graphical information and, in particular, from the sorts of charts produced using the S-PLUS Trellis graphical system, see Becker et al. (1996).

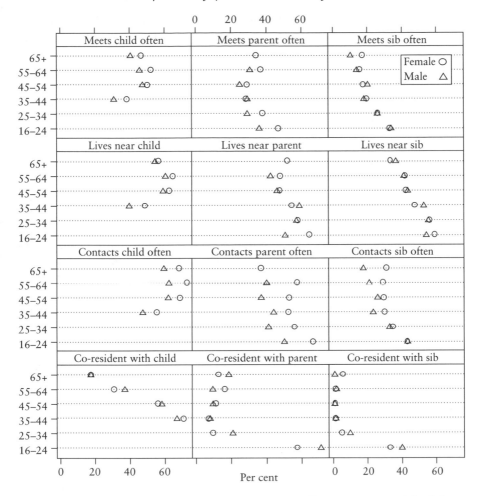

Fig. 2.2. Kin interaction by sex and age (ISSP 1986: All *N* >20 using weighted data 'often' meets/any contact with non-resident kin more than weekly; 'lives near' is within 30 minutes)

mother–daughter ties, were not replicated in his more recent ones, which show the possibility that this bond may be weakening (see also McGlone, Park et al. (1996)).

We expect considerable differences in kin interaction by age, since age is both an important factor in its own right and also because it is associated with changes in lifecourse stage (Leigh, 1982). At young ages, the volume of contact with mothers and fathers is broadly similar; unsurprising since visits will often be to the parental home.[3] Contact with sibs tends to decline with age,

---

[3] For this reason, visits to mothers and fathers are not distinguished, but consider the greatest frequency of contact with any parent considered (i.e. the more frequent of contact with mothers and fathers taken if they are both alive).

which may be due to the fact that when the sib with whom there was most contact dies, then there may be reduced contact with the surviving sibs; see Figure 2.1. However, women maintain constant levels of contact with sibs from the mid-30s, with about one third reporting contact at least weekly, whereas the figure for men is only about half of this level by age 65 and over.

The parent/child bond is stronger than those between other non-co-resident kin. Contact with direct descent kin, parents, and children, shows a rather different pattern from that with sibs. Contact with children peaks for both men and women around age 60, before declining at older ages. However, the data for the 35–44 group are not fully comparable to older age groups since at these ages most children will still be living with their parents whereas the contact variable relates only to those with all children away from home, and such families are likely to be atypical. These parents must have had children relatively early since children over 18 would have had to be born before the parent was aged 26 to be included, and the children will be at the lower end of the 16–24 age range. If allowance is made for these selection effects, the pattern of contact reported by parents is much more nearly constant with age. At older ages difficulty with mobility may inhibit visiting.

Children, on the other hand, report generally declining levels of contact with age. Reports from parents and children should reflect the overall level of parent–child contact from the viewpoints of the two generations. Parents report more contact than their children do: for example, just over 60 per cent of parents aged over 45 claim to have contact with their children at least weekly, whereas just under 50 per cent of children under age 35 report this level of contact with their parents. Since the parent respondent is asked about the child with whom they have *most* contact, whereas the child respondent is a *random* sib who will have less contact on average, the results are therefore consistent.

The event of marriage (and increasingly cohabitation) provides a new and important addition to the kin network and it is likely to lead to changes in interaction with the existing network, especially as partnership is often followed by birth of children. Figure 2.3 shows how contact varies by marital status of the respondent. Because there are relatively small numbers in some marital status groups, adjacent age groups have been combined. Those who are widowed have most contact with parents and children, presumably reflecting their need for support following bereavement, and they are also much more likely to live close to their kin. However, those whose marriages have ended in the alternative way of divorce or separation have considerably *less* contact, not only with their adult children (a proportion of fathers, in particular, are likely to lose contact relatively soon after breakdown), but also with their own parents, where rates of contact are only about half of those by the widowed group (Lye, 1996).

While the finding of less contact with their children by divorced and separated parents than those of other marital statuses holds across countries, this relationship reflects in part the fact that countries where divorce is common,

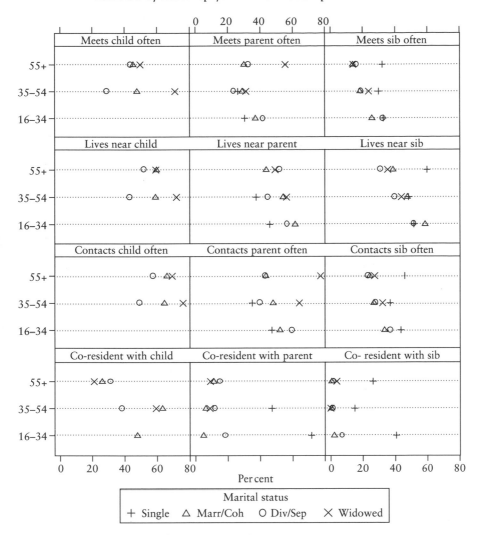

Fig. 2.3. **Kin interaction by marital status and age (ISSP 1986: All N>20 using weighted data)**

such as USA, Australia, and Britain, have lower overall rates of contact than do countries where it has been rarer, such as Italy and Austria.

Contact with sibs shows a different pattern by marital status, with single people having considerably more contact with their sibs than other groups, a finding common across all countries. In the absence of a spouse, sib relationships remain strong. Single people have about double the amount of contact with their sibs compared to ever-married people, but they do not have more contact with parents. Sib contact may provide interaction with people of the

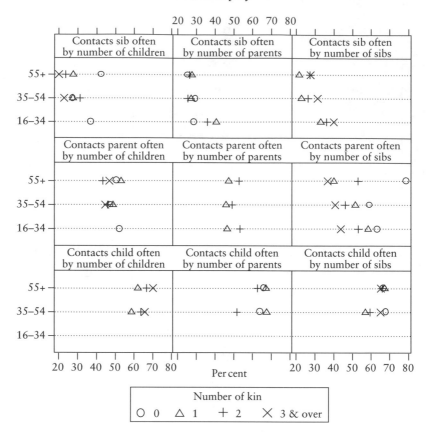

Fig. 2.4. Contact with kin by number of kin and age (ISSP 1986: All $N > 20$ using weighted data)

same generation as the respondent that would otherwise be available from one's partner, and sibling relations may become more important at old ages (Cumming and Schneider, 1961). Although the number of single people with children is small, they have less contact with their children than those of other marital statuses. In almost all cases, kin interaction by married/cohabiting people is intermediate between other marital status groups.

The constellations of kin may also affect patterns of contact. Figure 2.4 shows how this varies according to the numbers in the types of kin with whom contact is made (panels along the backward-sloping diagonal), and with other kin (all other panels). For reasons of space, only the frequent contact variable is shown; the 3+ category is irrelevant for the number of living parents. For contact with sibs, the main conclusions are that those without children at older ages have considerably more contact, in part related to the marital status differentials noted in Fig. 2.3, and that those with larger numbers of sibs have more contact with at least one sib than those with smaller numbers. Since they will, in addition, have contact with other sibs as well, the overall level of contact would appear to be more than proportionate with number of sibs. Although there is a tendency for one child to take on the primary caring role if there are two or more children, it seems unlikely that more general contact is so concentrated. Thus those parents with larger families are likely to have more contact with children in old age.

While there is little variation in contact with parents by number of children, from about age 35 there is more contact with parents when both parents are alive, although a bereaved parent is more likely to co-reside with her or his child and such cases are excluded from this analysis of non co-resident kin. A striking finding is that the pattern of contact with parents by number of sibs is bimodal, with those with no or three or more sibs being much more likely to have contact with parents at all ages than those with one or two sibs. The mechanisms may be different, in that an only child may have sole responsibility and hence require frequent contact, whereas overall kin contact is higher in 'kin rich' families. Conversely, the bimodal pattern is not found for contact reported by parents with children, but there is a steady rise with numbers of children, suggesting different mechanisms are at work in large and small families. Finally, there are no corresponding clear relationships in the patterns of contact with any of these types of relative according to number of children, apart from a tendency for contact with the one designated child in the survey to rise with the overall number of children.

Socio-economic Variations in Contact

Some of the studies discussed earlier and in later chapters, show that levels and patterns of interaction vary between different social status groups. However, the literature is mixed and the generalizability of these results is unclear. Among those of higher socio-economic status, young people may have more contact with parents because of longer periods of dependency, and at the other end of the age range, such groups may be better able to have elderly parents living with them. Upwardly mobile groups are less traditional in behaviour and more geographically mobile, so they have reduced face-to-face contact with kin as a consequence. However, this could be offset by alternative means of contact. Bell (1968) suggested that middle-class families are able to use greater financial resources to overcome distance, and Finch's (1989) tentative conclusion is that geographical mobility does not necessarily weaken family ties, though it may alter the type of interaction.

Figure 2.5 shows variations in kin interaction by relative educational status. Those with the lowest educational level both have most fact-to-face contact and live closer to their kin, while those with the highest level have the least contact, apart from interactions with children where the intermediate group has the highest rates. Differentials in face-to-face meeting and living nearby are very similar as would be expected. The highly educated live further from their kin, and even when all forms of communication are taken into account, they still have less contact, especially with sibs, where the differences tend to be

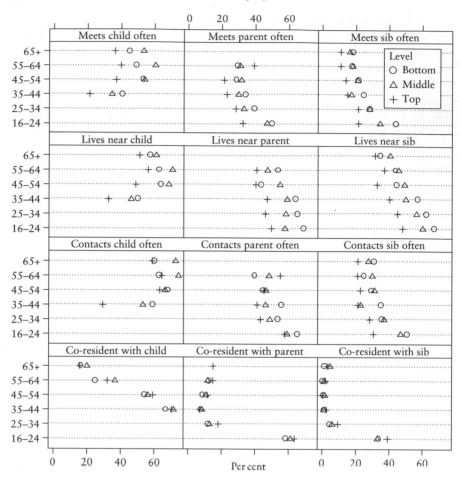

Fig. 2.5. Kin interaction by age and educational level (ISSP 1986: All $N > 20$ using weighted data)

greatest; the main exception is that there is more contact with parents among older well-educated people. Thus not only do the better educated have less contact, but they also have a narrower focus on direct kin in their contacts. The magnitude of educational differentials are at least as marked among young as among older groups, which is consistent with those theoretical arguments that suggest more 'modern' groups are less likely to maintain kin links. However, educational differentials are relatively small, especially when all forms of contact are taken into account, and they are generally much less than those found, for example, between men and women.

The relationship between social class and kin contact has been a topic of considerable interest. In the ISSP, respondents were asked for their self-assessed social class, apart from Hungary. The actual codes used varied, so that classes such as 'upper' or 'lower' were options in some countries but not in others. Therefore a broad dichotomy of lower/working and middle/upper has had to been used. The proportions in the former group were around 50 per cent in the Anglophone countries, but around 20 per cent in the other three countries, with Italy having the lowest value. Since patterns might be expected to differ between men and women, these have been shown separately. Figure 2.6 indicates higher levels of co-residence among the middle/upper class group (this holds even if the Italian

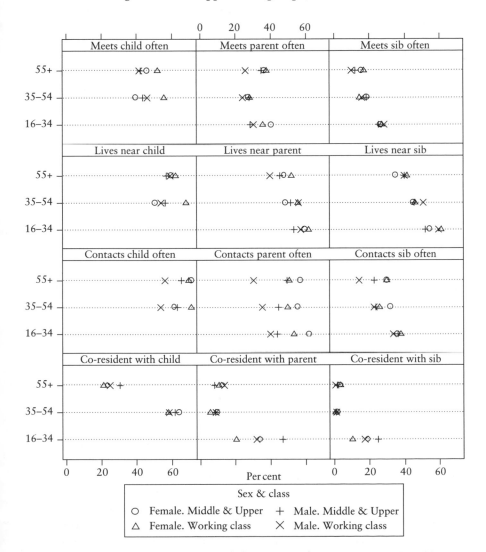

Fig. 2.6. Kin interaction by social class, sex, and age (ISSP 1986: N > 20 using weighted data)

data are excluded), possibly reflecting the longer period of dependency of the young people in this class. Those in the working class group are slightly more likely to live close to their kin, but while levels of a face-to-face contact are broadly similar, the middle/upper-class group has generally higher levels of all types of contact, and substantially so in the case of contact with parents. These findings appear to contradict the commonly held assumption that kin contact is more common in working-class families. The main difference between classes is accounted for by the much lower rates of contact by working-class men by means other than face-to-face meeting, where rates are typically only half of those of middle-class women. There is much greater similarity in the levels of contact of men and women in middle-class than in working-class families, suggesting less gender-stereotyped behaviour. However, once more, the main conclusion is that overall differences in kin contact by social class are relatively small. Some of the observed social class differentials arise from the fact that those in higher classes are more highly educated.

Variations in Contact According to 'Cultural' Factors

There is evidence that contact between kin varies substantially between different countries (Grundy, 1992) and between ethnic groups (Murphy, 1996) based on evidence about the specific case of co-residence. These differentials in co-residence cannot be explained by the differing socio-economic characteristics of the groups involved and may be regarded as 'cultural' in nature. It has been argued that country differences are of long standing, likely to be highly persistent, and to reflect two distinct European patterns (Reher, 1998). Figure 2.7 shows variations in kin contact by country. In order to maximize the visual information in these data, the countries have been ranked by increasing levels of contact averaged over the twelve indicators shown here. The most striking finding, and one that will also be stressed later, is the substantial differences between countries, so that, for example, half of those aged 35–44 in Italy see a living parent more than weekly, compared with around a quarter of those in Britain or the USA and one-eighth of those in Australia. In almost all cases, the ranking of countries is consistent with the Anglophone countries, Australia, Britain, and the US, having the lowest contact, West Germany next, followed by Hungary and Austria, and Italy has the highest level of contact on all twelve variables shown here. The range of variation is generally much greater than for other variables considered: for example, the overall proportions having contact with children, parents and sibs are 2.0, 2.9, and 1.7 times as large in Italy as in Britain respectively.

These data reinforce the findings from co-residence and country-specific studies that there are high levels of kin interaction in parts of southern Europe such as Italy (Barbagli, 1997). Contact is not only greater but also broader in that the largest differentials are found for the variable of contact with sibs; for which the Italian figure is three times that for Britain. However, the main

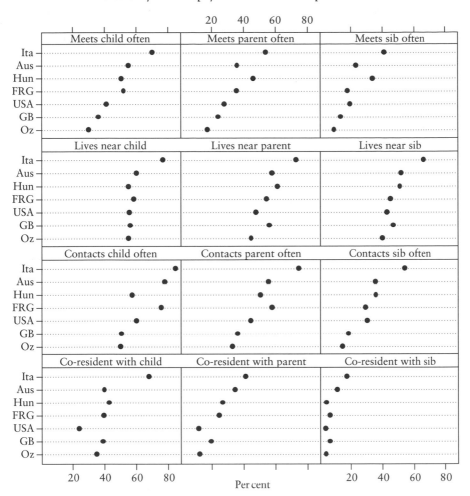

Fig. 2.7. Kin interaction by country and age (ISSP 1986: All *N* > 20 using weighted data)

conclusion is that there are not two well-defined kinship systems, but rather a continuum with Italy at on extreme and Australia at the other.

To investigate whether country retains an independent effect when other variables are considered simultaneously, a number of additional analyses were undertaken, and country was found to retain its importance. Figure 2.8 shows one such analysis, including the variable of frequency of church attendance as an alternative 'cultural' variable, which might be expected to be related to kin contact. In general, the higher the level of attendance, the more kin contact across all countries, but its magnitude is smaller than the country effect. Therefore, living in Italy rather than Britain tells much more about likely patterns of kin interaction than

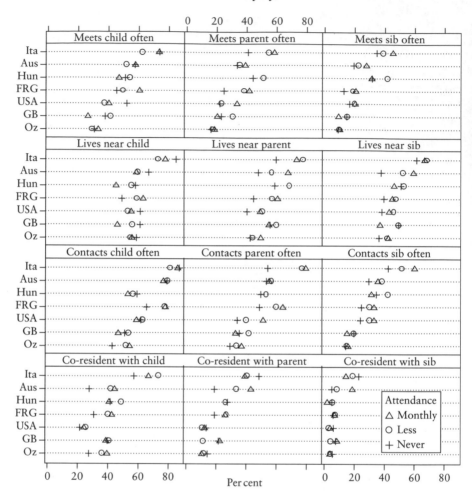

Fig. 2.8. Kin interaction by church attendance and country (ISSP 1986: All
N > 20 using weighted data)

whether a person is highly or poorly educated, working or middle class, or a
regular church attendee or not.

SUMMARY AND CONCLUSIONS

There has been a prolonged debate about whether kinship is 'weak' or not in
contemporary industrialized societies. However, 'weak' is rarely quantified
and to that extent, such labelling is arbitrary. However, given two or more estimates of kin interaction, it is usually clear which is the stronger. On this basis,
variation by country shows the most pronounced differences across all aspects
considered here. Variations by age are large, whereas those by socio-economic

characteristics are smaller. Existence of kin is a precondition for interaction, and availability of kin has importance for some patterns of interaction.

Segalen's (1997) opening sentence in a recent book, *Family and Kinship in Europe*, stated: 'family patterns in Europe are becoming increasingly indistinguishable', and that while it is not inescapable, 'there will come a time when we shall lose our national and regional distinctions and uniformity will reign with European families responding in the same way to a common policy'. On the other hand, Reher (1998) draws a sharp distinction between 'weak-family' societies; Scandinavia, the British Isles, the Low Countries, North America, parts of Germany and Austria, among which there are four countries in the ISSP sample (and Australia would presumably be included in this group also), and Mediterranean 'strong-family' societies (which includes Italy). He states that there is a major discontinuity between such societies: 'the elderly who do not maintain regular contact with their children are a small minority of the population [in strong-family societies such as Spain], much as are the aged in weak-family societies who receive regular weekly or daily visits from their children', although no evidence is cited for such a bold claim (Reher, 1998: 212). However, the figures for patterns of contact by the over-65s with their children shown in Table 2.2 suggest no evidence of a qualitative difference between Italy and the rest, but of a steady trend stretching from Italy to the USA and Australia (where, of course, geographical distances and population mobility are likely to inhibit face to face contact). In contrast to Reher's assumption, Austria is clearly closer to Italy in its kinship interaction pattern than to the Anglophone countries, and the assertion that elderly people who receive regular visits are a small minority in these latter societies is incorrect.

A number of authors including Reher have argued that contemporary kinship systems reflect patterns existing for many centuries. Few other aspects of contemporary society are believed to be so persistent, and it is implied that kinship systems will retain their distinctive nature in decades to come. However, it has been difficult to test this assertion, since few nationally representative data sets exist and therefore the possibility of making comparisons over time is very limited. However, Townsend's study in 1962 (Shanas et al., 1968) collected information about face-to-face contact by people aged 65 and over with any of their living children; similar questions to the ISSP ones were also included in the British Social Attitudes Survey in 1995 based on the child with whom there was most contact, and in the Omnibus Survey Kin Module (Grundy et al., 1999) based on contact with the eldest child reported by parents, and with parents by a random child.[4] Although the 1986 and 1995 surveys were the most comparable, their relatively small sample sizes and short time difference means that it is not possible to establish whether any statistically significant change took place, but the much larger sample size of the 1999 survey makes comparisons possible. These three

---

[4] The Omnibus Survey, unlike the British Social Attitudes Survey and ISSP, collected ages of parents, so making it possible to measure children's reported contact with their parents over age 65.

M. Murphy

Table 2.2. *Proportion of people aged 65 and over with children who interact with them at least weekly*

Country and date	Proportion of those with all living child(ren) outside the home seeing child weekly (%)	Proportion of those with living child(ren) living with a child (%)	Proportion of those with only one living child outside the home seeing weekly (%)	Proportion of those with only one living child outside the home having any weekly contact (%)	Sample size for co-residence column (weighted)
GB 1962	77	42	(58)		1,911
Australia 1986	61	10	55	75	121
Federal Republic of Germany 1986	67	16	53	83	471
GB 1986	69	13	60	87	180
USA 1986	62	10	50	80	224
Austria 1986	82	21	84	97	147
Hungary 1986	69	33	76	84	104
Italy 1986	88	38	93	100	96
GB 1995	61	16	49	85	345
GB 1999	48	4	54	76	2,232

Note: The 1962 Survey was based on contact with any living child; the 1986 and 1995 Surveys with the child with whom the respondent had most contact; and the 1999 Survey on contact with a random sib and with the eldest sib respectively.

Sources: 1986, ISSP; 1962 derived from Shanas et al. (1968); 1995, 1995 British Social Attitudes Survey; 1999 Omnibus Survey (Grundy, Murphy & Shelton, 1999).

additional nationally representative figures from Britain have been added to show one time trend. Over these three decades, contact appears to have fallen substantially. Although some of this will have been substituted by other means of contact, such as by telephone, nevertheless, the proportion not seeing a child at least weekly fell from one in four, to about four in ten over the period.

In 1986, there were three groups; Italy and Austria with proportions over 80 per cent; Australia and the US with values on the low 60s; and the rest intermediate between these two values. Therefore the difference between so-called 'strong-family' and 'weak-family' systems is about 20 per cent. The difference in the British figures over the 30-year period covered is also about 20 per cent. The argument that kinship systems are enduring is not borne out by this evidence. Over a relatively short period in historical terms, Britain, for example, has moved from a 'strong-family' to a 'weak-family' system. Of course, kinship systems are adaptable in that face-to-face contact is substituted by other means such as telephoning, but the possibility that these reflect a more fundamental weakening of kinship patterns should not be discounted on spurious arguments that—uniquely—kinship is unaffected by wider social trends.

3

One Happy Family? Sources of Intergenerational Solidarity and Tension as Contemporary US Society Ages

W. ANDREW ACHENBAUM

INTRODUCTION

In the 1830s a young French nobleman was commissioned to go overseas to assess innovations in the treatment of prisoners in the United States. Alexis de Tocqueville submitted his findings to the appropriate authorities upon his return to France. He then elaborated upon other impressions from his travels. De Tocqueville's real interest in visiting America was to judge for himself how relative conditions of economic, social, and political equality were transforming values, institutions, and comity in the New World. Having seen his grandfather guillotined during the Revolution, the Frenchman understandably had mixed feelings about mob rule. Still, he realized that the Age of Revolution was ushering in a new order, one eclipsing aristocratic regimes. De Tocqueville's two-volume masterpiece, *Democracy in America* (1836–40), remains a useful starting point for probing aspects of the history of American society and culture. This essay begins by analysing de Tocqueville's comments on family life and intergenerational relations during the Jacksonian era.

A sense of egalitarianism permeated domestic relations in the United States, in contrast to conditions in Europe, according to de Tocqueville:

In aristocratic families the eldest son, inheriting the greater part of the property and almost all the rights of the family, becomes the chief and to a certain extent the master of his brothers. Greatness and power for him; for them, mediocrity and dependence. ...Under democratic laws all the children are perfectly equal and consequently independent; nothing brings them forcibly together, but nothing keeps them apart; and as they have the same origin, as they are trained under the same roof, as they are treated with the same care, and no peculiar privilege distinguishes or divides them, the affection and frank intimacy of early years springs up between them. (de Tocqueville, ii. 206–7)

De Tocqueville hypothesized that true brotherly love and filial affections could spring from human nature wherever conditions of equality eroded aristocratic conventions. Once feudal institutions were abolished, the Frenchman deduced, new feelings would arise that would alter not only domestic politics but also the connections that bound people to society itself. 'Democracy loosens social ties, but tightens natural ones; it brings kindred more closely together, while it throws citizens more apart' (de Tocqueville, ii. 208). De Tocqueville in this account did not characterize the family as a little commonwealth—a place to teach the young skills for getting along in the meetinghouse and the marketplace. Rather, he portrayed it as a haven from a heartless, atomistic environment.

When the American retires from the turmoil of public life to the bosom of his family, he finds in it the image of order and of peace. There his pleasures are simple and nat-ural, his joys are innocent and calm; and as he finds that an orderly life is the surest path to happiness, he accustoms himself easily to moderate his opinions as well as his tastes. While the European endeavours to forget his domestic troubles by agitating soci-ety, the American derives from his own home that love of order which he afterwards carries with him into public affairs (de Tocqueville, i. 315).

The Frenchman no doubt exaggerated family differences that he perceived on both sides of the Atlantic. Historians of the colonial era and early American republic have documented many cases of domestic cruelty, abandonment, and greed across class, ethnic, and generational lines. Slave marriages were not recog-nized as legal unions under putatively democratic laws. Yet de Tocqueville's contrast rings true: Americans, more than their European counterparts, drew a line between the types of feelings and behaviour that they expressed at home and those that they shared with outsiders. Convinced that citizens in the New World distinguished sharply between public and private spheres, the Frenchman expected to find transatlantic variations in the ways siblings treated each other as well as in the manner in which parents and their off-spring interacted.

In de Tocqueville's view, families stood on an entirely new footing in democratic regimes: 'The distance which formerly separated a father from his sons has been lessened; and that paternal authority, if not destroyed, is at least impaired' (de Tocqueville, ii. 202). He linked the erosion of patriarchy to other traits that he discovered in the New World. 'Democracy... shuts the past against the poet' (ibid. ii. 78). As a consequence of the *individualisme* that animates new regimes, 'the woof of time is every instant broken and the track of generations effaced. Those who went before are soon forgotten; of those who come after, no one has any idea' (ibid. ii. 105). Since ancient times, of course, countless men and women had chosen their own independence and self-preservation above any concern for others. The 'novel' situation reported in *Democracy in America* resulted from *individualisme*'s effect on mass behaviour. De Tocqueville admired Americans' ability to seize the day, but he worried about the rootless behaviour that individuals expressed in the process.

The United States, in the Frenchman's opinion, was a land in which every generation acted as a new people. Connections between youth and age, he posited, could be easily severed in the New World. If his speculation were correct, only bonds of filial duty prevented the aged from being forsaken. Equally troubling to de Tocqueville was the spectre of American adults failing to make provisions for their futures:

In the United States a man builds a house in which to spend his old age, and he sells it before the roof is on; he plans a garden and lets it just as the trees are coming into bearing. . . . Death at length overtakes him, but it is before he is weary of the bootless chase of that complete felicity which forever escapes him.   (de Tocqueville, ii. 144–5)

To promote *Democracy in America* had unsettling effects on people. Conditioned to ignore the lessons of the past and to treat everyone warily, Americans sought ephemeral happiness, hoping to find it near the hearth. Nor did they tarry long, for they suspected that true felicity lay elsewhere. Only a genuine wellspring of emotions (including calculations of their natural self interests) made it possible for family life to exist and for generational relations to persist in the New World.

Historians, to be sure, have challenged and revised de Tocqueville's analysis of life in Jacksonian America. We now know, for instance, that the Frenchman exaggerated 'the general equality of condition among the people' (ibid. i. 3). The 1830s witnessed greater inequality than at any other moment in US history, except during the Reagan years. Surely there was greater oppression in parts of the South than in rural Europe; it is hard to imagine that the Irish shanties in New York City were demonstrably cleaner and better than lower-class dwellings in European urban centres. No reputable US historian, moreover, ignores changes in the structure and dynamics of family life on this side of the Atlantic (some are noted below) since the antebellum period.

Nonetheless, this essay dwells on *Democracy in America* because the text offers proof that, even before our Civil War, an astute observer discerned certain facets of intergenerational tension and intergenerational solidarity that prove salient today. Kin ties remain transient and malleable. Americans are constantly on the move. Yet most of us still act as if we believe that we are part of one happy family. Many Americans are hypocritical enough to call on kin on holidays. We (pretend to) claim that blood is thicker than water. Natural affection still binds many US families together.

To wit: several trenchant studies of domestic relations in the United States after World War II invoke themes that de Tocqueville enunciated. In arguably the finest historical treatment of American families during the Cold War era, Elaine Tyler May (1988: 15) emphasizes domesticity as 'the vision of the sheltered, secure, and personally liberating family toward which homeward-bound Americans set their sights'. Families provided a place where young and old could feel good about themselves in the face of a nuclear holocaust. Since only powerful leaders could keep the world from running amok, ordinary people defied Fate by having kids, buying new cars, and living in homes in the suburbs. Mass media and mass consumption defined the contours of the nation's middle class. (Postwar America fulfilled de Tocqueville's test of relative equality. May offers statistics [p. 228] indicating that 51 per cent of all workers earned between $5,000 and $10,000 in 1955; 80 per cent made between $4,000 and $15,000.) Magazines, movies, and television provided role models to show husbands and wives, brothers and sisters, and friends and neighbours how to accept, or at least endure, one another. Ministers and counselors offered advice on teenage crises and marital problems large and small.

Not every historian celebrated the state of the contemporary American family, to be sure. In one of the great jeremiads ever published in the US, *The Culture of Narcissism*, Lasch (1978) substituted a therapeutic label ('narcissism') for the de Tocquevillian signifier, *individualisme*:

The psychological patterns associated with pathological narcissism, which in less exaggerated form manifest themselves in so many patterns of American culture—in the fascination with fame and celebrity, the fear of competition, the inability to suspend belief, the shallowness and transitory quality of personal relations, the horror of death— originate in the peculiar structure of the American family, which in turn originates in changing modes of production. Industrial production takes the father out of the home and diminishes the role he plays in the conscious life of the child. The mother attempts to make up to the child for the loss of the father, but she often lacks practical experience of childrearing. ... Both parents seek to make the family into a refuge from outside pressures, yet the very standards by which they measure their success ... [come at] the expense of spontaneous feeling, a ritualized 'relatedness' empty of real substance. (Lasch, 1978: 176)

Lasch (1978) excoriated parents' reliance on experts who tried to impose social control on relations in which mutual love might be reciprocated. But the patterns that he identified—a sense of anomie, a present disconnected from both past and future—resemble those that de Tocqueville stipulated long before Freud reformulated our modern understanding of the meanings of 'love' and 'work'.

What follows does not pretend to be an exhaustive exegesis of the history of the US family. The next section highlights developments that have altered the context in which generational relations take shape. The final section reviews some likely consequences of population ageing on domestic politics.

HOW 'OUTSIDE' AGENCIES AND EXPERTS APPROPRIATED 'TRADITIONAL' FAMILY FUNCTIONS

Unlike Europe, where 'stem' families and extended kin networks have flourished in specific ecological settings during certain historical periods, nuclear families have always been the norm in America. Except during intervals of economic necessity, married people lived together, apart from (though often in close proximity to) their relatives. Home ownership was a working-class goal that US middle and upper classes took for granted. Children lived at home, or at least considered the family dwelling their primary residence, until they were capable of living independently.

Long-term demographic changes slowly transformed this general pattern. White, native-born fertility rates began to fall in the US after the Revolution. African-American fertility rates started to decline after the Civil War, and as is discussed in Chapters 1 and 10, a racial gap remains. Rates vary for other ethnic groups as well as for Native Americans, with, in each instance, a net drop over time. These declining fertility rates might have accelerated population ageing during the nineteenth century, but this trend was offset by a complex set of (inter)national migration patterns. Some people sailed back and forth across the Atlantic; others moved from one region to another in the United States. The relative proportion of older men and women in the population actually did increase, but rarely did the growing percentage of elders attract much public comment.

Americans instead worried about youth, whom they viewed as their prime investment in the future. Public school systems were quickly established in new communities. Lawmakers lengthened the school year and expanded classes beyond the elementary-school curriculum. Getting a good job increasingly required more than mastering the basics. 'Social, political, and industrial changes', declared leading experts in 1918, 'have forced upon the school responsibilities formerly laid upon the home' (quoted in Lasch, 1978: 154). By the end of World War I, a high-school diploma was a key to success; a semester or two of college gave applicants an added edge (Fass, 1977).

Schoolteachers and principals were not the only child savers. Besides erecting prisons, Americans during the first half of the nineteenth century built almshouses and all sorts of asylums—special facilities for the deaf, for veterans, for widows. Many of these institutions also accepted infants and youth. Benevolent groups created children's aid societies, established orphanages, and designed programmes for the recalcitrant. The juvenile court, which relied on the reformatory to provide basic elements of a good home, embodied 'organized altruism, the new therapeutic conception of the state, and the appropriation of family functions by outside agencies' (Lasch, 1978: 156). By the Great Depression, Americans depended on a large cadre of 'helping' professionals—educators, social workers, penologists, and psychologists—who complemented, and sometimes appropriated, parental functions (Lasch, 1977: 15). The public sector supplemented private initiatives for the young. States and the Federal government in the heyday of Progressivism (1900–20), for instance, enacted child-labour laws typically operating in concert with prevailing educational policies.

Families traditionally were expected to care for aged relatives, but precedents for extramural assistance date from the colonial era. Religious groups underwrote old-age homes. Many localities provided food and other charitable assistance. Through land bounties, pensions, and military facilities the

Federal government supported disabled veterans and those who in the twilight of life were impoverished. By World War I, funds for superannuated soldiers and sailors and their elderly dependents represented the single largest item in the Federal budget (Skocpol, 1992). The passage of the Social Security Act (1935) established a more comprehensive set of relationships among the aged, their families, and public and private bureaucracies. Policymakers tried to abolish poorhouses, for instance, by denying old-age assistance to residents in such institutions (Achenbaum, 1986). As was the case with advocacy and service agencies for children and youth, the elderly and their representatives grew more savvy over time in expressing their wants, demands, and expectations. Lines between autonomy and dependency became fuzzy, as did boundaries between responsible kin and professionals. Social workers acted as if they were family surrogates, offering advice on health, housing, and retirement options.

Historically, 'age' increasingly became a major criterion for allocating resources in contemporary America (Chudacoff, 1989). Birthdays increasingly marked rites of passages not only at home but in the public sphere. Children had to attend school until they reached a prescribed age. Licensing bureaus, voting registrars, and draft boards scrutinized proof of age. Older people had to be at least 65 (or, in some instances, 50, 55, 60, 62, 67, 68, 70, 72, or older) before they became 'entitled' to pensions, discounts, or some other service designated for 'mature' adults. Writing after the passage of Medicare, Medicaid, the Older Americans Act, and the implementation of a host of other Federal, state, and private initiatives, two distinguished gerontologists declared that 'the task is how to more effectively involve family and kin network in long-term care of the elderly and to do this without using the power of law and without destroying the internal dynamics of the particular family unit' (Shanas and Sussman, 1977).

In addition to these external structural changes, the growing insinuation of outside experts, bureaucracies, and public policies to supplement and sometimes control the behaviour of family members, US domestic relations since World War II have been significantly affected by two developments within the home. First, the option to divorce is now an escape clause in every marriage contract. Numbers fluctuate, but as Hughes and Waite discuss in Chapter 10, roughly half of all US marriages begun since 1970 ended in divorce within seven years. Married men and women have gone their separate ways since the colonial era, of course, but the act once brought shame to both parties unless it resulted from cruelty or promiscuity. Nowadays, divorce causes personal pain, especially if there are children involved, but little social opprobrium. This is not to minimize divorce's devastating financial and psychological impact. Women tend to suffer more than men in proceedings. If they have not been married to the same wage earner for ten years, for example, they lose all rights to their former spouse's Social Security benefits. Ex-husbands are notoriously irresponsible in meeting their court-required child support. The creation of new household units, with a confusing blend of stepchildren of various ages, makes for odd alliances, as explored by Dimmock et al. in Chapter 5.

Few kids are interested in committing to relationships that might not last through adolescence, much less into old age.

The subtle revolution in women's employment outside of the home has altered the dynamics of domestic life in other ways. Women have always worked hard in the US, but they rarely got compensated in cash for their efforts. Our founding mothers' primary tasks were to raise their children, to manage the household, and to take in boarders or piecemeal work if their husbands could not work or earn enough to cover basic needs. Various ethnic and racial groups devised rules that differed from the middle-class, native-born white norms described above but, in most instances, the domestic economy held sway under patriarchal control (Birnbaum, 1988: 74–5). Since World War II, the percentage of American females in the labour force has increased slowly yet steadily. Today, most US women between the ages of 18 and 55, significantly, including even those with children under the age of 7, work outside of the home. Economists report that women on average are still not paid as much as men on average for comparable jobs. Women of colour face double jeopardy in the marketplace. Most older workers encounter some form of age discrimination; its pernicious effects tend to be gendered. All that said, disparities in earnings on account of gender, race, and age are diminishing. There are cracks in the glass ceilings that still exist in corporate America and other sectors of the economy. Yet obstacles to female advancement once existing in relatively lucrative fields such as medicine, law, and engineering have decreased.

The ubiquity of two paychecks in a household has made an enormous difference in Americans' ability to consume and enjoy the prerequisites associated with living in an affluent society. The nation's richest have profited handsomely in recent years; there is a greater concentration of wealth in the US today than acquired by Rockefeller, Morgan, and the other Robber Barons. In contrast, the underclass has suffered disproportionately. Despite efforts made to improve educational opportunities and to create economic incentives, members of many minority groups lack access to decent educations and jobs, are frequently unemployed, and generally suffer more disabilities in middle age than afflict white men and women in their prime. Middle Americans now depend on that second income for house or car payments and other essentials. Being single in middle age is a risky business in the US. Ask any gay person who lacks spousal health benefits. Or, let a recently divorced person disclose her financial portfolio. Economically vulnerable Americans usually lack the support that makes married partners secure.

Enough has been said here about the significance of gender on changing the parameters of domestic relations in the US. Family dynamics look different depending on the gender lens deployed. Invoking matters of race and ethnicity, moreover, bring into play another set of arguments about the importance of paying attention to variations around the mean. The family choices made by Delaware Indians negotiating with William Penn, by Italian or Irish immigrants in steerage, and by slaves singing in their cabins, were not identical to those unfolding in shipbuilders' parlours or in Conestoga wagons. Race, ethnicity, religion, and region have long served as boundaries separating various groups of Americans' experiences from one another. Convergences have occurred, but only after people struggled to break down walls. 'Age' is not analogous to race or gender in its impact on people's lives over the life course. Congress finally abolished Jim Crow laws after decades of protest. Enacting and enforcing laws to fight age discrimination, which were based on the 1965 Civil Rights Act, have alleviated gross injustice yet rarely serve to extirpate prejudice. Divorce settlements can stipulate financial conditions and social arrangements that have yet to be negotiated very much in contracts between generations. There is another distinctive (perhaps more subjective) feature concerning perceptions of age and ageing that privileges individual sensibilities over sweeping generalizations. Americans tend to categorize various stages of life in black-and-white terms as if they essentially embody distinctive qualities. Child abuse makes headlines; many incidents of elder abuse go unreported. Teenage drinking and drug addiction are national scandals, but little attention is paid to alcoholism and pharmacological dependency in later years.

Ageing is dynamic. If we live long enough, we stand to gain insights from our experiences. We discern that the changes associated with ageing are often not as critical as the continuities in our attitudes and adaptability. With the passing of years we simultaneously appreciate that families also change in composition and tenor with each season. Nonetheless the ebb and flow of generational ties often diverge from individuals' pathways. The death of a family, after all, is dissimilar from a death in a family. Hence 'time' creates an anomaly in the way many Americans think about what lies ahead. On one level most of us acknowledge that biological, psychological, and physical change is inevitable. Yet cultural binders influence how people come to terms with such change. To the extent to which Americans make plans for the future (and many do not), they have difficulty envisioning their future selves as different from their presently transient selves.

Adults in other places have different perspectives on the generational social contract. According to Akiko Hashimoto (1996), the Japanese offer protective support to their elders, whereas most US citizens opt for a contingency approach to aid their parents when their capacity for autonomy and self-sufficiency wanes. Such cross-cultural comparisons may not isolate a trait unique to the US, but the difference is critical to understanding the impact of population ageing on the passage of generations and on the future of domestic relations. Current variations in Japanese and American responses to generational support hark back to a theme elaborated by de Tocqueville: Jacksonian Americans were so obsessed by the pleasures and insecurities of the present that they rarely worried about tomorrow. Forgetting traditional norms and presuming that their progeny could fend for themselves, they lived as if they could (and had to) care only for themselves.

The denial of ageing, in terms of ignoring its cumulative wisdom and inevitable demise, has led in the contemporary period to a paradoxical situation.

Cultural images clash with structural realities. On the one hand, the US press seizes on images of the 'greedy geezer': rich elders squandering thousands of dollars on cruises and vacation homes in Florida. On the other hand, few greedy geezers are plutocrats. Senior citizens in the richest nation in the world have actually made inadequate provisions for their later years. Federal statistics reveal that Social Security keeps more than two-thirds of all elderly Americans off the poverty rolls. The median bequest in the 1990s was $30,000, enough to cover outstanding hospital bills and to pay the lawyers, but not much to pocket (Peterson, 1999). Older Americans unquestionably are better off than they were in the Great Depression or even during Great Society. But senior citizens are not so affluent that they can afford to break their ties with their children.

Nor are the middle-aged children of today's elders likely to be spared the traumas and indignities of advanced age. Today's elders are healthier than any previous cohort in US history. But many parents over 60 already require help in dealing with multiple disabilities. Some mothers and fathers will end up living beyond their means. Even so, members of my cohort, born in the US between 1946 and 1964, expect to inherit a lot of money over the next two decades. Total generational transfers will exceed trillions of dollars, fuelling much speculation on Wall Street and in the press about whether the Baby Boomers will put this legacy back into the nation's infrastructure or indulge themselves in a fit of conspicuous consumption. But if this country fails to enact a national health care plan, it is possible that the US medical-bureaucratic complex will be the primary beneficiary of imminent generational transfers. This suggests that there are more immediate issues to be raised. How has population ageing affected family relations in the US? Are there salient variations by gender, race, ethnicity, or age? Who cares who cares for whom in later years? To what extent, if any, has the new politics of ageing, which capitalizes on intergenerational tensions, affected private domestic decisions?

THE IMPACT OF POPULATION AGEING ON FAMILY DYNAMICS AND GENERATIONAL RELATIONS

US sociologists and demographers did not systematically begin to analyse the impact of population ageing on family dynamics and intergenerational relationships until after World War II (Achenbaum, forthcoming). Specialists divided issues into disciplinary topics, such as family structure, kin relations, care giving, and role conflicts. Academic foci were further narrowed to explore variations due to differences in gender, race, and ethnicity. Ideological predilections sometimes lurked behind empirical analyses. Those who saw the family in decline worried about its capacity to support elders. Those who seized on the strengths of older women celebrated the capacity of individuals to survive adversity in later years.[1]

---

[1] See Bengtson, Rosenthal, and Burton (1996) for a summary of the literature.

As discussed in Chapter 1, extended longevity effects all sorts of horizontal and vertical relationships among family members. A century ago, it was probable that one or more parents would die before all the children were reared. Now the phrase 'until death do us part' has an ominous undertone: couples on average can expect to live together for four decades. Even if divorce occurs, former spouses often maintain some bonds through their children, grandchildren, and great-grandchildren. Similarly, the reciprocity implicit in ties across generational lines, notably between mothers and daughters, becomes more important with added years (Rossi, 1986). Women aged 55 are ten times more likely to have a surviving parent alive than was true two centuries ago. Not all US statistics augur well in this regard: a quarter of all births occur among single mothers, so in many families there is a significant deficit of potential kin ties at the outset. But insofar as friends become surrogate partners in raising children and caring for aged kin, the nuclear family no longer has to embrace all of the possibilities. This scenario becomes manifest in analyses of the diverse family structures in the US.

Ethnic variations fit the 'latent matrix' model. The Rileys (1993) refer to the importance of friends who serve as honorary aunts and uncles in the Asian American community, of the role of godparents among Spanish-speaking groups, and of the historical role that fictive kin have played among African Americans. Indeed, recent studies indicate that African-American elders have more extensive contact than their white counterparts with their immediate kin, extended families, and wider community. Participation in the local church enhances older people's sense of worth. Such bonds tend to reinforce one another, even if they do not necessarily add to increasing life satisfaction in later years (Coke, 1991). Even among the nation's very old, there seems to be great stability in support, both in terms of affection and potential support. Women are more likely than men to assist people over the age of 85, but that trend obtained at earlier ages. Nor are the nation's elderly being abandoned at advanced age. Investigators are inclined to depict family dynamics in terms of added generations loving and caring for their old. Yet researchers do point out that as the life course is extended, a significant proportion of elders do outlive their kin. Roughly a quarter of those over 85 who no longer maintain family relationships are childless. This means that only a quarter can count on a child for support as a caregiver (Johnson and Barer, 1997).

CONCLUSION

The increasing diversity of US family structures is in part a direct consequence of population ageing. Demographic realities challenge populist movements and political pundits who like to pit the current interests of age against youth's future claims on the commonweal. Had Americans for Generational Equity (AGE) not collapsed because of its own internal problems, its leaders would have succumbed as their ideological arguments were scrutinized. Generation

X surely differs, as claimed AGE supporters, from the dwindling cohort of World War II veterans. Yet both groups have a stake in the future well-being of boys and girls too young to vote, not to mention the happiness of the so-called 'sandwich generation' that matures between them. Similarly, presidential campaigns may flame dissent over long-term deficits in Social Security financing. But few Americans really wish to undermine the intergenerational principles that gird the programme. Social Security benefits more than senior citizens; its resources provide a vital but not the sole source of income security for children, young widow(er)s, and the disabled. Age differences exist, to be sure, but people of all ages are ageing. Therein lies the source of generational solidarity that outweighs age-specific tensions in contemporary America.

Features of US life resemble those that de Tocqueville reported. This still is a dynamic, enterprising land. As population ageing transforms the face of the US, as it has other advanced industrial societies, relations between spouses and parents and children (or their surrogates) will continue to serve as major sources of support in later years. Friends, neighbours, and a network of agencies will fill in the gaps. The US family in all of its forms remains a resilient, adaptable entity.

4

The Availability and Supportive Functions of Extended Kinship Ties in Later Life: Evidence from the Berlin Ageing Study

FRIEDER R. LANG

INTRODUCTION

Family relationships are an important resource of social adaptation in later life. Spouses, children, and siblings are typically among the most meaningful and supportive relationships of older adults. However, while there is much empirical knowledge about the role of close family members in later life, the functions of more distant relatives are not well understood. Unlike most other relationships, kinship ties may persist also in a 'hidden mode'. For example, relatives who never had contact may nevertheless know about each others' existence and their kinship. Although kinship ties are often loosely knit, they may easily be 'switched on' to become close and intensive, because next to kin individuals typically share a historical and family-biographical knowledge. However, there is not much empirical and theoretical knowledge about the specific functions and contributions of kin relationships in later life. Nonetheless, there is some empirical support for the idea that older individuals proactively engage in the continuation and discontinuation of relationships in accordance with their age-specific needs (e.g. Lang, 2000; Lang, Staudinger, and Carstensen, 1998).

In this chapter, the availability and supportive functions of extended kin relationships in later life are explored from two viewpoints: First, it is asked

The research reported was conducted within the context of the Berlin Aging Study (BASE). BASE is conducted by the Committee on Aging and Societal Development (AGE) of the Academy of Sciences and Technology in Berlin (1989–1993) and the Berlin-Brandenburg Academy of Sciences (since 1994) in collaboration with the Free University Berlin and the Max Planck Institute for Human Development and Education, Berlin. From 1989 to 1991 BASE was financially supported by the Department of Research and Technology. Since 1992, financial support has been awarded by the Federal Ministry of Family Affairs, Senior Citizens, Women, and Youth (314-1722-102/9 + 314-1722-102/9a).

how the structure and function of extended kin relationships differ from other social relationships in later life. A second perspective views kinship ties as resources in later life that may be activated in response to personal loss experiences such as widowhood or death of siblings. It is asked, in what ways older individuals activate extended kin relationships to relatives when nuclear family members are not available. Three compensatory mechanisms are distinguished: a relation-specific, a function-specific, and an outcome-specific compensation. Note that in the following, extended kin relationships are differentiated from nuclear family relationships such as spouses, children, or siblings. Note also that kinship here is not confined to 'bonds of blood' but also comprises legalized or in-law kin relationships as well.

STRUCTURAL AND FUNCTIONAL ASPECTS OF EXTENDED KINSHIP

Extended kinship networks may be seen as opportunity structures for social contact with relatives. While individuals do not have much control over how many relatives are available to them, they may well regulate whether they engage in active contact with their relatives. Not much is known though, to what extent individuals keep contact with all their relatives who are structurally available. In the following, *kinship availability* refers to the size of an individual's kinship networks, that is, the number of structurally available relatives. *Kinship activation* pertains to the extent to which individuals actually maintain personal (i.e. active) relationships with their relatives. Thus, kinship availability is defined as the objective structure (i.e. size) of kinship networks, whereas kinship activation may be seen as the individual's subjective use or realization of the available kinship network.

A central issue is to what extent activation of extended kinship ties depends on marital, parental, and sibling status. Do individuals make more use of their extended kinship after they have lost their spouse, sibling, or child? Are there differences when older individuals were never-married, childless, or siblingless throughout their lives? A second issue relates to the functional transactions with relatives. What are the functions of relatives in the personal networks of older adults? Are there differences between extended kinship ties, close family ties, or non-kin ties? A third, closely related issue asks for the outcomes of kinship availability and kinship activation on the social well-being of older adults. In specific, it seems relevant to what extent the activation of kinship protects against feelings of loneliness in later life, for example, when personal losses have occurred.

MODELS OF EXTENDED KINSHIP STRUCTURE AND FUNCTION

Few empirical and theoretical studies have explicitly addressed the structure and function of extended kinship ties in late life (e.g. Crohan and Antonucci, 1989;

Litwak and Szelenyi, 1969; Rossi and Rossi, 1990; Wellman and Hall, 1986). Typically, extended kinship ties are often conceived of as a latent resource or reserves in the social networks of older individuals. In this sense, extended kinship is viewed as serving a 'stopgap' function when close family members such as spouses, children or siblings are unavailable for older adults. As a consequence, the availability and functions of kinship ties in later life are often explored as a coping resource for older individuals who are confronted with the task of mastering social losses (Chatters, Taylor, and Jackson, 1986; Litwak, Messeri, and Silverstein, 1991; Simons, 1984). Without doubt, the experience of losing a spouse, a sibling, or one's child is a dramatic life event in later life that has far-reaching consequences for the social integration of the individual. Relatives may play a central role and contribute importantly in the process of coping with the many challenges associated with personal loss experience (Dykstra, 1993; Sussman, 1985). However, the role and function of extended kinship ties in such processes is not well understood. Two controversial, although not contradictory, models have explicitly addressed and elaborated the possible compensatory functions of kinship in later life. The one is the model of hierarchical compensation (Cantor, 1979; Chatters et al., 1986), and the other is the model of functional specificity (Litwak and Kulis, 1987; Litwak et al., 1991).

The Role of Extended Kinship Ties in Later Life according to the Model of Hierarchical Compensation

The model of hierarchical compensation builds on the premise that older people organize their social ties hierarchically with respect to the functions of social relationships (Cantor, 1979; Simons, 1984). Role relationships that serve a variety of functions such as companionship, confiding, intimacy, and supportive exchanges are expected to take a more central (i.e. higher order) position in an individual's personal network. In contrast, lower-order relationships are associated with few functions only. For example, marital relationships typically have more diverse functions than relationships with children, and than sibling relationships (Cantor, 1979; Chatters et al., 1986). Extended kinship ties assume a middle position in this hierarchy. They are typically associated with fewer diverse functions than close family members, but are functionally more multiplex than friendship or other non-kin relationships. A central assumption of the hierarchical compensation model is that individuals compensate for losses of relationships by extending the functional variety of those relationships which come closest in the functional hiearchy. For example, when nuclear family members are unavailable, it is expected that other relatives will take over their functional role. Some preliminary indication for such hierarchical compensation was already reported in the Kansas City study (Cumming and Henry, 1961) and in a separate study reported by Babchuk (1965). Empirical support for the hierarchical organization of social networks was reported from several studies (e.g. Rossi and Rossi, 1990; Shanas, 1979; Stoller and Earl, 1983).

According to the hierarchical compensation model, individuals activate their extended kinship ties when more central relationships such as a spouse, child, or sibling are not available in the personal network. The function of extended kinship is thus to substitute the roles of unavailable family relationships. Consequently, older adults who have lost their spouse, child, or sibling are expected more often to activate extended kinship ties as compared to most other older adults. Thus, the hierarchical compensation model suggests that relatives take over roles of hierarchically higher-order family relationships that have dropped out or were not available. In the following, this model is referred to as a *relation-specific compensation*. In the most general case, relation-specific compensation implies that activation of extended kinship ties is increased when family relationships are not available anymore in the personal network.

The Role of Extended Kinship Ties in Later Life according to the Model of Functional Specificity

The model of functional specificity emphasizes the uniqueness of functions associated with specific relationship types. According to functional specificity theory, different types of relationship may be defined with a set of specific and non-interchangeable functions that they fulfil to the individual (Litwak, 1985; Litwak, Messeri, and Silverstein, 1991). For example, marital relationships—consistent with the hierarchical compensation model—typically serve a variety of functions such as intimacy, confiding, supportive exchange, and social companionship. Generally, such functions have a unique character for the marital couple and cannot be fulfilled in other role relationships (e.g. by children). Consequently, it is argued that social losses of a spouse will result in a redistribution of functions across other available role relationships in the personal network. Following a social loss, individuals are expected to intensify those functions of their network members that were previously associated with the partner. For example, children may give more frequent emotional and instrumental support to their widowed parent than children of still married parents. Correspondingly, distant relatives of widows or widowers will be used more often as supporters and as companions. This means that following the loss of a close family member, transactions with distant relatives will be enhanced only with respect to a specific selection of functions.

In most general terms, the model of functional specificity suggests that following a personal loss, individuals make more use of already activated functions of their partners. The functional specificity model does not suggest a process of relation-specific substitution of lost family roles in the personal network. In other words, a lost spouse may not be completely substituted through other partners unless the widow or widower remarries. Quite in contrast, it is suggested that individuals compensate for social losses by reorganizing the specific functions of their remaining network partners. In the following, this model of functional specificity is referred to as *function-specific compensation*. In contrast to the relation-specific compensation model, function-specific compensation is expected to occur only with respect to a few functional transactions. For example, when older individuals experienced losses of a family member, only specific functions of kinship tie, for example instrumental support, are expected to increase.

Both models of hierarchical and function-specific compensation suggest that individuals make greater use of extended kin relationships following personal losses in the family. However, the specific compensation mechanisms described by the two compensation models differ with respect to their focus on either a relational or a functional specificity. Note that the described compensation mechanisms do not necessarily contradict each other. It seems plausible that there may be conditions in which a general substitution process (i.e. relation-specific compensation) as well as a function-specific compensation takes place in the personal networks of older people. However, the two described compensation mechanisms differ with respect to their basic predictions of what happens when family members drop out of one's personal network. The relation-specific compensation model implies an increased level of activated kinship ties when individuals have lost a close family member. The function-specific compensation model predicts that loss of a close family member is associated with an enhanced reliance on kinship ties.

Kinship Compensation: Integrating Different Compensatory Models. Both models of relation-specific and of function-specific compensation imply that social loss in the family can in principle be compensated with other kinship ties. Although both models contribute to the understanding of kinship ties in later life there are also open questions. At least three issues need further clarification with respect to possible compensation of unavailable close family ties: (*a*) the biographical uniqueness of life-long family relations; (*b*) the stability of compensation in the personal network; and (*c*) the affective outcomes of compensation processes.

Compensating Losses of Life-Long Family Relations. A central assumption of the relation-specific model is that kinship ties fulfil a substitute function when other family relationships are not available. In contrast, the function-specific compensation model suggests that individuals intensify functional transaction with relatives. Both compensation models imply that individuals who have experienced a personal loss seek to find other individuals who replace the position or the tasks of the lost family member. However, close family relationships are typically enduring over extended periods of the life span and are thus characterized by a unique relationship history. When experiencing such a loss, it seems clear that such emotional, meaningful functions of the lost partner, spouse, or sibling may not be replaceable at all. However, extended kinship ties are often characterized by a relationship history of life-long endurance. Thus, extended kinship ties may be comparable in many ways to close family ties as relatives share mutual biographical knowledge as well as their common family history (Landüschen, 1989; Vowinckel, 1995). It seems therefore plausible that extended kinship ties may provide meaningful social experiences when other more close family members are not available.

In contrast to the close family, however, there are less normative obligations with respect to the extended kinship system. For example, extended kin are not as much normatively obligated to care for their widowed relatives (e.g. Morgan, 1989). This means that the institutionalized task of extended kin relationships in later life are less clearly defined than they are for nuclear family relationships. This underscores some of the assumptions of the function-specific compensation model according to which functional transactions with existing extended kinship ties will be activated when close family members are not available. It seems questionable, though, whether such compensation is stable over longer periods of time.

Stability of Compensation. Both compensation models imply that compensation of family ties in the personal network is stable over time. According to this, relatives should take over positions or functions in the personal network for enduring periods of time when no spouse, child, or sibling is available. If there are such stable patterns of kinship compensation, no differences should be expected with respect to unavailability of close family members owed to loss experience or owed to life-long patterns of family structure (i.e. never-married, childless, single-child). It seems an open question, though, whether relatives have different functions for never-married or childless older people than for those older people who survived their spouse or children. In any case, when older individuals experience a personal loss of their spouse, child, or sibling, relationships with other relatives appear to become more important for the older adult. However, the course and endurance of such compensatory efforts may depend on the opportunities, habits, and needs of both relationship partners. Consequently, such compensation may only develop into a stable pattern when it reflects the communal and mutual interests of both partners.

Affective Outcomes of Compensation. A third issue pertains to the potential outcomes of compensatory mechanism in personal networks on everyday functioning and emotional stability of the older individual (e.g. Felton and Berry, 1992; Rook and Schuster, 1996). The experience of surviving one's spouse, child, or sibling entails much grief. In this situation, the availability of relatives in the personal network may contribute to social well-being, regardless of the specific functional transactions. Unlike most other social relationships, relatives are a unique resource in the process of grieving as relatives have experienced the same personal loss, but may have been more distant. Typically, relatives have known the deceased spouse, child, or sibling for a long time and share much biographical knowledge about the lost one with the older adult. This way relatives may contribute important support in the process of coping and readjustment of the older individual. Such compensatory functions of relatives pertain to an emotion-regulatory mechanism on the part of the mourning older individual. Such functions of relatives in the process of coping with social loss will be referred to as *outcome-related compensation* in the following. According to this notion of outcome-related compensation, older adults are expected to benefit from activated relationships with relatives in terms of affective outcomes after having suffered personal losses in the family. Kinship ties are expected to serve the compensatory function of helping older individuals back to positive functioning after a personal loss. This also implies that functions of relatives are temporary rather than stable over time. Note that the suggestion of an outcome-related compensation is not contradictory to the relation- and function-specific models of compensation. All three models emphasize different facets of the social compensation process and may well complement each other. Generally, the notion of an outcome-related compensation emphasizes the role of kinship ties in the process of adaptation to loss in later life.

In sum, three compensatory mechanisms can be distinguished with respect to structure and function of kinship ties, that is, a *relation-specific*, a *function-specific*, and an *outcome-related compensation*. Based on data from the Berlin Aging Study (BASE), three specific hypotheses on the role of kinship ties in later life were explored with respect to these three models of compensation. First, extended kinship ties are hierarchically organized: according to the first hypothesis, a greater proportion of structurally available kinship ties is currently activated when spouse, children, or siblings are not available in the older individual's personal network. Second, extended kinship ties are functionally specific: this second hypothesis states that kinship ties are activated for different functions (e.g. support, emotional closeness) in the personal networks, depending on what type of family relationship (i.e. spouse, child, sibling) is unavailable in the current personal network. Third, extended kinship ties are associated with a reduced risk of loneliness after social loss: this third hypothesis states that individuals feel less lonely the more kinship ties are activated in the current personal network.

THE BERLIN AGING STUDY (BASE)

Study Design and Sample Description

The Berlin Aging Study is based on a intensive and multidisciplinary 15-session interview with 516 Berliners aged between 70 and 103 years (Baltes and Mayer, 1999). The interview protocol covered a collaborative effort of four disciplines: internal medicine, psychiatry, psychology, and sociology. All participants were identified through probability sampling from the local registration office (in Germany each citizen is typically registered) stratified by age and sex. In total, 27 per cent of those contacted took part in all 15 sessions of BASE. In an analysis of representativeness of the final BASE sample compared to the parent sample of 1,908 older people, there is some indication that the final sample had a lower mortality rate after one year (see Lindenberger et al., 1999 for details). Of the 516 participants of BASE, 178 (34.5 per cent) were married or lived with a partner, 265 (51.4 per cent) were widowed, and 73 (14.1 per cent) were never-married or divorced. Most married participants had at least one living child (80.3 per cent). Only 68.3 per cent of widowed participants and 42.5 per cent of never-married participants had a living child. In total 135 participants (26.2 per cent) had always been childless and 355 participants (68.8 per cent) were parents with at least one living child. A total of 26 (5 per cent) participants have survived their children (referred to as 'survived parents'). About one-third of participants were 'siblingless', that is, they never had a sibling (or have lost their sibling more than 20 years ago; $N = 172$, 33.3 per cent). Nearly one-third of participants were 'survived siblings', that is, they have lost their sibling during the past two decades ($N = 154$; 29.8 per cent). Another third of the sample, had at list one living sibling ($N = 190$; 36.8 per cent).

Marital, parental, and sibling status was found to be closely associated with age of participants: married participants were, on average, 4 years older (i.e. 81.7 years, $SD = 8.2$) than widowed participants (87.3 years; $SD = 8.2$) but 2.5 years younger than never-married or divorced participants (84.1 Jahre; $SD = 8.6$; $Eta^2 = 0.071$, $p < 0.001$). Survived parents, on average were older ($M = 90.2$ years, $SD = 7.9$) than lifelong childless participants (86.9 years; $SD = 8.7$) and than parents with a living child (83.8 years; $SD = 8.4$; $Eta^2 = 0.037$, $p < 0.001$). Survived siblings were older (87.7 years, $SD = 8.2$) than participants with a living sibling (81.6 Jahre; $SD = 7.7$; $Eta^2 = 0.111$, $p < 0.001$), but were not significantly older than lifelong siblingless participants (86.1 Jahre; $SD = 9.0$, $Eta^2 = 0.007$, n.s.). In addition, their sex was associated with marital and with parental status. Only 14.6 per cent of all married participants were female ($N = 26$) in contrast to 66 per cent of widowed and 78.1 per cent of never-married or divorced participants. Survived parents were more likely to be female (69.2 per cent) than male (30.8 per cent).

Findings reported in the following refer to data assessed in two independent and separate sessions of the BASE interview protocol, that is, the sociological interview and the psychological interview on social relationships.

The biographical questionnaire on the life-course and the family assessed the structural availability of family and kin relationships within a structured interview. Participants reported all existing family relationships in their family. In addition to the spouse, children, and siblings, this pertained to relationships with grandchildren, great-grandchildren, children-in-law, nephews, nieces, brothers- and sisters-in-law, and grandchildren-in-law. On average participants reported 7.2 available relationships with relatives outside the nuclear family

($SD = 6.3$). Of these, 1.7 were grandchildren, and 1.0 were children-in-law. A total of 29 participants (5.6 per cent) did not report having any relatives available. Of these 21 participants also did not have any family.

The psychological questionnaire on social relationships assessed all currently activated relationships in the personal network with the circle diagram method (Kahn and Antonucci, 1980). The circle diagram consists of three concentric circles grouped around a small circle in which the German word 'Ich' ('I') is written. Participants first included names of network members in each of the three circles. The inner circle represents network members to whom the participant feels very close, so close that it would be 'hard to imagine life without'. The middle circle refers to those network members to whom the participant does 'not feel quite so close'. The outer circle lists those network members to whom the participants 'feels less close, but who are still important'. Participants, then, reported additional information on each network member such as sex, type of role relationship, age of partner, and frequency of contact. A second part of the questionnaire assessed supportive and tender exchanges with social partners. Participants named those social partners who have supported them over the past three months or who have received support. Note that participants listed full names of social partners including the type of relationship. Thus, all family members and relatives could be compared to the sociology questionnaire. In total, participants named 3.9 activated relationships with relatives ($SD = 3.9$) outside the nuclear family (i.e. spouse, children, siblings). This pertained to grandchildren ($M = 1$; $SD = 1.6$), children-in-law ($M = 0.5$; $SD = 0.8$) and other relatives ($M = 2.4$; $SD = 3.2$). Note that participants reported nearly twice as many relatives in the structured sociology questionnaire as compared to the circle diagram method. In the following, all relatives reported in the sociology questionnaire will be referred to as *available relatives* or *kinship availability* whereas all relatives reported in the psychology questionnaire (i.e. circle diagram) will be referred to as *activated relatives* or *kinship activation*.

Results

The availability of relatives (i.e. assessed with the sociological questionnaire) was found to be strongly associated with family status. Sibling and parental status together accounted for 23.2 per cent of the variance in the number of available relatives. That is, older people who had a living sibling reported about 1.4 more relatives than older people who have survived their sibling and 4.8 more relatives than older people who had remained life-long siblingless. Parents with a living child, on average, reported about 5 relatives more than childless people and 3.6 relatives more than parents who had survived all their children. Thus, social losses of close family members were found to determine the structure of kinship networks. However, most of the variation in the size of the kinship network does not depend on characteristics of the older individual. The structural availability of kinship was not significantly associated with age cohort, gender, marital status, number of medical diagnoses, education, or income. Older individuals do not have much influence on how many relatives are structurally available to them. However, they may to some extent influence with how many of their relatives they like to have active relationships. Table 4.1 gives an overview of the extended kinship availability and the proportion of activated family and kinship ties in the personal network. The proportion of activation refers to the percentage of activated relationships in relation to the number of available relationships. Activation, here refers to levels of emotional closeness and to supportive exchanges.

As shown in Table 4.1, most available marital relationships (96.6 per cent), relationships to children (91.0 per cent), sibling relationships (60.4 per cent) and kin relationships (53.9 per cent) were activated, that is reported as being more or less close or as support exchange partners. Note that the proportion of activation of relatives was significantly lower than among all other family relationships.

There were also differences with respect to which functions were activated across the different relationship types. For example, most spouses were associated with supportive exchanges, tenderness, and strong emotional closeness. On average, children did not differ much from spouses with respect to emotional closeness but were less often associated with supportive exchanges. Activated sibling relationships were characterized by few supportive exchanges but medium levels of emotional closeness. Relatives were mostly activated with respect to supportive functions while nearly one-third of all relatives were characterized as being less close to the older participant. However, there was great diversity across kin relationships. For example, most grandchildren and children-in-law were perceived as being very close. Relatives were closer than most friends. Also, supportive exchanges with relatives did not differ significantly ($p < 0.05$) from supportive exchanges with friends.

According to the relation-specific compensation model it is expected that non-availability of spouses, children, or siblings will be associated with increased, above average levels of activated extended kin relationships. Figure 4.1 shows the mean levels of activation across different family and extended kinship ties among widowed participants, never-married participants, survived parents, childless participants, lifelong siblingless participants, and survived siblings. In the figure, significant ($p < 0.05$) difference from average activation levels of the respective relationship type is indicated when the standard errors do not overlap with the grand mean (indicated by the dotted line). In this analysis, participants were excluded when they had not at least one of the respective relationships structurally available. Figure 4.1 shows that none of the comparisons groups differed significantly from the average activation level. This indicates that a central prediction of the relation-specific compensation model must be rejected. Levels of extended kinship activation did not differ from

Table 4.1. *Availability and activation of different types of relationships in general, depending on levels of emotional closeness and depending on type of support exchange (n = 516)*

Type of relationship	Availability (N)[a]	Proportion activated (SD)[b]	Type of activation					
			Emotional closeness[c]			Support exchange[c]		
			Very close	Close	Less close	Received	Given	Tenderness
Spouse[d]	34.5 (178)	96.1 (19.5)	89.9	5.1	0.6	79.8	80.3	63.6
Children[e]	68.8 (355)	91.0 (25.1)	82.4	15.8	4.8	56.6	33.5	33.3
Sibling[f]	36.8 (190)	60.4 (47.0)	27.7	31.0	6.5	10.5	16.8	10.5
Relatives	94.4 (487)	53.9 (37.8)	54.6	55.4	31.4	31.4	23.4	26.7
Children-in-law	63.0 (325)	52.4 (47.6)	40.3	16.0	4.9	16.0	8.6	3.4
Grandchildren	59.5 (307)	53.6 (44.6)	48.9	25.1	3.9	13.7	7.5	28.7
Other relatives	90.1 (465)	49.5 (42.8)	27.7	44.5	29.5	16.1	14.4	18.9
Friends[g]	—	54.7 (49.8)	24.1	60.3	57.5	29.8	34.4	27.3
Other non-kin[g]	—	85.7 (35.1)	9.3	35.8	60.2	56.1	38.9	16.3

[a] Percentage of participants with the respective type of relationship (unweighted percentage, number of cases in brackets).

[b] For relatives: the percentage is based on those relatives who were named in the circle diagram or as suport-exchange partners (SD in brackets).

[c] Percentage of participants, who reported to be close or to exchange support with at least one available partner of the respective type of relationship.

[d] Refers to marital relationships as well as to unmarried couples.

[e] Refers to biological as well as adopted children.

[f] Refers to the availability of living sibling. 14 participants had remained siblingless throughout their lives.

[g] Activated relationships with friends and other non-kin who were reported in the psychological questionnaire.

Activation of marital relationships (percentages, error bars)

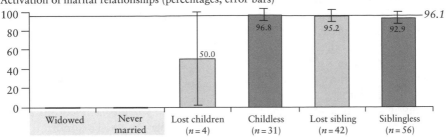

Activation of relationships with children (percentages, error bars)

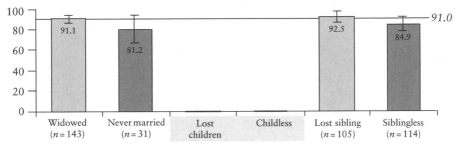

Activation of sibling relationships (percentages, error bars)

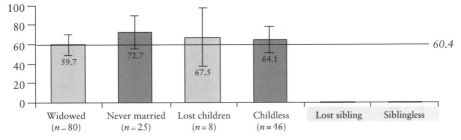

Kinship activation (percentages, error bars)

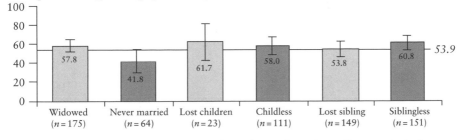

Fig. 4.1. Activation of family and kin relationships depending on marital, parental, and sibling status

Note: Shadowing indicates non-availability of the respective relationships in that group.

average neither with respect to life-long patterns of relationships (e.g. child-lessness, siblinglessness) nor with respect to social losses of family members.

A different picture emerged with respect to the specific contents of functional activation of extended kin relationships. Figure 4.2 shows the proportion of very close relatives and the proportion of relatives with whom participants exchanged tenderness. Figure 4.3 shows the proportion of relatives with whom supportive exchanges and social companionship was reported. Widowed participants maintained more often close, supportive, socially active, and tender relationships with relatives than non-widowed older adults. This indicates that widows or widowers seem to activate their extended kinship ties in very function-general ways across different domains of everyday functioning. Note also that never-married or divorced individuals made use of their extended kinship only with respect to supportive functions, but not in terms of emotional closeness or social companionship. Comparable patterns of extended kinship activation are also observed with respect to parental and sibling status.

Life-long childless older people reported fewer support exchanges and tenderness with relatives than survived parents, who have survived all their children. Similarly, surviving siblings reported more relatives who helped them than lifelong siblingless participants. Generally, relatives were typically the least activated for specific functions among those older people who have

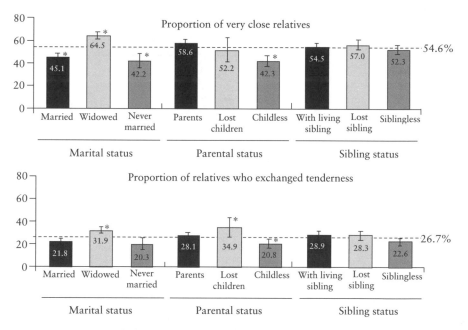

Fig. 4.2. Emotional closeness and tenderness with relatives depending on marital, parental, and sibling status

Error bars; dotted line = grand mean in total sample

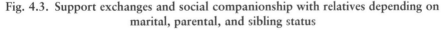

Fig. 4.3. Support exchanges and social companionship with relatives depending on marital, parental, and sibling status

Error bars; dotted line = grand mean in total sample

remained unmarried, childless, or siblingless throughout their lives (Figs. 4.2 and 4.3). Note again that there were no differences with respect to the general level of extended kinship activation between the family status groups (see Fig. 4.1). This means, that lifelong patterns of unavailability of close family members were associated with having generally fewer functional transactions with one's relatives. A reason for this finding is that older adults who are married, have a child or a sibling, have acquired stable behavioural patterns of supportive transactions with their family over the life-course and may therefore easily transfer these patterns to relatives in later life. In contrast, when having developed life long patterns of living without close family members, relatives may be more difficult to activate for specific functional transactions in later life.

In sum, results suggest that specific functions of extended kinship ties are more often used when social losses have occurred. These findings are consistent with the notion of function-specific compensation. However, with respect to widowhood, a more function-general extended kinship compensation was observed. This points to a 'hierarchy' of extended kinship functions in personal networks. Loss of a spouse or loss of one's children was associated with more domain-general activation than loss of one's siblings. Thus findings are also not completely inconsistent with the notion of relation-specific compensation processes. Findings also underscore that these compensation processes are associated with loss. When close family members were unavailable owing to life-long patterns of family status, less extended kin were often activated for specific functions in the personal network.

In a final step of this analysis, affective outcomes of the availability and activation of extended kinship ties were explored in association with family status. A four-factorial analysis of covariance of marital, parental, sibling status, and degree of kinship activation (low, medium, high) on feelings of loneliness was computed. Age, sex, education, and health were included as covariates. In order to avoid empty or small cells, only main- and two-way-interaction effects were tested. Table 4.2 shows the F values and partial coefficients of the analysis of covariance. As shown in Table 4.2, there was a positive association between age and number of medical diagnoses on loneliness. Older and less healthy participants felt more lonely.

In addition, there was also a significant negative effect of extended kinship availability and extended kinship activation on feelings of loneliness. Irrespective of the level of activation, having more relatives was associated with feeling less lonely. Moreover, activating relationships with relatives was also associated with a lower risk of loneliness. In addition, there was a significant interaction effect of level of activation and marital status (see Fig. 4.4). Levels of extended kinship activation was more strongly associated with feelings of loneliness among never-married or divorced older adults. Effects of extended kinship activation on loneliness did not differ between married and widowed participants. This was somewhat suprising, when considering the higher levels of function-specific kinship activation among widowed participants (see Figs. 4.2 and 4.3). Such function-specific kinship compensation does not seem to contribute to reduced risk of loneliness among widowed older adults. The finding that never-married older adults benefit from extended kinship activation, may thus reflect long-term patterns of compensation associated with the unavailability of close family ties. Older adults who live alone and never had a child or a sibling are better off when they manage to keep active contacts with their available relatives. This suggests that relatives also serve as an emotional 'reserve' for those adults who have lived their lives without close family members and thus appear to be at greater risk for experiencing loneliness in later life.

Table 4.2. *Effects of age, sex, health, education, kinship activation, and marital, parental, and sibling status on feelings of loneliness (Four factorial analysis of covariance; $n = 516$)*

Source of variation	Feelings of loneliness		
	F^a	b^b	Eta^2
Covariates (b^b):	12.2***		0.091
Age Cohort		0.13*	0.017
Sex (1 = men, 2 = women)		−0.08	0.006
Number of medical diagnoses		0.20**	0.047
Years of education		−0.13	0.020
Marital status	5.0**		0.020
Parental status	1.7		0.007
Sibling status	1.2		0.005
Availability of kin relationships	3.3*		0.020
Activation of kin relationships[c]	10.4***		0.041
Marital status × Kinship activation[c]	2.6*		0.021
Parental status × Kinship activation[c]	0.5		0.004
Sibling status × Kinship activation[c]	0.7		0.006

Note: *$p < 0.05$ **$p < 0.01$ ***$p < 0.001$.

[a] F values with df = 2,488 (resp. 3,488 for covariates and kinship activation; df = 4,488 for interaction effects). No further interaction effects between reported variables reached a critical level of significance.

[b] Partial coefficients of covariates also include information on direction of effects.

[c] For 29 participants who had no relatives available, kinship activation was set to zero. All reported results remain unchanged when excluding the 29 participants from the analysis.

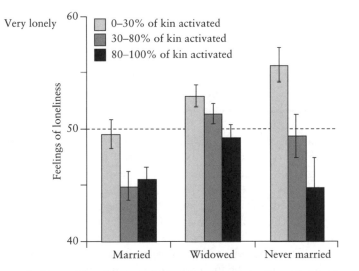

Fig. 4.4. Feelings of loneliness and kinship activation of married, widowed, and never-married older adults ($N = 516$)

Note: Figure is based on raw scores.

CONCLUSIONS AND OUTLOOK

In addition to close family ties, more distant relatives are found to be an important resource of social functioning in later life. An overwhelming majority of older adults had at least one relative. However, older adults maintained active relationships with only about one half of their relatives, on average. This means that a large proportion of kinship ties were not members of the older adult's personal (ego-centred) networks. Inconsistent with assumptions of the relation-specific compensation model, the extent of such activation of relatives in the personal network was not associated with marital, parental, or sibling status. However, specific functions of extended kin relationships differed depending on whether older adults had experienced the loss of their spouse, children, or siblings. Consistent with the function-specific compensation model, findings suggest that relatives may take over specific functions when central family relationships dropped out from the older adult's personal network (Litwak, 1985). For example, widowed older adults activated more relatives across more different functional domains than was the case for most other older adults. In contrast, childless, unmarried, or siblingless older adults reported less functional transactions than average. It seems that relatives are more willing to engage in functional transactions with older members of their kinship as long as there is a need for intensified contact. Extended kinship functions may also be differentiated depending on the type of loss experienced in the family. For example, widowhood and survival of one's children appears to generate a greater readiness for engaging in transactions among relatives than the loss of a sibling.

Moreover, extended kinship activation was observed to be generally associated with a reduced risk of loneliness, irrespective of whether relatives were also involved in specific functional transactions. Keeping in contact with one's relatives appears to contribute *per se* to social functioning in later life. One explanation may be that socially active and outgoing individuals typically experience fewer negative or depressive emotions (see Stokes, 1985, for a study with young adults). For example, keeping in good contact with one's relatives may be characteristic for extraverted and emotionally stable older adults. One may speculate that stable personality characteristics contribute to older adults ability to make more compensatory use of relatives when social losses have occurred. Further research may also acknowledge the possible dynamic interactions between personality and kinship activation and thus contribute more detailed information on the specific compensatory processes in personal networks (Rook and Schuster, 1996).

There is a caveat, though. Findings reported here relied exclusively on cross-sectional data. Therefore, inferring compensation processes from observed group differences ought to be interpreted with caution. Life-course patterns of family structures among older Europeans may also reflect cohort differences associated with two World Wars and economic crises during the participants' lifetimes (Maas, Borchelt, and Mayer, 1999). In general, findings suggest that extended kinship ties contribute to the social and emotional functioning of older adults. This is consistent with findings that suggest that older people do not only select social partners to fulfil instrumental support needs but also maximize intrinsic and emotional meaningful experiences in their personal networks (Lang et al., 1998; Lang, 2000). Extended kinship ties may have a greater potential for emotional meaningful contact owed to the shared and mutual biographical knowledge of most relatives.

Extended kinship ties of older people thus seem to entail a reserve potential of diverse functional transactions that can be activated in case of enhanced needs in later life due to social loss or owed to lifelong patterns of family structure. Findings are therefore also relevant to the understanding of future perspectives on the family, for example, with respect to possible increases of single housholds in some European countries. The tasks and functions of extended kinship systems appear to differ among baby-boomer generations as compared to birth cohorts that are characterized by single-child families or childlessness. Findings suggest that relationships to distant relatives may be an important source for continuity and long-term commitments in one's personal network. A possible consequence of this is that the quality and activation of extended kinship ties may be an important predictor of social adaptivity in later life. Rather than on the objective structure of the extended kinship networks, social adaptivity in later life is to some extent dependent on the older adult's activation of available relatives in the personal network.

5

Intergenerational Relationships among Stepfamilies in the UK

BRIAN DIMMOCK, JOANNA BORNAT,
SHEILA PEACE, AND DAVID JONES

INTRODUCTION

There is now considerable evidence that our understanding of family change in the UK is at a point of transition[1]. This is reflected in popular culture such as novels (Hornby, 1998), life-style magazines and soap operas, as well as academic discourse (Giddens, 1999). The tensions embodied in this transition are clear in the recent Home Office policy document *Supporting Families* (Home Office, 1999). In a foreword, the Home Secretary starts by saying that, 'family life is the foundation on which our communities, our society and country are built...They are as important now as they have ever been.' However, he is aware that traditional understandings of the family are changing due to high rates of cohabitation, children born outside marriage, divorce, lone-parenthood, and remarriage, and states that 'there never was a golden age of the family. Family life has continually changed—and changed for good reasons as well as bad' (Home Office, 1999: foreword). The final bow to the inevitable comes towards the end of this introduction when he states what the intentions of government policy are, or rather, are not: 'It is not about pressuring people into one type of relationship or forcing them to stay together.' This outbreak of pragmatism is based on a belief that marriage (particularly first marriage) is still the best hope for creating a stable context in which to bring up children. But it seems that government is not going to do much to discriminate in favour of marriage. Rather, the focus is on supporting 'parents' to make a better job of bringing up 'their children'.

It is quite remarkable that this is the first time any UK government has attempted to outline a coherent policy paper on 'the family'. It is intended to be 'sensible and pragmatic', and to encourage measures that will 'strengthen

---

[1] This chapter builds on work undertaken by the authors at the Open University as part of the Economic and Social Research Council (ESRC) Population and Household Change Programme (Wertheimer and McRae, 1999; McRae, 1999; Bornat et al., 1998*a,b*; 1999).

the family'. But is this really a policy for '*the* family', or is it a move towards a policy for the plurality of *families* (Bernardes, 1997)? Although the Home Secretary includes the definite article in his introduction, there is acceptance that government 'could not turn the clock back even if it wanted to'. This shift of emphasis is towards a more inclusive understanding of the diversity of family forms and away from seeing any family form not comprised of parents and their biological children as necessarily deficient. What is also evident, however, is a narrow focus on relations between parents and children, as if they are somehow synonymous with our understanding of family life. Seen in this way, family relations are 'de-gendered' (referring to parents rather than mothers/fathers), and in the absence of grandparents, 'de-generated'. Both of these tendencies are being challenged by other recent research (e.g. Smart, 1999; Smart and Neale, 1999; Dench et al., 1999) which is attempting to put both gender and generation back into the debate about family change and diversity.

'STEPFAMILIES'

This chapter draws on a small-scale, in-depth stepfamily study located in Luton, Bedfordshire. Using 1991 Census data, three wards were chosen which represented diverse areas, but with a high proportion of people aged 60 in common. Sixty life history interviews were carried out involving 28 men and 44 women (includes couples). Interviews focused on events surrounding family reconstitution and the impact on older generations within the family. There is a growing body of research that gives close attention to how ordinary people, as opposed to academics, journalists, politicians, and religious leaders, think and feel about family change (Gorell Barnes et al., 1998; Allan et al., 1999; Dench et al., 1999; Thompson, 1999), particularly as it affects relations between at least three generations. The stepfamily has become part of the mainstream agenda of funded academic research.

There are three reasons for this. First, a large number of people are experiencing post-divorce/separation family life, including the introduction of a new adult who adopts some parental roles (and that person's family) into the lives of children. There is some evidence that the process of creating a new family unit causes difficulties that are distinct from those of other types of family (Amato, 1994; Batchelor et al., 1994; Burchardt, 1990; Smith, 1990). Typically these involve parenting/step-parenting problems, adult conflict about child-rearing, issues around access to non-resident parents, and financial and legal problems. This is reinforced by statistics about the vulnerability of second/subsequent marriages and cohabitations. Second, there is a concern about the impact of family change on child-rearing, including evidence that children brought up in stepfamilies fare less well than those brought up in other types of family (Gorell Barnes et al., 1998; Kiernan, 1992; Rogers and Pryor, 1998; Safe on the Streets Research Team, 1999). Third, to this list must now be added a new concern, that is, the impact on older people when their children and grandchildren separate and recouple. This new concern is broadly of two types. Will children be deprived of the important influence of grandparents? Will the younger generations be able/willing to care for elders? Or, to be more precise, will elders with no female children be able to rely on former daughters-in-law, or new ones, to look after them in their old age? Will daughters who have remarried/coupled be overburdened by caring responsibilities? Does cohabiting induce the same intergenerational commitment as marriage? And are men likely to take on more caring responsibilities generally within the family, including care of their parents? This is all part of the current debate about the so-called 'burden of care', the impact of an ageing population and low overall birth rates.

Recently, the major campaigning organization for stepfamilies in England and Wales, the National Stepfamily Association, took the decision to merge with other organizations that focus on parenting, and lose its distinct identity and name. This decision was made because of the barriers created for many people in identifying with a word that seems irrevocably stigmatized and rooted in the past. Such reluctance to accept the 'step' label was well represented in our research. One of our respondents, a man in his late seventies who married a war widow with a daughter commented: 'I'm a great-grandfather step! But I don't—the word step doesn't come into my vocabulary now'. Another, a woman whose family is of Indian origin, had had two arranged marriages (the second following divorce). She and her new husband both have children from previous relationships (he is a widower):

But we do not like to use step-parent in our culture. We want to see the family bonding together. Although this step was being used in the beginning, but I'm afraid that was terribly upsetting for myself, and for my son, who hadn't been brought up to use the step word at all.

One important change thus facing older people is the move from seeing divorce and recoupling/remarriage as exceptional events to viewing them as now common—from their own experience of such changes as stigmatizing and shameful to where they are seen as, if not everyday and routine, at least unexceptional. However, such change is encompassed within an understanding of 'family'. Divorce and remarriage may impact on who is in, and who is out; but it does not merit a new conceptual tool, i.e. the stepfamily. Even the 'step' stem is rarely used in everyday discourse, and with reluctance. Indeed, researchers into step-relationships often encounter difficulties in finding people willing to respond to the label of 'stepfamily' (Allan et al., 1999; Bornat et al., 1996; Burgoyne and Clark, 1982). This is particularly the case when trying to engage with minority ethnic communities. Respondents trying to describe their complex family relationships do not want to have their experiences labelled and made subject to generalizations. It would appear that this message is getting home to those in government.

THE NEW EXTENDING FAMILY?

What emerges from the stepfamily study is a far more complex picture of family life than is usually reflected in popular debate. Although research subjects state strong views and principles, family change is seen as a complex issue not easily explained away by simple statements about changing moral values. The social context is changing and popular understanding appears to take account of this. Older respondents often acknowledge that even if they can't understand younger generations, they do realize that their lives are different from their own, and should not be judged solely by the standards with which they were raised. Indeed, to describe older respondents as having rigid views about the rights and wrongs of family life would be quite inaccurate. They used the research interviews as a way of reflecting on their experiences, and of balancing out the hopes they had for themselves and their children against the reality that confronts them. Older generations may not have experienced high rates of divorce, but they have endured other forms of disruption in their family lives, including violence, war, migration, unemployment, illness, and death. They are not strangers to family change and the arts of survival.

The rediscovery of grandparents and their importance in British literature (Dench et al., 1999; Allan et al., 1999) is highlighted by the impact of divorce. The role of the older generation in providing support to their children and grandchildren during divorce/separation continues the tradition of intergenerational solidarity whereby elders are called on during periods of crisis. The nature of the typical crises of family life may have changed (for example, from helping during daughters' pregnancy/illness or when men go off to war/look for work, to helping during divorce), but the role has remained similar. However, the part played by grandparents is not respected and acknowledged in the UK as it is in the US, where, according to the Census Bureau, 3.7 million children are being raised in their grandparents' home. This chapter examines grandparenting as a central facet of intergenerational relationships in stepfamilies, and also discusses caring for elders, gift giving and inheritance, and relationships with ex in-laws and step in-laws.

GRANDPARENTING

When trying to judge the importance of this aspect of intergenerational relations, there are a number of factors that have to be considered in post-divorce families. Grandparenting may not be very central to the identities of people in middle age. Grandparents may be hard-pressed to take on caring responsibilities when they themselves, particularly women, are often involved in heavy commitments to economic labour, and may also have caring responsibilities towards their own ageing parents. Of course, they are not immune from divorce and separation themselves. In addition there is a narrow time-window for grandparents to become important in the care of grandchildren during marital separation.

Intensive periods of involvement may be relatively short. Again, by the time the grandchildren are in their teens they will have a greater say in whether to continue a relationship with grandparents or not. Relationships between grandparents and their grandchildren are not entirely within the gift of the middle generation once children reach a certain age. The impact of divorce and remarriage on relations between grandparents and grandchildren is likely to be affected by the age of the grandchildren when the change occurs. Perhaps most important of all is that it is a highly complex matter not easily reduced to simple comparisons between the present and the past roles of grandparents.

According to Dench et al. (1999), family breakdown is associated with both the highest rates of grandparental assistance and the highest rates of dissatisfaction with the task. This is probably due to the fact that separation and divorce are more likely to occur when grandparents are relatively young. While, on the one hand, they are more capable of offering assistance, on the other, they are more likely to have other commitments and aspirations. This has an impact not just on the grandparenting role, but also on their parental roles in helping and advising their children during the crisis arising from separation. The older generation identify as much, if not more, with their parental role in supporting their children, as they do with their 'grandparenting' role of helping to look after their grandchildren. As one of our respondents memorably put it: 'you're never too old to be a parent.' The practical outcomes in terms of what parents do for their adult children in these circumstances will depend critically on the age of the grandchildren.

There is divergence in the pressures on paternal and maternal grandparents affected by the divorce and remarriage of their children. According to Dench et al. (1999), grandparents in the male line are frustrated in their inability to perform grandparental roles, while those in the female line may face excessive demands. When people recouple following separation from the birth parent of their children, it is tempting to think of the new partner's parents as 'step-grandparents'. Again, it may be argued that this is not a term that has much currency. Allan et al. (1999) argue that new 'in-law kin' created in stepfamilies are treated like any in-law kin, except that they are viewed as 'step-kin' in relation to children from earlier relationships. They see family solidarity in these circumstances as contingent, and not enduring.

With respect to 'ex-in-law kin', their study reveals some ambivalence. On the one hand, a desire to end involvement, and on the other, that being a 'good parent' to their children means not cutting them off from one set of grandparents, usually paternal. The potential of paternal grandparental relationships to survive separation of the grandchildren's parents would seem to be a very complex matter. A useful starting point may be the quality of the relationship between the grandparents and their grandchildren prior to the separation (Drew and Smith, 1998). Recoupling by the ex-daughter-in-law may create complications, but it would not seem that the step-grandparents take over, in any simple sense, from the paternal ones.

For Dench et al. (1999), parental relationship breakdown has two key impacts on the role of grandparents. First, it narrows the network of kin available to the parent with residence/custody of the children raising the importance of the role of the grandparents, usually maternal, and usually the grandmother. Second, grandparents lose their say and control over the situation. This loss of choice affects the quality of the relationship. Family solidarity becomes focused on survival rather than 'enjoying the grandchildren'. Children can often rely on the support of their parents during separation and recoupling, but they cannot rely on their approval. However, although disapproval may affect the quality of the relationship between the generations, it does not usually prevent help and support being offered. Finally, far from creating a new order of relationships between the generations, divorce and other family change may represent continuity with the past, whereby family solidarity is required for survival, rather than a matter of free will and life-style choice.

CARING FOR ELDERS

There is a range of ways apparent from the stepfamily study in which divorce/separation and the creation of step-relations appeared to affect the ability of adult children to care for their elders. Divorce/separation reinforced a strong desire among some older people to remain independent. It tended to strengthen intergenerational links between daughters and their parents, particularly their mothers. Some women have to try to reconcile both the traditional view of women as carers, and feminist discourses to do with independence. There is some evidence of older men living in relative isolation as a result of family change. Finally, divorce/separation and the creation of new families sometimes put greater geographical distance between relatives, and sometimes brings them closer together. This creates both closer intergenerational ties, but also families with little contact with their elders. In other words, there is no simple pattern available for policy makers to use when assessing the impact of family change on the availability of carers for older people.

As with the discussion of grandparenting above, multiple factors create considerable complexity when trying to understand how high rates of divorce and recoupling are affecting this aspect of intergenerational solidarity. It is significant that research into this matter frequently starts with a concern about the ability of children to care for their elders and the impact this will have on levels of taxation in a society with an ageing population. This has a tendency to distort research, starting as it does from an assumption that the family is 'breaking up'. David (1998) raises this issue when she asks if the family is 'changing, fragmenting, breaking up or down? And how do we know which, what or how?' Similarly, Haskey (1998), after summarizing the main demographic changes affecting the family in the UK in the twentieth century, concludes that it is not possible to make any sensible predictions about what will happen, but that it is possible merely to 'contemplate the rich complexity of family life!'

To date, the explanatory framework applied to understanding caring in these circumstances has tended to be based on ideas of a 'developmental stake' (Bengtson and Kuypers, 1971) or a notion of exchange-based behaviour (Finch and Mason, 1993). What is arising from recent studies, including the stepfamily study, is that applying an understanding of emotional attachment to adult parent–child relationships may add a crucial dimension. Parents' descriptions of their relationships with their children were usually more posit-ive than those children's accounts of their relationships with their parents. This seems to fit the dominant cultural norm that primary attachments are to chil-dren, and that these create stronger obligations than those to parents. This may be a useful starting-point on which to build complexity and divergence according to gender, class and culture/race. Historical analysis would support this view in that in the past, when couples had more children, the child most likely to act in a caring capacity to ageing parents would probably be an unmarried daughter. With much smaller families being the norm, rapid changes in the age at which women have children, and a rising life expectancy, there is more than enough complexity to convince us that understanding the issues that affect care of elders is no simple matter, without adding change created through divorce and remarriage.

It is also important to stress that caring responsibilities are not 'a one way street'. When faced with older relatives needing care, these needs have to be considered alongside other caring priorities, to children, grandchildren, or partners. The gender of the potential carer in question, her or his cultural background, *and* the complex individual history of relations with parents and parents-in-law will all play a part. Qualitative studies such as the stepfamily study have examples of respondents stating that their poor relationship with their parents will affect their response to their caring needs, and others saying that, despite problems, they still feel obligated. Most elders will usually state that they 'do not wish to be a burden' and value their independence above all else. These complexities are well illustrated by a 45-year-old white man liv-ing with a divorced woman, both having children but with none co-resident:

You have to live your own life. It becomes your responsibility. My mum and dad's not my responsibility. But if I can help them and love them and care for them. But I've got a family to look after as well...I'd make the choices which seem appropriate when the time came...I would make the decision. I wouldn't say they can come and stay with me, and then cause the breakdown of our family. Or, if it had to be a hard decision to make, to put them in a home. Because I believe sometimes we've got to make hard decisions in life.

What these types of complex, contradictory statements tell us is that what we think we might do, and how we actually behave in the given circumstances when a need for care arises, is not necessarily the same. Whilst there is a grow-ing awareness of the possibilities of looser-knit, divorce-extended families, when it comes to 'the crunch' the availability of care will usually depend on access to close 'blood ties'.

GIFT-GIVING AND INHERITANCE

As we will explore later in Chapter 9, it seems that whether it is gift-giving during life or intergenerational transfers of wealth through inheritance, the recourse to the 'blood is thicker than water' principle remains dominant in British families of all types. Numerous studies have shown that a desire to be 'fair' in stepfamilies has come up against the realities of emotional attachments and blood loyalty. Allan et al. (1999) examine this in the context of how grandparents deal with grandchildren and step-grandchildren when it comes to Christmas presents. These relationships were to some extent contingent on the age of the children when they acquired step-grandparents, and whether these step-grandparents had 'natural' grandchildren of their own. Although there was some evidence of an ideology of 'trying to treat them all the same', many indicated that they felt differently towards their 'natural' grandchildren. In practice, treating them differently with respect to giving gifts did not present problems, particularly if step and natural grandchildren were in different households. However, the fact that they had to find ways of justifying their behaviour suggests that there is awareness of a dilemma.

The stepfamily study, while generally supporting this finding, also revealed how, over many years, step-relationships across three generations can be stronger and more reliable attachments than those between blood relatives. One respondent, a man twice widowed and now living alone, had one child from his first marriage, three stepchildren, nine step-grandchildren and two grandchildren: 'my stepdaughter. I see her more than all the others put together.' He also had close and regular contact with his stepson, while his stepdaughter and daughter co-operated in ensuring that he was safe:

And she [his daughter] gets on extremely well with my stepdaughter as well. And she knows she keeps an eye on me, so. She says, I know [stepdaughter]'ll let me know if you're in any trouble.

Again, this would suggest that examining the factors that create secure attachments and applying these across the full range of blood, in-law, and step-relationships may offer better chances of understanding and predicting behaviour than making generalizations based on the label attached to any particular relationship. In this example, these step-relationships have come about as a result of death rather than divorce, and as several authors note (Robinson and Smith, 1993; Batchelor et al., 1994), there can be differences in stepfamily dynamics in these circumstances. However, there are other examples of similar attachments created through divorce-extended families.

With respect to inheritance, the search for 'fairness' is also apparent. With increasing divorce and separation it may be the case that the blood relationship between parents and children will become more reliable and important than those between spouses/partners. New partners will not be able to assume that they take a prime position with respect to inheriting their partner's' property.

The growing tendency to replace marriage with cohabitation, and life-long partnerships with serial monogamy may indicate a developing separation between matters of partnership with respect to emotions and issues of property. However, the evidence at present suggests that who inherits what from whom appears to depend both on the traditional 'blood' relationship, and the history of contact and maintenance/child support, particularly between fathers and their children. Although we have now had thirty years of rapidly rising divorce rates and increasing numbers of 'stepfamilies', it is probably still too early to be clear of the impact this trend will have in this area. The cost of divorce and of care of elders may be impacting on the available estate of many people, countering the growing trend for more people to have significant personal wealth in the form of property. There is from the stepfamily study evidence of respondents questioning traditional beliefs about inheritance patterns as a result of divorce and remarriage in the family, although most said that they will follow traditional patterns, if reluctantly on occasions. There may also be a growing tendency for women to have power over the disposal of wealth, both because of greater independence, and a tendency to live longer.

RELATIONS WITH EX IN-LAWS AND STEP IN-LAWS

The funeral of Diana, Princess of Wales in 1997 illustrates some of the complexities involved in intergenerational relationships in stepfamilies. She herself had parents who divorced and remarried, and was, as is well known, separated from the Prince of Wales at the time of her death. This separation involved infidelity on both sides. Her death in the company of a male companion brought yet another grieving family into the equation. The British royal family are well known for their ability to deal with public rituals. But at this emotional moment in the history of the country there did not appear to be any rules to guide how an ex-mother-in-law should respond to the death of her ex-daughter-in-law, let alone how to respond to the family of her ex-daughter-in-law's boyfriend. Not surprisingly, the Queen looked and behaved as if she was ignoring the reality of what had happened. Criticism of the royal family about their handling of this tragic event shows how the gap between the established ideology of the family has been brought up against the reality of how families actually function at the turn of the century. Not even a skilled practitioner in etiquette could write a set of rules that could encompass the complex permutations and combinations that might arise in these circumstances. Listening to the commentators at this funeral was an object lesson in the way that the English language, usually so adept at changing quickly, continues to stumble over words that might convey what a stepmother's relationship is to her stepdaughter's ex-mother-in-law. Indeed, do we need words for such relationships?

In a family that can trace itself back many generations, and where the precise location of second and third cousins once removed can be found in an instant, how are the future royal genealogists going to do justice to the relationship between Diana's oldest son and future King, and his father's devoted consort? Is she his 'stepmother' and what meaning do we attach to such labels? Smith (1990) would argue that they are irrevocably stigmatized because the role of the stepmother is associated with the death of an idealized mother; indeed, the word derives from Old English 'steop' and Old High German words linked to bereavement: 'If you have a stepmother, you have mother-loss, total or partial, in terms of the ideal we hold of an ever-present mother.' Although the vast majority of step-relationships now come about through divorce, this association with loss endures. It now applies to the loss of an idealized notion of *the* family comprising two married parents and their biological children. What many of the British public cannot forgive in the present royal family is that they, like so many of their 'subjects', have failed to live up to this myth. Genealogists can draw on experience of chronicling the changes brought about by Henry VIII in the sixteenth century through divorcing and executing his spouses. However, modern researchers using genograms to track and analyse complex families are certainly reporting drafting difficulties when remarriage occurs across generations (Allan et al., 1999; Bornat et al., 1999).

One of the reasons that we must return to an intergenerational focus on families across at least three generations is that grandparent–grandchild relationships create blood ties. This trans-generational link creates different dilemmas when separation and recoupling occur because a parent's ex-in-laws are a child's blood relatives. In the UK, the point of strain is usually on the man's side, as in most instances women have residence/custody, and continuity is more easily maintained with maternal grandparents. In any type of family there are likely to be differences in the degree of solidarity with kin. For example, a child's relationship with her maternal grandmother is likely to be much closer than her father's relationship with his mother-in-law. In this sense, as Allan et al. (1999) point out, stepfamilies differ only in the degree of different members' commitments within and outside the household and into the wider, divorce/separation extended family. As all those involved in trying to understand and work with stepfamilies constantly point out, they are just families, but with greater complexity (Robinson and Smith, 1993; Visher and Visher, 1996). Contact with ex-in-laws often ceases after separation/divorce. However, though older respondents usually remain loyal to their own children who have separated and re-partnered, some take a strong moral position on their behaviour, and the damage this has done; loyalty does not imply approval. If ex-in-laws are close by, then certain aspects of the pre-separation relationship may continue, particularly if close relationships with daughters-in-law have developed over long periods prior to divorce. Another of our respondents, a woman in her thirties with three children, is separated from her husband, who was judged to be at fault by his mother: 'My [ex] mother-in-law. Yes, she's brilliant . . . she's more of a mum to me than my mum was.'

We would question that there is much evidence yet for Stacey's (1998) conception of the 'divorce extended family'. Nevertheless, there is some evidence that a common strategy dealing with the creation of new divorce-based step-families making a fresh start through the exclusion of the absent parent, usually the father, is being challenged by a new orthodoxy. This argues that maintaining blood ties between children and their absent father, and his family, is usually 'a good thing'. The focus on the alleged best interests of children is consistent across both of these strategies, but radical change has occurred in defining how these 'best interests' are served. In just thirty years or so, child-care orthodoxy has gone from encouraging permanence and predictability for children, the stepfather replacing the father, to maintaining blood ties at almost all costs, embodied in The Children Act 1989, and creating parental responsibility that transcends marriage after separation, divorce, and recoupling. This new enlightenment has been criticized by some feminist writers (Smart, 1999; Smart and Neale, 1999) as neglecting the fact that the quality of the relationship between children and their father prior to separation should be the focus of what is in the child's best interests with respect to contact after separation. They argue that this cannot be separated from the sacrifices made by most mothers who take on the lion's (lioness's) share of the care of children in most circumstances, whether unmarried, married, divorced, or remarried. The reason that these arguments are important with respect to relations between ex-in-laws and step-in-laws is that they are likely to be contingent on relationships between children and their absent parents, absent grandparents, and the arrival of step-parents and step-grandparents.

CONCLUSION

Current concerns about dealing with family change and its intergenerational consequences are not new, even if a major cause of change, divorce, and remarriage on a mass scale, is. It should also be noted that part of the concern is created by assumptions that family life is significantly less stable now than it was in the past. There are arguments on both sides in this area, but it is a contested matter, not a fact. Unfortunately, there has been a tendency for some research to start from an assumption that family change and discontinuity is somehow new, or on a new scale. This may have distorted the way in which research questions have been framed and contributed to a sense of 'crisis' and moral panic. There are several older respondents within the stepfamily project for whom dealing with family disruption caused by absent fathers represents continuity as they themselves had parents who died, left home for work or war, or became incapacitated. For these previous generations of men and women denied access to divorce, many families were de facto (matrilineal) lone parent families as the men concerned played little or no part, even in providing reliable finance. They are now experiencing a second or third generation of such family change. To these families, divorce and remarriage represent a form of continuity.

There is a growing tendency towards smaller households, including single-person ones. However, this does not mean that their solitary occupants are not in some senses living in a family, even an extended one. Confusing family and household has always been a misleading thing to do in the UK context. The primacy of the attachments formed between parents and children appear to be surviving beyond the attainment of adulthood for many people, particularly for those whose partnerships/marriages do not endure. The much heralded arrival of the 'new man' (Dench, 1996; 1997) does not yet appear to be making an impact on these matters, but this does not mean that such changes are not occurring. Rather, it may be some time before evidence for significant change in the caring roles of men becomes apparent, particularly in relatively small-scale studies.

As yet, the evidence for the arrival of *divorce-extended families* whereby a modern 'tribe' arises through enduring connections with ex-partners and new ones is very limited. Like the interest in the impact of the new, caring man, we must wait and see if this change becomes significant. Families are becoming more adept at including stepchildren/grandchildren, added in-laws and step-parents at any life-stage. However, when demands are created by very high dependency, then parent–child relationships, particularly those between mothers and their children (including adult children) appear to be the default position. It is tempting to see this evidence of greater matrilinearity as the result of feminism, but this is not without its ironies. Some feminists are questioning the benefits of the association between work and liberation for women, par-ticularly the working class (Smart, 1999; Smart and Neale, 1999), and it is arguable that women as the maintainers of family solidarity and the strength in adversity represents continuity rather than a radical change. The stepfam-ily study has evidence that women are struggling to reconcile feminist dis-courses of independence with attachments to parents and children. What may be most questionable in this light are the benefits of marriage to women. However, by narrowing the network of people available to help with the rais-ing of children, it is placing yet more emphasis on maternal grandmothers to provide support to their daughters at a time when their expectations may also be changing.

There is a need for a greater awareness of the conditions required for secure and enduring attachments to survive and thrive, and much more priority given to those who play a part in raising children. Clearly the role of marriage in securing these attachments is being questioned as never before. It is quite pos-sible for the care of the vulnerable to be shared more widely, but in the absence of a collective sense of responsibility for the needs of others, particularly the young and the old, the default position is not the 'nuclear family', but mothers. Two final considerations are relevant. First, as we saw in Chapter 1, divorce and repartnering are not confined to younger people. It is emerging among older adults as well, the consequences of which will be discussed in Chapter 10. Second, for this and other reasons it cannot be assumed that older generations will always put the needs of their children and grandchildren first, indeed Finch in Chapter 9 argues the opposite for the English case. They are being courted, as consumers, and many have relatively large disposable incomes. They may react, in time, to any policy assumptions that the childcare problems created by divorce and remarriage among their children can be solved by mobilizing grandparents through appeals to family solidarity.

6

Working Carers in the European Union

ROBERT ANDERSON

INTRODUCTION

This chapter reviews the situation of the carers of dependent older people in the European Union, specifically with regard to those carers who combine eldercare with paid employment. It considers the rationale for attention to the relationship between caring and working, and how this is addressed in the policies, programmes, and official documents of the EU institutions, as well as in member states.

When the chapter turns to look at the characteristics of, and problems faced by, working carers, it extends coverage by drawing material from research outside the EU, particularly from North America. So, too, when the focus is upon policy developments and workplace measures to improve the situation of working carers, the analysis is informed by experiences both in and outside the EU. It is paradoxical, when more and better data highlight the need for action to improve opportunities for working carers, that systematic documentation and research on these improvement initiatives is largely missing.

While the debate on the reconciliation of childcare and employment has moved forward quite vigorously with corresponding developments in public policies, collective bargaining, and workplace initiatives, the motor for action on eldercare appears to have stalled. The chapter concludes with a series of proposals for measures to address the evident challenge of working and caring in the EU and to improve the opportunities for those who want or need to combine eldercare with employment.

WORKING CARERS AS AN ISSUE

The reconciliation of employment with care responsibilities is, first and foremost, a problem for carers, as subsequent sections on the financial, emotional, and professional costs of caring should make clear. These personal costs of care have, however, been marginal to most of the policy debate on employment, and even to much of the analysis of care for dependent older people.

As Reichert and Naegele (1999) point out, the extensive information available on general aspects of home care in Europe (Hutten and Kerkstra, 1996) and on care policies in different countries (Bettio and Prenchal, 1998; European Commission, 1999*a*) dwarfs the meagre research into the situation of working carers.

In most EU member states, particularly in southern Europe, difficulties in resolving work–care conflicts have been managed within the family or (for example in Greece) by recruiting private help. Care policies in nearly all countries are built around the cornerstone of family care and depend more or less explicitly upon it. Specific consideration of carers' preferences or priorities in relation to employment has been neglected, although it is increasingly noted as an issue in reflections upon the sustainability of family care. There are increasing needs and pressures for people of working age, and particularly for more women, to be in employment. At the same time, employees appear increasingly determined to establish a better balance between work and non-work life. Such trends are current in Europe and may well generate greater conflicts between family care commitments and paid work (European Commission, 2000*a*; European Commission, 2000*b*). Over the last year EurolinkAge, a non-governmental organization, has brought together groups representing carers' interests from Finland, Belgium, the Netherlands, Ireland, and the UK. Although this initiative found little documentation of good practice in reconciliation of care and employment, it elaborated a strategy to meet carers' needs.

The implications of eldercare for the employers of working carers have been examined in a small number of European studies, as well as more extensively in research in the US and Canada (Reichert and Naegele, 1999). While Johnson and Lo Sasso in Chapter 7 describe mixed findings for the US from the perspective of labour productivity and caregiving, a recent US study of the costs of caregiving, in terms of lost productivity, estimated that US businesses were losing between $11.4 billion and $29 billion every year; and the trend will be for these costs to rise, as the number of employed caregivers is growing (Metlife, 1999). No comparable assessment has been made in Europe, but the business argument for attention to eldercare issues has been articulated for nearly a decade (Berry-Lound, 1994). The Industrial Society in the UK has recently drawn a clear picture of the costs of failure to support working carers in terms, for example, of employee performance, absenteeism, and recruitment costs (Daniels and McCarraher, 2000). More generally, arguments for a better work–life balance (e.g. DfEE, 2000) underline employers' needs to maintain their experienced, motivated, and productive workforces. There are many similarities to the business case for older workers (Walker, 1997) and clearly most working carers are in these older age groups. Apart from initiatives in the UK (e.g. Carers in Employment, 1995), employers in the EU do not appear to have established any formal networks to address the issue.

Governments in EU member states are primarily responsible for the organization and financing of care for dependent older people. The World Health Organization (2000) emphasizes that support to informal caregivers should be among the key principles for development of care policies; high priority should be given to considering workers who are carers, and to the protection of care-givers' rights and opportunities for employment. However, in most countries, the focus of care policies upon carers is generally vague and peripheral (Phillips, 1996). Furthermore, policies for care, while acknowledging the importance of family care, have tended to develop in isolation from policies for employment or for equal opportunities (Pearson, 1996). This limited approach to policies for care of older people is changing as countries such as Finland and Denmark develop more integrated approaches to ageing issues and, for example in the UK, where a national carers strategy is being developed (Department of Health, 1999). These are, however, relatively isolated examples: as an element of the European Employment Strategy, national governments are required to report upon developments to improve reconciliation of employment with care responsibilities—very few have identified new services or policies to support the carers of older people; the focus is upon developments for childcare (European Commission, 1999*a*).

The scale and pace of demographic change in Europe (European Commission, 2000*c*) demands rethinking of all those policies and institutions that originated in an era when population structure and outlook were very different. Other trends in family formation, household size and composition, female employment and mobility have for some years pointed to the changing prospects for family care of older people, even if it is difficult to make firm statements about the future (Salvage, 1995; Allen and Perkins, 1995; Nocon and Pearson, 2000). However, in the debate about the future of work and non-work life, childcare has dominated the agenda of governments and social partners in Europe. For many of the parties involved, the challenge remains to address eldercare and employment more explicitly as an issue for policy and practice.

THE EUROPEAN UNION AND WORKING CARERS

For nearly a decade key European Union policy documents have drawn attention to the employment problems of workers with caregiving responsibilities and have encouraged the development of measures to facilitate the reconciliation of care and employment (European Commission, 1993; 1994). Both Directives and Resolutions from the Council of Ministers, as well as agreements between the social partners at European level have contributed to the promotion of family-friendly employment. The focus is, however, upon childcare rather than eldercare, as reflected in the first formal social partner agreement at European level, which was for parental leave.

This agreement was signed at the end of 1995 following a process of consultation in which the Commission had proposed to widen the debate beyond the question of parental leave. The Commission believed that a more extensive approach to reconciling work and family life, specifically including the development of more flexible work patterns, would not only promote equality of opportunity between women and men, but would also contribute to boosting training and employment. During negotiations the issue of leave to care for dependent older relatives was introduced but did not attract adequate support. In essence, the final agreement guarantees workers a minimum of three months unpaid parental leave; it also includes an element to cover unforeseen absences from work for pressing family reasons.

The same emphasis upon childcare can be seen in the Resolution on the balanced participation of women and men in family and working life which was agreed by the Council of Employment and Social Affairs Ministers in June 2000. The text is overwhelmingly concerned with working fathers and mothers; there is only passing reference to the general need for measures to encourage a balanced sharing between working men and women of the care to be provided 'for children, elderly, disabled or other dependent persons'.

The Amsterdam Treaty put employment at the centre of the economic policy agenda of the Union, while also reinforcing attention to the reduction of inequality and the promotion of equal opportunities, in all aspects of work and non-work life. The member states agreed, in 1997, to develop and implement a European Employment Strategy which adopted a series of guidelines to increase employment rates in Europe—specifically through the promotion of employability, adaptability, entrepreneurship, and equal opportunities. The 1999 guidelines mainstream equal opportunities between women and men into all the guidelines largely because of the weaknesses found in this dimension in the annual reports from the member states. In the specific guideline on reconciliation of work and family life, there is a call for attention to measures that would support working carers—affordable, accessible, and high quality care services, and flexible working conditions. On the whole, though, these measures have failed to materialize, or at least to be reported, in policy or practice initiatives. Commitment to the promotion of family-friendly employment varies widely between the member states; as the most recent Annual Report on Equal Opportunities observes: 'Few Member States mentioned care facilities for the elderly and concrete initiatives on care for all other dependents (than children) are lacking in all of the National Action Plans' (European Commission, 2000a: 13).

These National Action Plans for employment and the reports of developments are prepared by the public administration in each member state. As such they do not, generally, reflect the results of systematic research, but the highlights of recent measures. Nevertheless, the highlights in relation to initiatives for working carers are sparse. In its analysis of the 1998 reports, the Commission identified new measures for childcare and eldercare in Greece, as well as new legislation in Sweden to improve access to, and quality of, care for the elderly, with increased budgets to local authorities for both childcare and eldercare. Effectively all measures reported to improve reconciliation of work and family life were directed to childcare, even though the same report emphasizes the changing nature of dependency in Europe with increasing numbers of older people and fewer children 'which will have significant implications, not only for the participation of women and men in the labour market, but also for the supply of both paid and unpaid care services' (European Commission, 1999*b*: 17). Various analyses from the Commission, on equal opportunities and employment, on the labour market and local development, have identified the need for the creation of formal employment in care services, arising at least in part from a concern that the 'care gap' will not be filled, as it has been in the past, by the informal and unpaid care of women. The tension between increased female unemployment and care responsibilities for older relatives has also raised concerns about the prospects for further increasing female employment rates (European Commission, 2000*c*).

In the EU social policy arena, the established priority of employment is fast being joined by initiatives to modernize social protection. In this area there is particular interest in the health and care needs of dependent older people, and a clear understanding that 'Support services...for people with disabilities or who are elderly and frail are of the utmost importance for improving the income security of people with families, especially women' (European Commission, 2000*c*: 4). The major trends that are regarded as being significant for the social protection systems are all directly related to the issue of working carers: the ageing of the European population; the changing gender balance in employment and the increasing numbers of women; the persistence of long-term unemployment, particularly among older workers; the trend to earlier retirement; and the rise in the number of single-person households (European Commission, 2000*b*). However, the key trends and the major issues—of social exclusion, the sustainability of pensions or the quality of health care services—tend not to be linked in any explicit way to the tensions around eldercare and employment.

The relative neglect of working carers is somewhat surprising given that the 1995 report on social protection (European Commission, 1995) looked specifically at the social protection arrangements of those who had given up paid work for a time or reduced their working hours 'due to the need to look after young children, disabled adults or elderly invalids' (p. 20). The report acknowledges that most of the focus has been upon the problems faced by those caring for children and that the situation of those caring for disabled adults and older people has been relatively neglected. It argues that the work problems people face in respect of caring obligations are both increasingly important and increasingly recognized in member states. In fact the evidence appears equivocal regarding the attention given to this issue in member states and even the Commission's interest has hardly been maintained in the social protection field. The issue of working and caring receives explicit attention primarily in the area of equal opportunities for women and men, under the umbrella of reconciling work and family life. In the next year or two the issue should, however, receive more priority as the conclusions of the Lisbon (2000) Summit of Heads of State called for more attention to the relationship between social protection and employment policies. Meanwhile, a number of key trends in European society do appear to underline the increasing importance of attention to the work and care problems of working carers, and of carers who would like to be in employment.

DEMOGRAPHY, DEPENDENCY, AND THE LABOUR MARKET

Many of the key trends are discussed elsewhere in this volume; this section will only address changes and developments directly related to the prospects and challenges for working carers in Europe.

Both the general population and the working age population in Europe are ageing. The growth in the number of people aged 65 and over is set to accelerate over the next 10–15 years as the post-war baby boom generation reaches their late sixties. Of particular interest is the increasing proportion of older elderly people, since these are those most likely to have health and care needs. Currently 3.8 per cent of the EU population is aged 80 or over ranging from 2.5 per cent in Ireland to 4.8 per cent in Sweden. Over the next decade it is projected that the number of people aged 80 and over will rise by 36 per cent (European Commission, 2000d). Of course, there are very significant regional and country differences, but Belgium, Greece, France, Italy, and Luxembourg are expected to experience the largest increases of around 50 per cent in a decade. Between 1995 and 2025 it is expected that there will be twice as many people aged 85 or over; and nearly three times as many people aged 90 or over. Bettio and Prenchal (1998) propose that by the year 2010 Europeans will probably comprise 1.5 children below age 10 for every person aged 75 and over, compared with 1.8 children in 1995—so people aged 75 and over will constitute 45 per cent of 'core' dependants compared with 35 per cent in 1995. The question is whether this notion of dependency will have practical meaning; in the context of discussing care needs it is easy to forget that most older people are fit, active, and living essentially independent lives.

A study which examined dependency at the European level found that just under two-fifths of people aged 60 and over reported some functional limitation (Walker, 1993). The variations were quite wide between countries, from 53 per cent in Greece to 22 per cent in Belgium suggesting that, apart from 'true' differences, some variations occur in interpretation of the question. There was the expected association between age and disability: 32 per cent of those aged 60–64 reported a limiting long-standing illness or disability compared with 47 per cent of those aged 80 and over. Such data, of course, say little about the extent to which help may be required and may underestimate the significance of some conditions such as dementia, the prevalence of which increases with age. In Walker's (1993) report, slightly less than one-third of people aged 65 and over reported receiving regular help with personal care or household tasks. There appear to be no precise data on the number of older people in Europe dependent on long-term care; it has been estimated that up to 5 per cent of people aged 65 and over are dependent upon regular social care and 15 per cent are partly dependent; these proportions increase with age so that 10 per cent of those aged 75 years and over are directly dependent, with around 25 per cent partly dependent (European Commission, 1999*a*).

The ageing of the population and the rapidly increasing numbers of older elderly people point to a corresponding increase in the need for care. Of course, effective demand for care will depend upon many factors, such as housing and technology (Salvage, 1995) as well as the health of the older population. There are some indications that the relationship between age and dependency is changing for the better with increased life expectancy and some delay in the onset of dependency until later in life (European Commission, 1999*a*; Jacobzone, 2000), especially with favourable trends in the duration of severe disability (Mathers and Robine, 1997). The recent OECD analysis indicates that in most of the advanced countries, disability-free life expectancy at age 65 is increasing (Jacobzone, 2000). However, this is a picture of general health improving, not that eventual need for care is avoided; and 'moderate' levels of disability may be particularly demanding of support from family carers. Furthermore, overall health and social needs are unlikely to decline significantly until effective treatments or interventions for cognitive impairments become available (Medical Research Council, 1999).

While not supporting the notion of a demographic 'time-bomb', these health and disability trends equally offer no substantial reason to expect diminishing demand for support from family carers. Other factors such as, for example, the increasing number of older people who live alone suggest increased demand for care from those with moderate disabilities. As other chapters have discussed, there are also important changes in family and household structures which complicate and possibly intensify demands upon family carers: people are marrying less and at later stages in their lives; divorces are more frequent; people are choosing to have children at a later stage in their lives; and family sizes are smaller (Salvage, 1995; European Commission, 2000*d*). In stark demographic terms, the probability of becoming a family carer is increasing.

The average age of the European workforce is increasing, but also patterns of labour-force participation, of entry and exit, have changed markedly over the last two decades. The female employment rate has increased from 44 per cent in 1975 to 50 per cent in 1996, and it appears that most of the growth in employment in recent years, and probably into the future, has been accounted for by women. This growth will include older as well as younger women; between 1986 and 1997, the proportion of men aged 55–64 participating in the EU workforce fell by 6 per cent while the corresponding figure for women rose by 4 per cent (European Commission, 2000*d*). Altogether some 42 per cent of the EU workforce is female, but the proportion is still below 40 per cent in Spain, Greece, Italy, and Luxembourg (European Commission, 2000*a*). It is also important to note that 6 per cent of men but about 1 in 3 women work part-time, with particularly high rates in the Netherlands (67 per cent of female employment) and in the UK (44 per cent) but with very low rates of part-time female workers in Greece (8 per cent), Italy, and Portugal (both 12 per cent) (European Commission, 1999c). This employment picture has complex links to family care, which are discussed next.

FAMILY CARERS AND EMPLOYMENT

Any review of this issue is blighted by methodological difficulties in comparing data from different studies, which have used a range of definitions of 'carer' and, to a lesser extent, of 'employment'. Data come from two main sources—surveys of carers which ask about employment and surveys of employers or workers which ask about caregiving activities. Few of these sources present nationally representative data but may be based upon workers in a company, or carers of people with particular conditions, or the recipients of a given service or benefit (Phillips, 1999). Most of the company-based studies are based in larger enterprises, and so far none of the community-based studies have reported any longitudinal analysis, although the European Community Household Panel Survey may be a source in the near future. The definition of a working carer varies in terms of criteria such as the number of hours of paid work to be defined as employed, the tasks and time commitments of the carer, and whether the carer and dependent person live together. The net result is that studies within as well as between countries produce non-comparable results on basic data such as the prevalence of working carers (Martin-Matthews, 1999).

The situation of family carers in the European Union has been documented in European surveys (Walker, 1993) as well as in a range of national studies (Jani-Le Bris, 1993). Even with the rapid social and economic changes of the last two or three decades, the family remains the main provider of care and support to older people. In both the original Eurobarometer survey and in a repeat of some questions in 1999, approximately one in ten Europeans aged 15 and over were providing care to someone within their household, and one in seven were providing care to someone outside the household—as a result of long-term illness, disability, or old age (Walker, 1999). Of course, these data say nothing about the character of the care activities, their intensity or duration. New data from the 1995 wave of the European Community Household Panel Survey (European Commission, 2000d) indicated that only 6 per cent of adults in the EU were providing care to sick or disabled adults and older people (in the same household and outside)—but carers were spending a high average of 21 hours per week on this care.

The extent of in-house care depends significantly upon the composition of the household: it is, for example, much more common for families in Spain, Italy, and Greece to share the same household as the dependent older person, and therefore to provide care within the household. Walker's recent (1999) analysis shows that the proportion who reported providing non co-resident care to a relative aged 60 and over (mainly parents) varied markedly between EU member states broadly on a north–south axis: it ranged from 20 per cent in Finland and around 12 per cent in Denmark, Sweden, the Netherlands, and Ireland to 4 per cent or less in Italy, Spain, and Portugal. Evidently, the availability of other forms of support, especially from public services, is also a key consideration (Salvage, 1995; Walker, 1993). While acknowledging the significance of country differences, the basic finding of the Eurobarometer survey is that two-thirds of the care provided to older people comes from within the family.

In all countries, the majority of carers are women, even if the proportion varies between Member States and depends upon the nature of the care provided. Overall, differences between women and men in reporting that they provide some care may not be very large. Corti and Dex (1995) examined data from the 1991 British Household Panel Survey and found that similar proportions of men and women were co-resident carers, but women were more often non-resident carers. Among the co-resident carers, one-third spent at least 50 hours a week on caring while more than half of non-resident carers devoted less than 5 hours a week to these activities. Women report more time spent caring than men; in the European Panel Survey (European Commission, 2000*d*) women averaged 22 hours per week compared with 18 hours for men. People of working age, particularly women, appear most likely to take on the care of older relatives (Walker, 1999; Corti and Dex, 1995), with the peak among those in the second half of working life (Bettio and Prenchal, 1998). In the European Panel Survey (European Commission, 2000*d*) the prime age for caregiving to sick, disabled, or frail adults was 50–59. In Great Britain (DfEE, 2000) it has been estimated that 22 per cent of women and 17 per cent of men aged 45–64 give care to a dependent adult. However, male carers may be more likely to be sharing caregiving with others (Jani-Le Bris, 1993) and may define their role more in management of caregiving than direct personal care (Phillips, 1994; Berry-Lound, 1994).

Among carers of working age, a considerable proportion are in employment. There are no published EU data, but figures from national studies indicate that up to half of carers under age 65 combine care with employment. A survey of carers in Germany (Schneekloth and Potthoff, 1993) reported that 72 per cent of the main carers of those in need of nursing care were not employed, but among carers aged 18–64, nearly half were combining care with paid employment. Similarly, in the United Kingdom, it is reported that just under half of carers are working full-time or part-time (DfEE, 2000). Among people of working age responding to the 1991 British Household Panel Survey, 62 per cent of male carers were in employment, compared with 77 per cent of all men in the age group 16–64; and 43 per cent of married women carers of working age were in employment compared with 60 per cent of all married women (Corti and Dex, 1995). So, among people of working age, both men and women carers are less likely to be in employment than non-carers and carers are more likely to work part-time. These data also show that the proportion of men among working carers is higher than in the general population of carers; and this has been found elsewhere (Hoskins, 1993). Other factors influencing the likelihood that a carer will be in employment include whether the carer lives with the dependent person, nature of dependency, and availability of other support (Phillips, 1999).

Many of these data on carers are nearly a decade old. More recent and perhaps more practical data have been derived from surveys of workers. Martin-Matthews (1999) has estimated that between 12 and 16 per cent of employed Canadians are active in care for older people (comparable with a figure of 15 per cent for Great Britain in 1990—Carers in Employment Group, 1995).

A recent survey carried out by the European Foundation for the Improvement of Living and Working Conditions provides unique data. The survey involved telephone interviews in the summer and autumn of 1998 with more than 30,000 people aged between 16 and 64 years across the fifteen member states and Norway. Among those in employment, 9 per cent of men and 12 per cent of women reported 'care responsibilities' for elderly relatives or other adults who need assistance due to ill-health or incapacity' (Fagan et al., forthcoming). The corresponding figures were higher for people outside employment but seeking work—13 and 16 per cent respectively, reinforcing the point that care responsibilities act as a barrier to the labour market. Care responsibilities are, as in other studies, related to age: among people aged 50 and over who were employed or job seekers, 20 per cent of women and 15 per cent of men reported adult care responsibilities compared with 16 per cent and 12 per cent respectively among workers in their 40s. So, giving care to older people occupies a significant proportion of the workforce particularly among the growing numbers of older workers. There are, of course, important country differences and the proportions of workers with eldercare responsibilities were twice as high in Greece, Portugal, Spain, and Italy as in the UK, Denmark, and the Netherlands. Data from the first wave of the European Household Panel Survey likewise show relatively high proportions of working women aged 35–64 involved in eldercare in Greece, Spain, and Italy (Van Solinge, 1998).

Men and women who were employed and reported eldercare responsibilities worked similar hours to men and women without these responsibilities (although significant differences, especially for women, have been reported elsewhere, e.g. Phillips, 1999). The differences in working time were between men and women. Among those with eldercare responsibilities, 17 per cent of women and 2 per cent of men worked less than 20 hours a week, 29 per cent of women and 6 per cent of men worked 20–34 hours, and only 54 per cent of women but 92 per cent of men worked full-time (Lilja and Hämäläinen, forthcoming). The workers without eldercare responsibilities were more satisfied with their hours of work than those who had these care duties. Among workers who report care responsibilities many will share at least some of the tasks with a spouse, if not with siblings (Jani-Le Bris, 1993). Interestingly, among the wives of employed men aged 45–64 only a quarter worked full-time in Spain, Italy, and Ireland compared with half or more in the Nordic countries. This is suggestive of the role of spouses in care and an association with the availability of services for home care of older people.

There is a lack of detailed knowledge about the relationship between the number of working hours and the number of caring hours and the tasks involved. The European Foundation survey shows that in general carers work as many hours as non-carers, but carers with particularly high care responsibilities appear less likely to be in employment (Lazcko and Noden, 1992). It appears that carers in employment are less likely to contribute high numbers of hours per week to caring (European Commission, 2000*d*; Corti and Dex, 1995). This raises the question though, whether carers with high care demands are people who were never in full-time paid employment or those who had to leave or reduce employment because of caring responsibilities.

There are a number of studies that indicate the extent of reduced labour market participation among people who take up care responsibilities. The representative survey of carers in Germany has been referred to, in which two-thirds of carers of working age were in employment when caring began; subsequently at least one quarter had given up work and a similar proportion had reduced working hours (Schneekloth and Potthoff, 1993). In the 1991 British survey (Corti and Dex, 1995), twice as many carers, compared with all working women, reported that they had had to leave their job or cut down on working hours; the data show a similar, if not worse, situation for the male carers. Data from a survey of carers in Spain (Duran, 2000)—among whom half provided 5 or more hours of support daily—indicate that 12 per cent had left employment and 12 per cent reduced working hours. Other less representative surveys in Ireland (O'Connor and Ruddle, 1988) and in the Ile-de-France region (Jani-Le Bris and Luquet, 1993) have found that about 1 in 8 carers had left employment because of care responsibilities.

The factors influencing the decision to give up work or reduce hours are complex and will involve factors such as the carer's household income, gender, marital status, and stage in the life cycle, as well as the nature of dependency. Evidently, changes in employment—leaving the job, reducing hours, rejecting promotion—have professional, financial, and personal consequences. In the European Foundation survey (Fagan et al., forthcoming), among those providing care to adult dependants, one-quarter of the women and 15 per cent of the men felt that this care limited their employment opportunities. The proportion who expressed this view ranged from less than 10 per cent in Sweden and Finland, to more than a third in the UK and Ireland. There was also a link between early exit plans and care responsibilities—among those aged 50–59 who are currently employed but who think they will not be employed five years hence, more than 40 per cent of women and 20 per cent of men think they will be caring for an elderly relative (Lilja and Hämäläinen, forthcoming).

While care responsibilities may be a factor in early retirement (Phillips, 1999; Lazcko and Noden, 1992) especially where these are heavy, for some carers employment is a key condition for sustaining the role of carer (Jani-Le Bris, 1993). Employment can offset the trials and tribulations of caring; it provides an alternative focus for daily life and may offer contacts with colleagues who can provide advice and support. It also obviously provides an income and pension rights to reduce the risk of poverty in old age. Nevertheless, missed career opportunities, the need to forego overtime, lost pay from unpaid time off, or reduced hours of work may contribute to the finding that carers in paid employment had lower incomes than households of all people in paid employment (Corti and Dex, 1995).

Two studies of the longer-term effects of being a carer point strongly to adverse impacts on career and income-earning prospects. Hancock and Jarvis (1994) looked at the experiences of more than 1,000 past carers. They reported that both male and female carers had lower incomes from employment as well as reduced occupational and personal pensions. People who had cared for more than ten years were worse off financially compared with people who had cared for shorter periods. The Metlife (1999) study involved 55 caregivers aged 45 and over who had made some adjustment to work because of caregiving. Again a significant proportion, 40 per cent, reported missed career, training, or promotion opportunities, while two-thirds reported loss of earnings; the lifetime impacts on income and retirement benefits were substantial.

When the caring is over, carers may experience difficulties in finding a job, perhaps because of age discrimination (Walker, 1997) or because they lack the confidence or the skills to return to work, or because, in their circumstances, there are financial disincentives to return to work (Jacobzone, 2000). The relationship between caring and employment is complex and dynamic. It appears though that many carers, in fact most, continue in employment. While there is no necessary conflict between working and caregiving, carers often experience reduced opportunities in employment and may, particularly where their care responsibilities are heavy, have no option but to give up work altogether.

CARERS IN EMPLOYMENT AND THEIR NEEDS

The financial disadvantages of being a carer are only one amongst a range of problems that carers face. Carers often fail to appreciate the time commitment they will make (Metlife, 1999) as well as the intensity of demands, pressures, and disappointments they will encounter. Not surprisingly, relatively high levels of burden are often reported by the general population of carers (Schneekloth and Potthoff, 1993) with deterioration in relationships, in family life, in morale, and social participation found in a series of country studies in Europe (Jani-Le Bris, 1993). The health of carers may suffer, with stress-related conditions (O'Connor and Ruddle, 1988) as well as widespread fatigue and tiredness (Duran, 2000). However, the general population of carers is older than the working population, as well as including more spouse carers. The following assessments are restricted to studies of working carers, regrettably nearly all from the UK; knowledge of working carers' needs and preferences is still very patchy at least in the published literature (and there appear to be few company-based audits in Europe).

Employment is, as referred to earlier, not only a source of tension and conflict, but for many working carers, an essential balance or counterweight to caregiving roles (Jani-Le Bris, 1993; Hoskins, 1994). However, while work may have a favourable influence on caring, the reverse seems rarely to be the case, even if patience, managerial skills, and a sense of responsibility acquired as a carer may be valued (Lazcko and Noden, 1992). This impression may be one shared by many carers who are reluctant to identify themselves as such and may feel a certain stigma (DfEE, 2000), generating some hesitation to use support services or entitlements.

Information on the problems faced by working carers tends to come from surveys in specific workplaces or enterprises. Response rates are a problem and generally it should be expected that a higher proportion of carers than non-carers will complete a questionnaire on caring experiences. Nevertheless, some such surveys can usefully indicate the nature of problems and preferences even if exact figures are misleading.

The CARNET study (Martin-Matthews, 1999) surveyed more than 8,500 employees in large Canadian companies—45 per cent of employees reported giving some care to an older person in the previous 6 months, most of which was instrumental care (shopping, driving, etc.), but 12 per cent reported help with personal care such as washing and dressing. Although only 13 per cent of women workers and 8 per cent of male workers provided care for 5 hours or more every week, a high proportion of all working carers (41 per cent) had experienced one or more unpredicted crises in the previous 6 months. The burdens of caring were higher for both men and women who provided help with personal (cf. instrumental) care. Women carers also reported more sickness and absenteeism, and participated less in company events or non-essential activities. Women carers also appeared to be much more disadvantaged in terms of promotion and career opportunities.

Surveys of employees in a private and public sector organization in England (Berry-Lound, 1994), showed many similarities in the extent of caring and care responsibilities. Surprisingly, a high proportion of carers in both workplaces were under 45 years of age, and a number of employees in both organizations who worked full-time also provided more than 20 hours of care every week. Only a minority of respondents were providing direct personal care. Half of the almost 400 employee carers worried about their caring responsibilities while at work. A quarter reported that they had arrived late to work and a similar proportion that they had left work early because of their caring responsibilities. Forty per cent of the employee carers had taken time off work to care, and one in five had co-ordinated care services while they were at work, presumably involving time on the telephone. Employees also reported lost opportunities for training and promotion and almost 10 per cent had considered leaving the job because of difficulties combining work with caring. Among the most common demands from the working carers was raising of awareness among managers and other employees about how caring for older people affects staff at work. A majority of respondents said they would find training courses on 'preparation for caring' useful. Specifically, they would value information on services in the area and how to access them. Among the services which were not available, there was demand for respite care in the evenings, weekends, and holidays.

In other studies, carers have emphasized the unpredictability of caring and the need for flexibility in working times and organization of work, for time off for emergencies, retraining after a career break and part-time work (Carers in Employment, 1995). The relative lack of part-time posts in traditional male employment as well as cultural expectations and traditions may contribute to particular problems for men in reconciling work and care. Phillips (1994) has identified a range of factors—in the caring situation and relationship, the availability of alternative support and in working conditions—that affect the problems facing carers. Pearson (1996) has emphasized the location of the dependent person relative to the caregiver and their degree of dependence. The response to these problems will be influenced by resources available, but also by the values and attitudes of the key players in the workplace and public policy.

DEVELOPMENTS FOR WORKING CARERS

The European Union's employment policy guidelines have highlighted the care issue as an important element influencing the ability of workers to remain in and to return to employment. However, our picture of developments to support the working carers of older people is poor and incomplete. There has been no systematic survey of initiatives in the workplace, even in larger enterprises, although there are efforts to collect examples of positive developments (Hoffmann, 1992; Phillips, 1996). Some information is available from a volume of experiences in Europe and North America (Reichert and Naegele, 1999) and from a study of collective bargaining agreements in the EU (EFILWC, 1999). More tangential material on relevant developments in policy and public services has recently been published in reports sponsored by the European Commission (Bettio and Prenchal, 1998; European Commission, 1999a; European Commission, 2000e). However, there are relatively few examples of initiatives, particularly in the workplace, that have been designed specifically for carers of older people.

It has been argued that corporate America has woken to the pressures that its (valued) employees face in caring for elderly relatives. To retain skilled employees and to maintain productivity, it does appear that a growing number of US companies, albeit mainly the bigger household names (e.g. AT&T, IBM, Hewlett Packard, Bank of Boston), are providing support. These developments are usually characterized as: policies—for work organization and working time, particularly for different forms of flexible working hours and flexible location, such as homeworking; services—typically for information, advice, and referral, but also including support to develop community services, transport for dependent relatives, and some workplace-based care provision; and benefits—such as preferential rates for long-term care insurance that covers the older person, or cash compensation for time taken off to care.

Even in the United States, however, 'Few companies have employer-sponsored programmes or eldercare services which formally support caregivers and minimize productivity losses' (Metlife, 1999: 8). In fact, it is estimated that somewhat less than a quarter of companies with 100 or more employees have programmes in place to support carers. Some initiatives have been abandoned after failing to meet carer needs because the schemes were too inflexible, or in the wrong place at the wrong time; for example, the footwear company StrideRite opened a daycare centre but closed it due to lack of demand from dependent older people many of whom lived too far from the facility and were not interested by the service. Other initiatives have been strained by low take-up by carers, particularly of information and care services. Some workers are hesitant about the impression they will create as lacking in motivation or the capacity to cope; others are simply unaware of the available resources, while as Phillips (1996) notes, for others care is a private matter to be resolved by private solutions. This last may also be the view of other staff at work and it seems clear that the success of developments for working carers will depend upon support from line managers and colleagues. The various schemes and opportunities should be seen as fair, accessible to all and of benefit to more than one group of employees.

The United States and the European Union of course present different contexts and prospects for reconciliation of working and caring. In general, Europeans have more extensive support through social protection schemes and related community and care services—accepting that these are highly variable and may not be directed to the support of carers. Some of the private company initiatives from the US may be neither necessary nor appropriate in the European context and, although specific measures have been developed for carers in European workplaces (Phillips, 1996; Hoffmann, 1992), company-sponsored services are not widespread. In Europe, the emphasis has been upon working time and organization, good communication and explicit management support, rather than the development of special eldercare initiatives (Daniels and McCarraher, 2000).

Over the last decade, at least in the UK, the family-friendly agenda has moved somewhat from direct help with childcare to a range of benefits and flexible working practices designed to support a wider range of employees with caring responsibilities—at least in those enterprises with formal policies or pro-grammes. A survey of leading organizations (Industrial Relations Services, 2000) found that part-time working, family/emergency leave, and jobsharing were the most common approaches; flexitime and homeworking tended to be reserved for certain employee groups and there was little opportunity for tem-porary reduction of working time. Some specific assistance with eldercare, such as establishing a self-help forum for carers (by a local authority employer), was evident but not common. Formal schemes to support carers have usually been investigated, though seldom evaluated, in large businesses, but there is evidence of some support to carers in smaller and medium-sized enterprises (Bevan et al., 1999). The main strategy to enable workers to combine their employment with caring was some form of flexitime arrangement. Again, Bevan and colleagues (1999) emphasize the importance for success of positive attitudes from col-leagues and managers; they underline the need for support from senior man-agers and for clarity of information on schemes and eligibility conditions. It is also clear that the existence of supportive policy statements should not be mis-understood to represent meaningful options in practice.

Many, if not all, workplace initiatives will be developed by employers in consultation with their workers. More formal collective bargaining agree-ments also play an important role, especially in improving arrangements, for example for leave, that go beyond legally required minimum standards. The European Foundation's (1999) report identified many examples of agreements on short- or medium-term family leave to care for children and dependent family members, some few of which specifically benefit carers of dependent older relatives—for example: an agreement in the Dutch insurance sector allows unpaid leave to care for a seriously ill partner or parent, if dependent, for up to 6 months; in Spain, an iron and steel industry agreement provides voluntary leave of absence to care for a relative with serious disability, for not less than one year and not more than five years, accompanied by an entitle-ment to keep the job open. There are considerable differences between sectors in the duration of leave allowed, in conditions for entitlement, and in the extent to which leave is paid. For carers, such leave entitlements may be helpful, but also too inflexible to meet regular and unpredictable care needs. In gen-eral, these collective agreements to provide leave or part-time work to care for an older person cover rather few carers, and the take-up appears to be low (Bettio and Prenchal, 1998).

Government action to support carers is considerably more extensive than reflected in the reporting of National Action Plans for employment. However, many of the initiatives are recent and most pay little attention to improving employment opportunities for carers. The following section focuses upon measures more significant for working carers; again the initiatives can be con-sidered in terms of policies, services and benefits for working carers.

Public policies may serve to increase awareness and recognition of the contribution and rights of working carers even when they offer little direct support with either employment or care tasks. Among policy measures, those that enable carers to take time off, albeit unpaid, are important. Eligibility to leave for family care may depend upon the relationship to the dependent person or to the terms of employment, and is generally recognized only when the older person is severely ill or for very short periods (Bettio and Prenchal, 1998). Sweden grants the longest duration of 60 days leave in cases of very severe illness, while in Finland and Belgium, longer periods off work can be taken in the framework of multi-purpose career break schemes (European Commission, 1998) in which rights to sickness, pension, and unemployment benefits are maintained. Paid leave to care for family members is possible in Italy and Finland (European Commission, 2000e). Nevertheless, take-up of these leave entitlements appears to be low (Bettio and Prenchal, 1998) and there may be concerns about how employers and colleagues will react when leave is taken. Currently, in Ireland, a Carers' Leave Bill is under discussion which would entitle carers to take unpaid leave to provide full-time care for up to 65 weeks. The National Carers' Association has argued that jobs should be kept open for longer on the grounds that the average period of care for recipients of the carers' allowance is more than three years.

The Austrian government has developed an information and advisory service for carers (European Commission, 2000e) and similar support may be available in other member states through initiatives involving voluntary and carers' associations. Services to help the dependent person, whether transport, day care, home help, or respite care, will often, of course, benefit the carer. The rights of older persons to residential and home care services vary across the member states as do levels of provision (European Commission, 1999a; European Commission, 1998). The presence or availability of informal support may influence the provision of formal services; and this clearly may impinge upon the carer's rights to continue in employment.

Direct financial support to carers may come from a range of benefits including specific allowances or continued payment of social benefits during leave. In general, the introduction of allowances directly to carers is not relevant to working carers as those in employment are ineligible for the allowance. Where the allowance has been designed to be paid at a higher level, for example in Finland, as reimbursement for work, this may be an incentive to leave employment. Similarly, the development of care insurance schemes in Germany, Austria, and Luxembourg or of other schemes, such as dependency benefit in France, which enable older people to employ family members as carers, may influence employment decisions. However, of course, this will depend upon the scheme's criteria and level of payment as well as upon the employment and working hours of the carer. Other aspects of these schemes may be of assistance to some working carers: for example, those workers in Germany who, as a result of care demands, are not gainfully employed more than 30 hours per week, may have their contributions paid to the statutory pension insurance (European Commission, 2000e). Although the impact of financial benefits on the carer's employment requires more study, the numbers who have, for this reason, left formal employment to provide care are likely to be low (European Commission, 1999*a*).

CONCLUSION

It is widely acknowledged at EU level (e.g. European Commission, 1999*d*; European Commission, 2000*d*) and in some member states that the ability to combine employment with care for a dependent older person will increase in importance. Across Europe, family care persists as the cornerstone of measures to support older people in need, while female employment has been growing. Although many factors will influence the scale of care demands (Salvage, 1995), these are not likely to decrease, while the general policy objectives in employment involve increasing both women's employment rates and those of older workers. The resolution of these trends requires that care for older people, both at home and in the community, is organized in such a way that caregivers can participate in the labour force. This will involve the development of more support services in the workplace and in the community, as well as rethinking of the division of labour within households.

Trends in employment towards a more flexible workforce may have both positive and negative implications for carers. On the one hand, flexible hours or part-time employment may enable time for caring; on the other the uncertainties of some novel contracting, temporary, and 'on-call' employment may make employment hours less predictable and care arrangements less sustainable. There may be concern too about the opportunities for continuous training and career development of those in more flexible employment. As employers develop 'family-friendly' policies, it remains to be seen if these extend to workers in part-time and temporary employment, or those working in small and medium-sized enterprises.

Although the effects of changes in work contracts and conditions have been emphasized in their effects on women, increasingly men too are engaged on atypical contracts, working part-time and from home, and entering self-employment. This may facilitate care-giving and is often a feature of the employment of older workers who are also those most likely to have responsibilities for elderly parents. However, men may be more involved in care tasks which are independent of time while women are more constrained to perform personal care and other tasks which are dictated by or dependent upon performance at particular times.

Notwithstanding the importance of working and caring as an issue for employers and policy makers, there remains a significant deficit of direct information— on the situation of carers, their numbers, concerns, and preferences, presented in ways relevant to those concerned with policies for social protection, equal opportunities, and employment. There is a lack of systematic information on how family care and its relationship with employment is changing across

Europe. The conditions under which carers are able to seek and sustain employment, or else have to quit work or care, are not well known. More detailed analyses of these changes or of the potential effects of policy interventions may contribute to the focusing of policy interest among governments, employers or unions. For example, there is a need for analysis of: the impact of care insurance; the costs and benefits of the introduction of workplace support to carers; the prospects for good quality employment in the care sector; factors influencing take-up of services, leave opportunities, and benefits. There is also the need to examine the patterns and prospects in the different EU member states.

This chapter has pointed to a large agenda for research, practice, and policy. It has underlined the relatively low profile of working carers in the debates on employment, on social protection, on equal opportunities, and on reconciliation of work with family life. While lessons can and should be learnt from the debate on childcare and employment, eldercare is different in important respects: more men and older workers are involved; most working carers reside in a different household from the older person; care needs are unpredictable and the final outcome is not usually independence; carers may feel they had little choice about their responsibilities. There are a range of potential opportunities to improve the situation of working carers—in policies, services, and benefits (e.g. Salvage, 1995; Phillips, 1996)—many of which are not relevant to childcare. There is, therefore, a need for more explicit attention to the links between eldercare and employment; and for more direct incorporation of working carers into the current debates on the future of employment and the future of care.

7

Family Support of the Elderly and Female Labour Supply: Trade-Offs among Caregiving, Financial Transfers, and Work— Evidence from the US Health and Retirement Survey

RICHARD W. JOHNSON AND
ANTHONY T. LO SASSO

INTRODUCTION

Women's increasing participation in the labour force has transformed family relations over the past thirty years. Much attention has been focused on the changing role of women as mothers and how the rise in employment rates for married women affects fertility, childcare, and child development. The impact of women's growing involvement in the labour market on eldercare has received less attention. However, the effects may be substantial. Adult daughters have traditionally served as the primary caregivers for their frail parents, but their growing employment responsibilities may be incompatible with their traditional caregiving role. In this chapter we explore how women at mid-life balance support of their elderly parents with their responsibilities in the workplace.

Caring for frail elderly parents can interfere with paid employment. Adult daughters may need to take time off from work or retire altogether in order to care for their parents or to help them with chores or errands. Some elderly persons who are very frail need constant care and cannot be left alone, making paid work virtually impossible for family members who serve as primary caregivers,

Financial support was provided by grant 7R03AG15525-02 from the National Institute on Ageing and by the Retirement Project, a multi-year research effort at the Urban Institute funded by the Andrew W. Mellon Foundation. The opinions expressed are those of those authors and do not necessarily reflect the views of the Urban Institute, its board, or its sponsors.

unless the care is shared among several family members. Parents who require less intensive care may still need assistance that can interfere with work schedules, such as help with the preparation of meals or with transportation to doctors' offices.

An alternative means of supporting frail parents would be to provide them with financial assistance. Instead of providing care to their parents themselves, which can interfere with paid employment, some workers may choose to help their parents financially. Parents could then use the cash transfers to purchase formal home healthcare services or to defray the cost of nursing-home care. Substituting financial support to parents for time help would allow some children to help their parents without reducing their hours of work, which may be especially attractive to workers who earn high wages. Some adult children might even increase their labour supply in order to provide more generous financial support to their parents.

This chapter examines the relationship between labour supply, time help to parents, and financial assistance to parents for a nationally representative sample of American women aged 53 to 63. Because parents who reside in nursing homes or co-reside with their adult children may need different amounts of help from those living independently, we also modelled the effects of parental living arrangements on transfers to parents. We found that women who helped their parents with personal care assistance worked significantly fewer hours than those who did not help their parents, while those who provided financial assistance worked significantly more hours.

BACKGROUND

As described for Europe in Chapters 6 and 8, the family has traditionally been an important provider of care to the frail elderly people in the US as well. Despite the attention focused on the high cost of nursing-home care, most eldercare is provided informally at home by family members. In 1996, just 4.2 per cent of persons aged 65 and older were in nursing homes (National Center for Health Statistics, 1998), but many more elderly persons living in the community required care. For example, 10.5 per cent of the non-institutionalized elderly in 1996 were unable to complete basic personal activities such as getting out of bed or dressing without help and another 11 per cent were limited in their ability to perform these basic activities unaided (National Center for Health Statistics, 1998). The help that frail elderly persons receive at home generally comes from close relatives. For example, 57 per cent of primary caregivers for impaired, community-dwelling persons aged 70 and older are either the spouses or adult children of the care recipients (McGarry, 1998). For unmarried elderly care recipients, adult children account for 42 per cent of all caregivers. Recent evidence indicates that a large minority of elderly persons receive informal care, particularly once they reach very advanced ages, and that the personal characteristics of both the elderly and their adult children, including gender, race, marital status, and health, are important determinants of the amount of care received by parents and provided by children (Cicirelli, 1983; Ettner, 1996; Mui, 1995; Silverstein and Waite, 1993; Sloan et al., 1997; Spitze and Logan, 1989; 1990; 1992; Stern, 1995; Stoller and Earl, 1983; Wolf and Soldo, 1994).

However, ongoing demographic and socio-economic trends are increasing time pressures for women with frail parents who attempt to fulfil both their traditional caregiving responsibilities and their emerging responsibilities in the workplace. Over the past generation, women have assumed a much larger role in the labour market, limiting the amount of time they are able to devote to other responsibilities, including caring for their frail parents. Only 36 per cent of married women aged 45 to 64 were employed in 1960, compared with 65 per cent in 1997 (US Census Bureau, 1998). The increased work responsibilities of women, who have historically been the primary caregivers for the frail elderly, may become incompatible with their caregiving responsibilities.

At the same time, the demand for help with personal care by the elderly has been changing. It is difficult to assess long-term trends in the need for care. Increases in longevity and declines in fertility have raised the number of elderly Americans over time, but improvements in health have decreased disability rates among the elderly since at least the mid-1980s.[1] Elderly disability rates may have begun to fall much earlier, but reliable data do not extend back beyond twenty years. One way to assess long-term changes in the number of elderly persons who need care is to compare over time the proportion of the population that is in the final year of life, since the need for care often increases dramatically as an individual approaches death. Based on census data on the size of the American population by age and vital statistics data on the probability of death by age in 1960 and 1997 (Anderson, 1999; National Center for Health Statistics, 1963), we computed the number of Americans aged 65 and older in the last year of life, per 10,000 persons in the total population. The rate increased from 53 per 10,000 in 1960 to 64 per 10,000 in 1997. As the number of elderly persons who may need care rises and the number of married women in the labour force increases, time pressures on families will intensify. How families respond to these pressures will have important implications for retirement and long-term care policies.

Relationship between Caregiving and Labour Supply

Economic theory predicts that individuals will reduce their labour supply when they devote time to the help of their parents. When workers choose to help their parents, they can either reduce the amount of time they devote to

---

[1] Disability rates among the elderly in the US declined from 24.9 per cent in 1982 to 21.3 per cent in 1994 (Manton, Corder, and Stallard, 1997).

paid work or they can reduce the amount of time they devote to leisure. Under standard assumptions about individual preferences, the theory predicts that persons will reduce both their hours of paid employment and their leisure time when they devote time to their parents.

The available evidence on the relationship between caregiving and labour supply is mixed. Whereas some researchers have concluded that hours of paid work reduce hours of time assistance or that hours of time assistance reduce hours of work, others have been unable to find statistically significant relationships between caregiving and labour supply. Most bivariate comparisons of hours of work and time assistance have found that they are negatively related. In early work, Muurinen (1986) reported that caregivers suffered income losses because their caregiving responsibilities often forced them to withdraw from the labour force or to reduce their work hours. Brody and Schoonover (1986) found that working daughters of disabled elderly widows provided less personal care and help with cooking than non-working daughters (but that the shortfall was made up by purchased help). More recently, Boaz (1996) reported that primary caregivers who worked full time in 1989 provided less time assistance than primary caregivers who did not work at all (19.9 hours per week vs. 41.8 hours). Soldo and Hill (1995), examining data from the first wave of the Health and Retirement Study (HRS), found that work hours and hours of time help were negatively correlated. Stone and Short (1990) found that some adult children caring for their parents were forced to rearrange their work schedules to accommodate their caregiving responsibilities, but that their caregiving duties did not appear to affect the probability of employment.

Results of more sophisticated multivariate analyses have been less consistent, however, and appear to depend on the ways in which the analytic samples were constructed and on the choices of estimating techniques. For example, one study using data from the National Survey of Families and Households (NSFH) found that the provision of care to parents had no significant effect on the labour supply of men or women when the caregiving indicator entered the hours of work equation directly (Ettner, 1996). However, when using instrumental variable techniques that account for the fact that individuals choose whether or not to provide care, the study found that providing non-coresidential care to elderly parents reduced the number of hours of paid work for women but not for men, while co-residing with frail elderly parents had large negative but insignificant effects on work hours for both men and women. Using cross-sectional data from the Survey of Income and Program Participation (SIPP), Ettner (1995) found when not instrumenting for caregiving that the provision of more than 10 hours per week of parental assistance and co-residence with a disabled parent both significantly reduced hours of work; when instrumenting for caregiving, only co-residence had a significant effect. Panel data from the National Longitudinal Survey of Mature Women indicate that women who start providing care to disabled family members report significantly fewer hours of paid employment than women who never provided care (Pavalko and Artis, 1997). Doty, Jackson, and Crown (1998), who used data from the 1989 National Long Term Care Survey (NLTCS) and its companion Informal Caregivers Survey, found that paid employment by female primary caregivers significantly reduced the hours of care they provided. However, virtually the entire shortfall was made up by secondary caregivers, including paid helpers, who increased their time assistance when the primary caregiver worked. Total hours of assistance provided by all parties to the care recipient fell with hours of paid work only when the female primary caregiver worked more than 17 hours per week.

Other researchers have concluded that the provision of care to frail parents does not significantly reduce hours of paid work. For example, a study based on the NSFH found that caring for either elderly parents or parents-in-law had a negative but insignificant effect on the work hours of married women (Wolf and Soldo, 1994). Using data from the NLTCS, Stern (1995) also found that the effect of hours of paid work on the receipt of informal care from children was insignificant when he employed instrumental variable techniques but significant when he did not instrument. Another study, which treated the level of informal care as an exogenous variable, found that caring for spouses encouraged women to retire from the labour force, but that parental care had no effect on labour force withdrawals (Dentinger and Clarkberg, 1999). Pezzin and Schone (1999) estimated a simultaneous, multi-equation, endogenous switching model of informal care, parent–daughter co-residence, and female labour supply based on data from the 1986–7 matched Hebrew Rehabilitation Center for the Aged (HRCA) Survey of the Elderly in Massachusetts and HRCA–NBER Child Survey. They found that the correlation between informal care and labour force participation was negative but small, and concluded that the trade-offs between labour supply and parental caregiving decisions were modest for adult daughters.

Financial Transfers

In addition to providing caregiving services, adult children can support their elderly parents by providing financial assistance. In 1992, for example, an estimated 7 per cent of persons aged 51–61 with surviving parents transferred at least $500 to their parents during the previous 12 months (McGarry and Schoeni, 1995). Those who helped their parents financially transferred on average $2,100 per year. An elderly person is more likely to receive help from an adult child than an adult child is to provide help, because most elderly persons have more than one child. In 1988, 12 per cent of all elderly persons in the NSFH, and 15 per cent of those with at least one non-co-resident adult child, reported receiving regular financial assistance from their children (Freedman et al., 1991).

The ways in which families choose among different types of support for their elderly members and how these different types of support affect labour supply are not well understood, although a few recent studies have begun to explore some of these trade-offs. Using data from the 1988 wave of the Panel Study of Income Dynamics, Couch, Daly, and Wolf (1999) estimated a joint model of time use and monetary transfers to examine how adult children supported their elderly parents. They found that money transfers to parents responded positively and significantly to the wage rates of married and unmarried men and women. Time transfers, in contrast, responded negatively to the wage rates of unmarried men and women and married men, but not to those of married women. In general, households with individuals earning high wages relied relatively more on cash transfers and relatively less on time transfers than did lower-wage households. The researchers also found evidence consistent with an unmeasured tendency of some families to provide multiple sources of support. However, they did not directly model the trade-offs among labour supply, time transfers, and money transfers.

Boaz, Hu, and Ye (1999) estimated a simultaneous-equations model of financial help to parents, time help to parents, and co-residence with parents, using data from the 1992 wave of the HRS on individuals aged 51–61 with at least one frail parent. They found that economic employment generally reduced hours of caregiving. In addition, their results indicate that financial assistance and co-residence increase hours of caregiving, suggesting that families do not trade-off one type of support for another. Borsch-Supan et al. (1992), using data from the HRCA Survey of the Elderly in Massachusetts and the HRCA-NBER Child Survey, also found that children who made financial transfers to their parents spent more time with their parents. The study did not, however, model financial transfers to parents. Instead, it treated the provision of financial help as an exogenous characteristic of adult children.

DATA AND MEASURES

To measure the relationship between labour supply and the support of elderly parents, we examined data from the second wave of the HRS. Designed and fielded by the Institute for Social Research at the University of Michigan, the HRS provides detailed information on labour supply, family structure, intergenerational transfers, health, income, and assets for a large sample of Americans at mid-life. Because it surveys many individuals with elderly parents, it is particularly well suited for a study of the trade-offs among caregiving, financial transfers, and work.

The HRS consists of data collected from personal interviews with a nationally representative sample of non-institutionalized individuals born between 1931 and 1941 and their spouses. Baseline interviews were completed for 12,654 individuals in 7,702 households in 1992. When married couples were interviewed, only the financially knowledgeable spouse was questioned about income, assets, pensions, and health insurance coverage, and only the spouse more knowledgeable about family issues was questioned about family structure, social networks, and social support—though in the baseline interviews, only the wife was questioned about family matters. Blacks, Hispanics, and Florida residents were sampled at twice their rate in the general population. Respondents are being re-interviewed every two years. Information was collected from 11,602 respondents at wave 2, conducted in 1994.

The sample was restricted to non-proxy age-eligible female respondents (aged 53–63 in 1994) with at least one living parent, since only persons with living parents are 'at risk' of providing care to their parents. Only biological parents, not step-parents were considered; very few HRS respondents reported having surviving step-parents, however. Only 43 per cent of HRS respondents had a surviving parent at wave 2. Men were excluded because women are more likely than men to provide care to their parents (Dwyer and Coward, 1991; Marks, 1996) and because previous studies have documented that women's labour supply is more elastic than men's, at least for women in this cohort (Killingsworth, 1983). After eliminating cases with missing data, the sample consisted of 1,747 women.

Labour Supply

At each wave of interviews, HRS respondents were asked whether they were currently working for pay. Respondents who were working were then asked about the number of hours per week they usually worked on their main job and the number of hours per week they usually spent at any other paid work, such as a second job or military reserves. They were also asked the number of weeks they usually work per year (including paid vacations) and the number of weeks of paid vacation they receive. Labour supply was measured as total annual work hours, computed by multiplying usual number of hours worked per week by number of weeks worked per year (net of paid vacations), for all jobs.

Time Assistance to Parents

Information was collected from all single respondents and from 'family-knowledgeable' spouses, generally wives, among married couples about the amount of care they provided to their parents and, if married, the amount of care their spouses provided to the spouses' parents. Married respondents were also asked about care provided by themselves and their spouses to parents-in-law. In wave 2, respondents were asked whether they or their spouses spent a total of 50 or more hours in the past 12 months helping their parents 'with basic personal activities like dressing, eating, and bathing'. Respondents who reported providing care were then asked who was helped, mother, father, both parents, step-parents, etc., and how many hours of care were provided to each recipient by the respondent and by the spouse. In addition, respondents were asked whether they or their spouses spent a total of 50 or more hours in the past 12 months helping their parents 'with other things such as household chores, errands, transportation, etc.'. Questions about help with chores were not asked in the baseline interviews of the HRS, which is why we did not use the first wave of data in our study. Respondents who reported providing this type of care were then asked who was helped and how many hours of care were provided to each recipient. Respondents who were unable to estimate the precise number of hours of help were asked whether they provided more than 100 hours of help in the past 12 months.

Two dichotomous measures of time assistance to elderly parents were computed: an indicator of the provision of at least 100 hours of personal care assistance during the past 12 months and an indicator of the provision of at least 100 hours of help with chores and errands to parents during the past 12 months. Estimates of the precise number of hours of time assistance in the models were not used because response rates were quite low for these questions. The amount of assistance provided to parents-in-law was also not examined.

Financial Assistance to Parents

Information was also collected about financial transfers to parents. Family-knowledgeable spouses and single respondents were asked whether they and their spouses gave financial assistance to their parents in the past 12 months that totalled $100 or more (not counting any shared housing or shared food). Because response rates were low, estimates of the precise amount of money that was transferred were not used, neither was financial assistance to parents-in-law examined.

Other Respondent Characteristics

The HRS also includes detailed information on a number of respondent characteristics that are likely to be important determinants of labour supply and transfers to parents. Information was collected on the respondent's age, race, education, country of birth, current marital status, health, income (broken down by source), and own children. Education was measured by a series of binary variables, indicating whether the respondent never attended high school, attended high school but did not complete it, completed four years of high school, attended some college but fewer than four years, and completed four or more years of college. Health was measured by the respondent's self-assessment of their current health status (excellent, very good, good, fair, or poor), which has been shown in many studies to be a reliable indicator of health problems and mortality (Greiner et al., 1996; Idler et al., 1990). Non-wage income was measured as the sum of income from rent, dividends, interest, trust funds, royalties, alimony, and child support, expressed in constant 1993 dollars. Because of concerns about possible endogeneity, non-wage income was lagged from the first wave. Measures of family responsibilities and resources were also created. The number of own children aged 22 and younger was computed. In addition, an indicator of spousal poor health was constructed, defined as having a spouse who had at least some difficulty performing an *activity of daily living*.[2]

Parental Characteristics

Available parental characteristics in the HRS that were examined included vital status, age, marital status, home ownership, financial situation, number of children, living arrangements, and health. Parental health was measured by two dichotomous variables, indicating whether either parent (if both were alive) needed help with basic personal activities such as dressing, eating, or bathing, and whether either parent could not be left alone for one hour or more. The financial situation of the parent was measured by two dichotomous variables, indicating whether the finances of the parent were better than the respondent's and whether parental finances were worse than the respondent's. Parental age was measured by the age of the older parent when both were alive. The total number of sons and daughters, who could provide alternative sources of support in place of the respondent was computed for the parent. Living arrangements were measured by four dichotomous variables, indicating whether the parent lived in a nursing home, with the respondent, in the community separately from the respondent but within 10 miles of her, or more than 10 miles from the respondent. Most community-dwelling parents who lived separately from the respondents lived independently, but some of them lived with other children or relatives or in group situations. For very few (45) respondents, both parents were alive but not married to each other. In these cases, the variables for home ownership, financial situation, living arrangements, and marital status indicated whether either parent owned a home, had better or worse finances than the respondent, lived in a nursing home or with the respondent, or was married. All parental characteristics were reported by the respondent, who was either the adult daughter or the daughter's husband.

STATISTICAL METHODS

A three-stage triangular system of equations was estimated to represent the factors affecting parental living arrangements, time and money transfers from adult daughters to their elderly parents, and the labour supply of women at mid-life. Broadly speaking, it was assumed that elderly living arrangements (such as nursing home residence) are determined primarily by parental need. Living arrangements, in turn, influence the decision of the adult child to provide assistance to the parent (in the form of personal care assistance, help with chores, financial assistance, or some combination of the three). Lastly, it

---

[2] Activities of daily living include walking across a room, getting in and out of bed, bathing, eating, and dressing without help.

was assumed that assistance to elderly parents affected the adult daughter's labour supply. By imposing the direction of causality in this manner, it was possible to explore sequentially parameter estimates of interest in each group of equations and control for the potentially simultaneous relationship among the various outcomes of interest.

To model the living arrangements choice, a multinomial logit (MNL) equation was specified. With the MNL model, the choice between two or more mutually exclusive alternatives can be estimated. In this case, the alternatives were different living arrangements of the parents, whether they resided in nursing homes, with the respondents, in the community separately from the respondents but within 10 miles of them, and in the community but more than 10 miles from the respondents. Following Greene (1997), the general form of the MNL model can be expressed as:

$$\Pr(Y = j) = \frac{\exp(\beta_j' x_i)}{1 + \sum_{k=1}^{J} \exp(\beta_k' x_i)} \qquad \text{for } j = 1, 2, ..., J, \tag{1}$$

where x is a vector containing parent and adult child characteristics and where there are $J + 1$ alternatives, implying J log-odds ratios each of which can be represented:

$$\ln \left[\frac{P_{ij}}{P_{i0}} \right] = \beta_j' x_i. \tag{2}$$

Put differently, the J estimated sets of coefficients from the MNL model represent the effect of the independent variable on each of the J outcomes *relative to the base outcome*, which in our case was when parents lived in the community more than 10 miles from the respondents.

Using the estimated coefficients from equation (1), it is straightforward to generate the predicted probabilities for each parent of residing in a nursing home and of co-residing with the respondent. In the context of our estimation problem, the probabilities can be expressed as:

$$\hat{p}_{NHi} = \Pr(Y = NH) = \frac{\exp(\hat{\beta}_{NH}' x_i)}{1 + \exp(\hat{\beta}_{NH}' x_i) + \exp(\hat{\beta}_{CR}' x_i) + \exp(\hat{\beta}_{10mile}' x_i)} \tag{3}$$

$$\hat{p}_{CRi} = \Pr(Y = CR) = \frac{\exp(\hat{\beta}_{CR}' x_i)}{1 + \exp(\hat{\beta}_{NH}' x_i) + \exp(\hat{\beta}_{CR}' x_i) + \exp(\hat{\beta}_{10mile}' x_i)} \tag{4}$$

$$\hat{p}_{10mile} = \Pr(Y = 10mile) = \frac{\exp(\hat{\beta}_{10mile}' x_i)}{1 + \exp(\hat{\beta}_{NH}' x_i) + \exp(\hat{\beta}_{CR}' x_i) + \exp(\hat{\beta}_{10mile}' x_i)}, \tag{5}$$

where *NH* indicates nursing home residence, *CR* indicates co-residence with the respondent, and 10*mile* indicates residence within 10 miles of the respondent. The beta-hats represent estimated coefficient vectors. Because these estimated probabilities are based only upon observable attributes of the parent and adult daughter, they do not have an unobservable component that could be correlated with unobservable factors affecting assistance from adult children to their parents. If living arrangements had not been modelled as probabilities, and instead included actual living arrangements in the model, the potential correlation between unobservable factors affecting actual living arrangements and unobservable factors affecting assistance could have biased the estimates.

The predicted probabilities from (3), (4), and (5) were used to measure the effect of parental living arrangements on the provision of assistance from adult children. The following series of probit regressions were estimated:

$$Pr(PCA) = F(\alpha_{NH1}\hat{p}_{NHi} + \alpha_{CR1}\hat{p}_{CRi} + \alpha_{10mile1}\hat{p}_{10milei} + \beta'_{PCA}x_i) \tag{6}$$

$$Pr(Chore) = F(\alpha_{NH2}\hat{p}_{NHi} + \alpha_{CR2}\hat{p}_{CRi} + \alpha_{10mile2}\hat{p}_{10milei} + \beta'_{Chore}x_i) \tag{7}$$

$$Pr(FIN) = F(\alpha_{NH3}\hat{p}_{NHi} + \alpha_{CR3}\hat{p}_{CRi} + \alpha_{10mile3}\hat{p}_{10milei} + \beta'_{FIN}x_i), \tag{8}$$

where PCA indicates personal care assistance, $Chore$ indicates help with chores or errands, and FIN indicates financial transfers. Each of the dependent variables was measured as a dichotomous outcome. Note that the alpha coefficients measure the effects of nursing home residence, co-residence, and residence within 10 miles of the daughter on each mode of support from adult daughters, controlling for other observable factors and the potential endogeneity of parental living arrangements.

Because we were interested in the effect of each support mode on the labour supply of adult children, the estimated probit regressions from equations (6), (7), and (8) were used to generate predicted probabilities for each type of support, $\hat{p}_{PCA}$, $\hat{p}_{Chore}$, and $\hat{p}_{FIN}$. Again, these predicted probabilities were based entirely on observable attributes, eliminating any potential unobserved correlates that could also affect work hours and thus could bias the coefficient estimates in our labour supply regression.

Finally, how each type of support affects annual hours of work for women at mid-life was investigated, specifying the following regression:

$$Hours_i = \alpha_{PCA}\hat{p}_{PCAi} + \alpha_{Chore}\hat{p}_{Chorei} + \alpha_{FIN}\hat{p}_{FINi} + \beta'x_i. \tag{9}$$

Because the focus was on women's labour supply and many women have zero work hours, labour supply regression in (9) was estimated with a Tobit model. The Tobit specification allows for censoring in the distribution of hours worked in the form of a mass of observations at zero. Again, the alpha coefficients indicate the effect of each type of support on hours worked controlling for the observable adult child characteristics in x and the potential endogeneity of the support variables.

RESULTS

Table 7.1 reports the percentage of women aged 53–63 with at least one surviving parent who assisted their parents in 1994. Only 8.5 per cent of women

Table 7.1. *Assistance from women to their parents, by personal characteristics, 1994*[a]

	Percentage of sample	Percentage who help with basic care[b]	Percentage who help with chores or errands[b]	Percentage who provide financial help[c]
All	100.0	8.5	22.5	15.1
Age				
53–55	44.3	6.4	21.9	15.6
56–59	33.4	9.4	22.9	16.8
60–63	22.3	11.2	23.2	11.4
Race				
White and other	85.4	8.3	23.0	13.9
Black	9.0	8.6	19.5	18.2
Hispanic	5.5	11.2	19.6	28.2
Marital status				
Currently married	66.7	6.7	22.2	15.5
Divorced or separated	18.0	10.5	21.4	13.2
Widowed	11.9	12.8	23.1	10.4
Never married	3.4	18.2	33.3	33.0
Education				
Did not finish high school	20.5	11.0	19.3	13.0
High school graduate	40.2	8.3	26.0	15.8
Some college	22.1	4.7	17.6	11.4
College graduate	17.2	10.7	24.6	20.6
Health				
Excellent	21.8	6.5	21.6	15.9
Very good	33.0	8.0	21.8	13.3
Good	26.5	8.0	25.9	19.3
Fair	12.5	11.4	20.5	11.7
Poor	6.2	14.3	18.9	10.1
Own children aged 22 or younger				
No	80.0	8.7	23.2	15.9
Yes	20.0	7.6	20.0	11.9
Any living sisters				
No	31.6	8.6	30.6	13.8
Yes	68.4	8.4	18.8	15.7
Any living brothers				
No	29.7	8.4	25.3	14.4
Yes	70.3	8.5	21.4	15.4

Table 7.1. (Contd.)

	Percentage of sample	Percentage who help with basic care[b]	Percentage who help with chores or errands[b]	Percentage who provide financial help[c]
Parental living arrangements				
Nursing home	9.4	12.6	14.4	20.5
Co-reside with respondent	6.4	30.1	65.2	27.9
In the community separately from respondent, but within 10 miles	33.1	9.1	32.6	11.6
More than 10 miles from respondent	51.2	4.7	12.2	14.7
Parent needs help with care				
No	73.8	3.0	21.2	12.0
Yes	26.2	24.1	26.2	23.7
Parent cannot be left alone				
No	86.3	6.4	22.6	14.2
Yes	13.7	21.9	21.9	20.5
Parent's financial situation				
Better than respondent's	30.1	6.3	19.6	5.7
Worse than respondent's	38.3	10.1	24.5	24.6

[a] The sample includes 1,747 women from the second wave of the HRS, aged 53–63 in 1994, with at least one surviving parent. Estimates are weighted to reflect the oversampling of blacks, Hispanics, and Florida residents in the HRS.
[b] Includes only time assistance of at least 100 hours in the past 12 months.
[c] Includes only financial assistance of at least $100 in the past 12 months.

devoted at least 100 hours in the past 12 months to helping their parents with basic personal care. Help with chores or errands was much more common, with 22.5 per cent of women spending 100 hours or more helping with these activities. However, help with personal care was more time intensive than help with chores and errands. Among women who provided help and for whom complete data on hours were available, mean annual hours spent on help with personal care was 649, compared with 345 for help with chores and errands.

Fully 15 per cent of women in 1994 reported providing at least $100 in financial assistance to their parents in the past 12 months, among those with at least one surviving parent. Among those who transferred at least $100 to their parents, the mean annual transfer was $696. Hispanics were somewhat more likely to help with basic care and to provide financial help than whites or blacks. Women who never married were substantially more likely to provide all types of help than women who had been married at some point (although only 3 per cent of women never married). Currently married women were especially unlikely to provide basic personal care assistance to their parents. Women who completed college were more likely to help their parents financially than women with less education.

Parental characteristics had some important effects on the probability that women provided help. Parental health was strongly associated with the likelihood that women provided help to their parents. Among women who reported that their parents needed help with care, 24.1 per cent provided at least 100 hours of personal care assistance and 23.7 per cent provided at least $100 in financial assistance. Differences by parental health in the probability of providing help with errands and chores were small, however. Women who reported that the financial situation of their parents was worse than their own were more likely to provide monetary support and time help than those who reported that their parents' financial situations were better than their own. Women were also much more likely to provide help when their parents lived with them than when they lived elsewhere in the community. For example, almost two-thirds of women who resided with their parents helped them with chores or errands, and 30 per cent of them helped with basic personal activities. In addition, women were more likely to help with personal care when their parents lived in nursing homes than when they lived nearby in the community but separately from the daughters themselves, but they were less likely to help with chores or errands. This probably reflects the fact that nursing home residents generally do not have to maintain their own households. Daughters were especially unlikely to help with personal care or with chores or errands when they lived more than 10 miles from their community-dwelling parents. Finally, women without any sisters were more likely to help their parents with chores or errands than women with sisters. Differences by the presence of brothers in the probability of providing help with chores or errands were much smaller. These findings suggest that the type of help provided by children may often be gender-specific, with daughters in this cohort, for example, perhaps providing help with meal preparation and sons providing help with household repairs. Thus, help provided by same-sex siblings may be more substitutable than help provided by opposite-sex siblings.

Table 7.2 reports the combination of modes of parental support by women in 1994. About 65 per cent of women with at least one surviving parent did not provide significant help to their parents in any form—not help with personal care, help with chores or errands, or financial help. Women who did help

Table 7.2. *Combinations of modes of parental support by women, 1994*[a]

Help with personal care[b]	Help with chores or errands[b]	Financial help[c]	Percentage of sample
No	No	No	64.7
Yes	No	No	2.9
No	Yes	No	13.9
No	No	Yes	9.3
Yes	Yes	No	3.4
Yes	No	Yes	0.6
No	Yes	Yes	3.6
Yes	Yes	Yes	1.6

[a] The sample includes 1,747 women from the second wave of the HRS, aged 53–63 in 1994, with at least one surviving parent. Estimates are weighted to reflect the oversampling of blacks, Hispanics, and Florida residents in the HRS.
[b] Includes only time assistance of at least 100 hours in the past 12 months.
[c] Includes only financial assistance of at least $100 in the past 12 months.

their parents generally provided only one type of assistance. Only 9.2 per cent of women provided more than one type of help, and only 5.8 per cent of women combined financial help with some form of time assistance.

Table 7.3 explores the relationship between work status and help to elderly parents. Overall, 60 per cent of women aged 53–63 with at least one surviving parent worked for pay in 1994. Labour force participation rates for women increased with education and decreased with age and health problems. Hispanic women and women with parents who could not be left alone for one hour or more were also less likely to work than other women.

Women who worked for pay were somewhat less likely to help their parents with basic personal care than women who did not work. Fully 10 per cent of women who were not working helped their parents with personal care, compared with only 7 per cent of working women. Within each of the personal characteristics examined, working women were less likely to provide care than women who did not work. The exception was for college graduates, women in excellent or poor health, and women with parents in nursing homes. Among Hispanics, women who never married, and women who lived with their parents, working women were especially less likely to provide basic care than non-working women. Differences by work status in the probability of helping with chores or errands and of providing financial assistance to parents were small.

Estimates from Multivariate Models

Table 7.4 presents multinomial logit estimates of parental living arrangements, with standard errors reported in parentheses and odds ratios reported in brackets. Estimates indicate the effect of a given characteristic on the likelihood

Table 7.3. Assistance from women to their parents, by work status and other characteristics, 1994[a]

	Percentage who work	Percentage who help with basic care[b]		Percentage who help with chores or errands[b]		Percentage who provide financial assistance[c]	
		Workers	Non-workers	Workers	Non-workers	Workers	Non-workers
All	60.0	7.3	10.3	22.7	22.2	15.8	14.0
Age							
53–55	69.0	6.2	6.8	21.4	23.2	15.2	16.4
56–59	60.0	8.1	11.4	24.1	21.1	17.8	15.3
60–63	42.0	8.9	12.9	24.5	22.2	13.4	10.0
Race							
White and other	60.8	7.3	9.9	23.2	22.8	14.6	12.9
Black	58.9	7.8	9.7	19.1	19.9	22.2	12.6
Hispanic	48.7	5.9	16.2	21.2	18.0	27.5	28.8
Marital status							
Currently married	58.0	6.0	7.7	22.6	21.6	16.2	14.5
Divorced or separated	68.2	8.7	14.2	22.8	18.4	15.6	7.9
Widowed	57.9	10.2	16.3	21.8	24.8	11.3	9.2
Never married	62.3	12.8	27.0	28.5	41.1	23.6	48.6
Education							
Did not finish high school	41.1	10.0	11.7	21.0	18.2	13.1	13.0
High school graduate	59.6	5.9	11.9	27.0	24.5	17.6	13.2
Some college	69.5	4.3	5.7	17.2	18.7	10.9	12.5
College graduate	71.2	11.8	7.9	22.8	29.1	20.4	21.0

Table 7.3. (Contd.)

	Percentage who work	Percentage who help with basic care[b]		Percentage who help with chores or errands[b]		Percentage who provide financial assistance[c]	
		Workers	Non-workers	Workers	Non-workers	Workers	Non-workers
Health							
Excellent	69.6	6.9	5.5	21.6	21.7	14.6	19.0
Very good	67.4	6.8	10.5	19.8	26.1	13.5	12.9
Good	62.3	7.2	9.4	27.3	23.7	20.9	16.7
Fair	40.8	8.8	13.2	21.0	20.2	12.4	11.2
Poor	15.3	17.1	13.8	42.1	14.7	17.9	8.6
Parental living arrangements							
Nursing home	57.1	13.2	11.7	10.2	19.9	20.0	21.2
Co-reside with respondent	66.4	19.8	50.4	61.9	71.7	22.8	37.8
Within 10 miles of R	59.5	8.4	10.0	32.6	32.5	13.4	9.0
More than 10 miles away	60.0	3.8	6.1	13.3	10.7	15.7	13.3
Own children aged 22 or younger							
No	59.8	7.6	10.4	23.4	22.8	16.9	14.4
Yes	60.6	5.9	10.0	20.2	19.7	11.6	12.4
Any living sisters							
No	62.6	8.3	9.1	31.9	28.6	12.9	15.3
Yes	58.8	6.8	10.8	18.3	19.5	17.3	13.4
Any living brothers							
No	62.8	7.3	10.3	26.8	22.8	15.4	12.7
Yes	58.8	7.3	10.3	20.9	22.0	16.0	14.4

Parent needs help with care							
No	63.2	2.9	3.1	21.8	20.3	13.5	9.5
Yes	51.0	22.6	25.6	26.1	26.2	23.8	23.5
Parent cannot be left alone							
No	61.8	5.6	7.5	23.4	21.4	15.2	12.6
Yes	48.3	20.4	23.3	17.6	26.0	21.0	20.1
Parent's financial situation							
Better than respondent's	61.8	5.0	8.3	20.5	18.3	4.6	7.4
Worse than respondent's	59.8	8.4	12.7	24.3	24.8	25.5	23.3

[a] The sample includes 1,747 women from the second wave of the HRS, aged 53–63 in 1994, with at least one surviving parent. Estimates are weighted to reflect the oversampling of blacks, Hispanics, and Florida residents in the HRS.
[b] Includes only time assistance of at least 100 hours in the past 12 months.
[c] Includes only financial assistance of at least $100 in the past 12 months.

Table 7.4. *Multinomial logit estimates of parental living arrangements, 1994*

	Lives within 10 miles	Co-residence	Nursing home
Characteristics of parents			
Age of older parent	0.021*	0.044**	0.032
	(0.012)	(0.022)	(0.025)
	[1.021]	[1.045]	[1.032]
Parent needs help with care	−0.094	0.792***	3.405***
	(0.168)	(0.268)	(0.416)
	[0.910]	[2.207]	[30.105]
Parent cannot be left alone	−0.445*	0.220	1.981***
	(0.250)	(0.349)	(0.292)
	[0.641]	[1.246]	[7.252]
Parents are married	−0.180	−1.366***	−0.472
	(0.136)	(0.394)	(0.362)
	[0.836]	[0.255]	[0.624]
Parent owns a home	−0.185	−0.947***	−1.337***
	(0.125)	(0.231)	(0.288)
	[0.831]	[0.388]	[0.263]
Finances of parent are	−0.101	−0.454	0.513
better than respondent's	(0.140)	(0.285)	(0.386)
	[0.904]	[0.635]	[1.671]
Finances of parent are	0.006	−0.354	1.024***
worse than respondent's	(0.136)	(0.255)	(0.313)
	[1.006]	[0.702]	[2.785]
Mother is alive	0.467***	0.412	−0.191
	(0.176)	(0.368)	(0.389)
	[1.595]	[1.509]	[0.826]
Number of daughters	−0.158***	−0.029	−0.100
	(0.038)	(0.083)	(0.092)
	[0.854]	[0.971]	[0.905]
Number of sons	−0.158***	−0.339***	−0.344***
	(0.038)	(0.084)	(0.089)
	[0.854]	[0.713]	[0.709]
Demographic characteristics of the daughter			
Age	−0.074	0.845	1.336
	(0.689)	(1.362)	(1.633)
	[0.929]	[2.327]	[3.806]
Age squared	0.001	−0.008	−0.011
	(0.006)	(0.012)	(0.014)
	[1.001]	[0.993]	[0.989]
Black	0.441***	0.210	−0.211
	(0.169)	(0.300)	(0.376)
	[1.554]	[1.234]	[0.810]
Hispanic	0.437*	0.779*	−0.453
	(0.254)	(0.446)	(0.644)
	[1.548]	[2.179]	[0.636]

Table 7.4. (Contd.)

	Lives within 10 miles	Co-residence	Nursing home
Currently married	0.213	0.043	1.923
	(0.801)	(1.711)	(1.941)
	[1.237]	[1.044]	[6.845]
Foreign born	−1.641***	−1.217**	−2.341***
	(0.290)	(0.476)	(0.695)
	[0.194]	[0.296]	[0.096]
Number of children aged	0.188**	0.062	−0.197
22 and younger	(0.084)	(0.180)	(0.256)
	[1.207]	[1.064]	[0.821]
Education of the daughter			
[Reference: No high school]	—	—	—
Some high school	−0.022	−0.106	−0.363
	(0.263)	(0.496)	(0.545)
	[0.979]	[0.900]	[0.695]
High school graduate	−0.052	0.231	0.459
	(0.251)	(0.473)	(0.510)
	[0.949]	[1.260]	[1.582]
Some college	−0.340	0.200	0.327
	(0.269)	(0.506)	(0.569)
	[0.712]	[1.222]	[1.387]
College graduate	−0.936***	0.153	−0.920
	(0.289)	(0.509)	(0.600)
	[0.392]	[1.165]	[0.398]
Health status of the daughter			
[Reference: Excellent]	—	—	—
Very good	−0.157	0.252	0.300
	(0.158)	(0.341)	(0.387)
	[0.855]	[1.286]	[1.349]
Good	0.039	0.696**	0.261
	(0.165)	(0.330)	(0.394)
	[1.039]	[2.006]	[1.299]
Fair	−0.095	−0.029	−0.179
	(0.204)	(0.420)	(0.460)
	[0.910]	[0.972]	[0.836]
Poor	−0.195	−0.130	−0.359
	(0.263)	(0.510)	(0.562)
	[0.823]	[0.878]	[0.699]
Age of spouse of daughter	−0.001	−0.020	−0.038
	(0.013)	(0.029)	(0.032)
	[0.999]	[0.980]	[0.962]

Table 7.4. (Contd.)

	Lives within 10 miles	Co-residence	Nursing home
Non-labour income of daughter ($000)	−0.002 (0.005) [0.999]	−0.004 (0.011) [0.999]	−0.0001 (0.0114) [1.000]

Note: The multinomial logit model is based on 1,747 observations of women aged 53–63 with surviving parents in 1994, from the HRS. Estimated coefficients are relative to parents living in the community more than 10 miles away from the respondents. Standard errors are reported in parentheses, and odds ratios are reported in brackets. The estimating equation also includes a constant term.
* $0.05 < p \leq 0.10$ ** $0.01 < p \leq 0.05$ *** $p < 0.01$.

of a particular arrangement (nursing home residence, co-residence with the respondent, or living in the community separately from the respondent but within 10 miles of her), relative to the parent living in the community more than 10 miles from the respondent. Odds ratios that exceed 1 indicate that the variable increases the likelihood of the given parental living arrangement, while odds ratios less than 1 indicate that the variable decreases the likelihood of the given arrangement. Asterisks denote odds ratios that are significantly different from 1.

Parental living arrangements appeared to be determined primarily by the needs of the parents. Frail elderly parents, who needed help with basic personal care or could not be left alone for one hour, were much more likely to live in nursing homes than parents who were in better health. Parents who needed help with personal care were also more likely to live near the respondent than to live more than 10 miles away from her. Controlling for health, parental age increased the likelihood that parents lived with or near the respondent. Parental finances were also associated with living arrangements. Parents whose financial situations were worse than the respondents' were more than twice as likely to live in nursing homes. Not surprisingly, parents were also less likely to live in nursing homes or with the respondents when the parents were homeowners, and they were less likely to live with the respondents when they were married. There was some evidence that social support influenced living arrangements. Parents were less likely to live in nursing homes as the number of children increased, perhaps because the help that children provide to their parents could enable them to live in the community for longer periods of time. The number of children also decreased the likelihood that the parent lived with or near the respondent, although it did not necessarily decrease the likelihood that the parent resided with or near any child. Only the number of sons, not the number of daughters, had statistically significant effects on nursing home residence and co-residence, however. Mothers were significantly more likely than fathers to live near their daughters.

With a few exceptions, characteristics of the daughter generally were not important determinants of parental living arrangements. Race, education, and health of the daughter generally had insignificant effects on parental living arrangements, except that blacks and Hispanics were more likely than whites to live near the respondent, and college-educated daughters were less likely to live near their parents than daughters who did not attend or complete college. Foreign birth had important effects on each of the types of living arrangements we considered. Parents of foreign-born daughters were substantially less likely to live with or near their daughters than parents of native-born daughters, probably because the parent often remained in the daughter's origin country. They were also less likely to live in nursing homes, perhaps because nursing homes may be less prevalent in the daughter's origin country than in the US. Even when parents lived in the US, cultural differences between immigrants and native-born Americans may have led low rates of institutionalization for the parents of foreign-born women.

Table 7.5 reports probit estimates of assistance to parents by women aged 53–63 in 1994. The models were estimated separately for personal care assistance, assistance with chores and errands, and financial assistance. Marginal effects are reported in brackets. Parental health and living arrangements had important effects on the likelihood that children provided assistance. Daughters were more likely to provide all types of help, including financial assistance, when their parents needed help with basic personal activities. Proximity also played a large role. Daughters were 90 per cent more likely to provide help with chores and errands when they lived within 10 miles of their parents, and 62 per cent more likely to help with chores when they lived in the same household, than when they lived more than 10 miles away from their parents. Daughters were also more likely to provide financial assistance when they lived with their parents, even though respondents to the HRS were asked to exclude the value of shared food and housing when they reported the level of financial assistance to their parents. Controlling for parental health, however, nursing home residence did not significantly affect the probability that daughters provided time or financial assistance to their parents.

Parental finances also influenced the likelihood that daughters provided financial help to their parents. Daughters were significantly more likely to provide money transfers when the financial status of their parents was worse than their own and less likely to provide money transfers when the financial status of the parents was better than their own. Parental finances did not significantly affect time transfers, however. Other parental characteristics that might reflect the availability of alternative means of support generally did not influence the probability that women helped their parents. Daughters were not less likely to help their parents when the parents were married or had other daughters or sons, even though these spouses and other children could provide assistance in place of the help provided by the respondent.

Table 7.5. *Probit estimates of assistance to parents for women, 1994*

	Personal care assistance	Assistance with chores	Any financial assistance
Characteristics of parent			
Predicted probability of	1.845	4.452***	1.207
living within 10 miles of R	(1.675)	(1.309)	(1.363)
	[0.077]	[0.900]	[0.144]
Predicted probability	1.644	3.050***	2.793**
of co-residence with R	(1.513)	(1.169)	(1.222)
	[0.068]	[0.616]	[0.334]
Predicted probability	0.032	1.168	0.646
of nursing home residence	(0.942)	(0.719)	(0.766)
	[0.001]	[0.236]	[0.077]
Age of older parent	0.012	0.007	−0.005
	(0.012)	(0.009)	(0.010)
	[0.001]	[0.002]	[−0.001]
Parent needs help with care	1.364***	0.409***	0.383***
	(0.178)	(0.132)	(0.138)
	[0.057]	[0.083]	[0.046]
Parent cannot be left alone	0.348	0.240	−0.093
	(0.212)	(0.173)	(0.178)
	[0.014]	[0.048]	[−0.011]
Parents are married	−0.226	−0.062	−0.200
	(0.186)	(0.120)	(0.134)
	[−0.009]	[−0.013]	[−0.024]
Parent owns a home	0.061	0.053	0.168
	(0.166)	(0.113)	(0.122)
	[0.003]	[0.011]	[0.020]
Parent financial	−0.043	0.104	−0.216*
status better than R	(0.150)	(0.099)	(0.124)
	[−0.002]	[0.021]	[−0.026]
Parent financial	0.040	0.042	0.587***
status worse than R	(0.136)	(0.090)	(0.098)
	[0.002]	[0.008]	[0.070]
Mother alive	−0.115	−0.248	0.468**
	(0.206)	(0.160)	(0.185)
	[−0.005]	[−0.050]	[0.056]
Number of sons	−0.070*	−0.006	−0.028
	(0.041)	(0.028)	(0.030)
	[−0.003]	[−0.001]	[−0.003]
Number of daughters	−0.003	0.018	0.088*
	(0.064)	(0.050)	(0.050)
	[0.000]	[0.004]	[0.011]
Adult child characteristics			
Age	0.543	0.186	0.834
	(0.653)	(0.439)	(0.525)
	[0.023]	[0.038]	[0.100]

Table 7.5. (Contd.)

	Personal care assistance	Assistance with chores	Any financial assistance
Age squared	−0.005	−0.002	−0.008*
	(0.006)	(0.004)	(0.005)
	[0.000]	[0.000]	[−0.001]
Black	−0.384**	−0.355**	0.241
	(0.190)	(0.145)	(0.152)
	[−0.016]	[−0.072]	[0.029]
Hispanic	−0.090	−0.191	0.169
	(0.262)	(0.196)	(0.201)
	[−0.004]	[−0.039]	[0.020]
Currently married	−0.488	−0.210	0.423
	(0.796)	(0.513)	(0.594)
	[−0.020]	[−0.042]	[0.051]
Foreign born	−0.230	0.461	0.945**
	(0.500)	(0.395)	(0.405)
	[−0.010]	[0.093]	[0.113]
Number of children aged	−0.014	−0.139*	−0.201**
22 and younger	(0.101)	(0.075)	(0.087)
	[−0.001]	[−0.028]	[−0.024]
Education of daughter [Reference: No high school]	—	—	—
Some high school	−0.143	−0.121	−0.224
	(0.224)	(0.171)	(0.190)
	[−0.006]	[−0.024]	[−0.027]
High school graduate	−0.045	0.147	0.069
	(0.212)	(0.159)	(0.175)
	[−0.002]	[0.030]	[0.008]
Some college	−0.063	0.195	−0.075
	(0.250)	(0.185)	(0.201)
	[−0.003]	[0.039]	[−0.009]
College graduate	0.348	0.765***	0.357
	(0.335)	(0.271)	(0.280)
	[0.014]	[0.155]	[0.043]
Health status of daughter [Reference: Excellent]	—	—	—
Very good	0.076	0.129	−0.033
	(0.160)	(0.109)	(0.122)
	[0.003]	[0.026]	[−0.004]
Good	−0.051	0.120	0.050
	(0.171)	(0.111)	(0.123)
	[−0.002]	[0.024]	[0.006]
Fair	0.233	0.082	−0.141
	(0.182)	(0.133)	(0.152)
	[0.010]	[0.016]	[−0.017]

Table 7.5. (Contd.)

	Personal care assistance	Assistance with chores	Any financial assistance
Poor	0.220	0.166	−0.283
	(0.227)	(0.175)	(0.208)
	[0.009]	[0.034]	[−0.034]
Age of spouse of daughter	0.004	0.002	−0.005
	(0.013)	(0.008)	(0.010)
	[0.000]	[0.000]	[−0.001]
Non-labour income of daughter ($000)	0.005	0.007**	−0.006
	(0.004)	(0.003)	(0.004)
	[0.0002]	[0.0014]	[−0.0001]
Constant	−19.321	−8.273	−24.757*
	(18.676)	(12.521)	(14.940)

Note: Probit regressions were based on a sample of 1,747 observations of women aged 53–63 with surviving parents in 1994, from the second wave of the HRS. Standard errors are reported in parentheses and marginal probability effects (calculated at the means) are reported in brackets.
* $0.05 < p \leq 0.10$ ** $0.01 < p \leq 0.05$ *** $p < 0.01$.

Personal characteristics of the daughters generally had smaller effects on the likelihood of helping parents than parental characteristics. Education, health, age, and marital status of daughters did not significantly influence transfers to elderly parents, except that college graduates were significantly more likely to help with chores or errands than daughters who did not complete college. Blacks were also less likely than others to provide help with personal care and help with chores or errands. In addition, foreign-born women were more likely to provide financial assistance to their parents than native-born women, perhaps because many parents of foreign-born women lived outside the US, making hands-on assistance impractical.

Table 7.6 reports Tobit estimates of the number of hours of paid employment in 1994 for women aged 53–63. Marginal effects are reported in brackets. The models incorporate the predicted probabilities of helping parents, derived from the equations reported in Table 7.5. As expected, the predicted probability of providing help with personal care was associated with substantially fewer hours of work. The results indicate that women who helped their parents with basic personal activities worked 751 fewer hours per year than those who did not help their parents with basic care. In contrast, women who provided financial assistance worked 519 more hours per year than women who did not transfer money to their parents. Helping parents with chores or errands did not significantly affect hours of paid employment, however. Because women who helped with personal care activities devoted more hours

Table 7.6. *Tobit estimates of women's labour supply, 1994*

Independent variable	Estimated coefficients
Predicted probability of providing help with personal care	−1134.41**
	(492.72)
	[−751.35]
Predicted probability of providing help with chores	51.92
	(494.19)
	[34.39]
Predicted probability of providing financial assistance	783.72**
	(400.56)
	[519.08]
Demographic characteristics of the daughter	
Age	1653.59***
	(504.57)
	[1095.21]
Age squared	−15.30***
	(4.42)
	[−10.13]
Black	−65.56
	(120.06)
	[−43.42]
Hispanic	41.00
	(179.80)
	[27.15]
Currently married	584.20
	(575.81)
	[386.93]
Foreign-born	−283.83
	(191.94)
	[−187.99]
Number of children aged 22 and younger	−87.74
	(62.95)
	[−58.11]
Education of daughter	
[Reference: No high school]	—
Some high school	24.39
	(195.63)
	[16.16]
High school graduate	212.08
	(182.76)
	[140.47]
Some college	530.47***
	(188.37)
	[351.35]

Table 7.6. (Contd.)

Independent variable	Estimated coefficients
College graduate	530.11***
	(199.22)
	[351.10]
Health status	
[Reference: Excellent]	—
Very good	15.54
	(108.94)
	[10.29]
Good	−118.24
	(117.53)
	[−78.31]
Fair	−896.23***
	(149.48)
	[−593.59]
Poor	−2143.00***
	(228.76)
	[−1419.36]
Number of ADL limitations of spouse of daughter	−43.14
	(180.09)
	[−28.57]
Age of spouse of daughter	−19.47**
	(9.60)
	[−12.90]
Non-labour income of daughter ($000s)	−5.63*
	(3.37)
	[−3.73]
Constant	−43370.70***
	(14349.60)

Note: Tobit regression was based on a sample of 1,747 women aged 53–63 with surviving parents in 1994 from the second wave of the HRS. Standard errors are reported in parentheses, and marginal effects (calculated at the means) are reported in brackets.
* $0.05 < p \leq 0.10$ ** $0.01 < p \leq 0.05$ *** $p < 0.01$.

on average to their parents than those who helped with chores or errands, it is not surprising that providing care had larger effects on labour supply.

Other results from the model were consistent with past findings on women's labour supply. Annual hours of work increased with education and health and decreased with non-wage income. Labour supply increased with age up to age 54, and then began to decline with age. Hours of work also decreased with the age of the husband, perhaps because husbands and wives co-ordinate their retirement decisions, so women with older husbands are less likely to work than women with younger husbands.

CONCLUSION

Families can support their frail elderly members in different ways. Elderly persons may choose to live independently in the community, and their adult children may visit on a regular basis to provide care, or their children may provide them with financial assistance that would defray the costs of purchasing formal home healthcare services. Alternatively, frail elderly persons may live with an adult child and receive personal care and financial assistance in the shared home. Another option is for elderly parents to move into nursing homes, where their children can still provide hands-on care and/or help with financial costs.

Most women who currently provide help to their parents offer time assistance, either with basic personal activities or with chores and errands. In the analysis 26 per cent of women aged 53–63 with surviving parents provided at least 100 hours of time help during the previous 12 months, whereas only 15 per cent of women provided at least $100 of financial help. In addition, only 9 per cent of women provided financial help without also providing time help.

However, as more women assume important roles in the labour market, providing time-intensive personal care assistance will become increasingly more difficult. The findings from the study suggest that devoting time to the informal care of elderly parents may be incompatible with full-time paid employment at mid-life. Women aged 53–63 who helped their parents with personal care activities cut back their hours of paid work by 751 hours, or by about 70 per cent. Although additional research is needed to determine whether these reductions in labour supply come about through early retirement or reduced weekly hours of work, our results suggest that special work arrangements, including flexible work schedules and part-time work, may be necessary if persons with frail family members are to balance successfully their work and caregiving responsibilities.

At present few persons at mid-life spend substantial amounts of time helping their elderly parents in any given year. We found that about one in four women aged 53–63 in 1994 with surviving parents helped their parents during a 12-month period, but only 43 per cent of persons in this age range had surviving parents. In other words, only about 11 per cent of women at mid-life devoted more than 100 hours per year to assisting their parents in 1994. However, for those who do provide informal care the costs are high. The loss of 751 annual work hours for women translates on average into about $12,750 in pre-tax lost wages per year in 1994 dollars. Those who cut back their labour supply to care for frail family members also lose retirement savings because they accumulate fewer credits towards future Social Security and private pension benefits. Others may lose health insurance benefits if they drop out of the labour force before they become eligible for Medicare benefits.

Given the growth in women's employment rates and the difficulties that working women encounter when they provide hands-on personal care, formal home healthcare is likely to become an increasingly important option for frail elderly persons in the near future. Liu, Manton, and Aragon (2000) have documented a shift towards paid caregivers and away from family caregivers over the past two decades. They estimated that between 1982 and 1994, the proportion of elderly persons with disabilities who relied only on informal helpers declined from 74 to 64 per cent, while the proportion with paid helpers increased. Adult children may play important roles in helping their frail parents finance the costs of formal home care, particularly since third parties, such as Medicare, Medicaid, and private insurance, often do not cover home healthcare services. In 1994, 57 per cent of disabled elderly persons who received formal home care paid their caregivers themselves (Liu, Manton, and Aragon, 2000).

Women who provided financial help to their parents worked 48 per cent more hours than women who did not assist their parents financially, among those with surviving parents. Women with high earnings capacity may choose to focus their efforts in the workplace and help their elderly parents financially, rather than divert time from their paid work to provide personal care assistance to their parents. These results are consistent with the findings of Couch, Daly, and Wolf (1999) that men and women with high wages give their parents more money help and less time help than those with low wages.

Although most of the concerns raised about the high cost of caring for the frail elderly have focused on the costs of formal care, the financial costs incurred by families who provide informal help to the frail elderly are also high. Pressures on families will likely mount in the near future as falling mortality and fertility rates continue to increase the proportion of the population that is very old and as women continue to play more important roles in the labour market. How families react to these pressures will have important implications for the welfare of the frail elderly population in coming decades.

8

Social Care for Older People: The Growth of Independent-Sector Provision in the UK

MARTIN KNAPP, JULIEN FORDER,
JEREMY KENDALL, AND LINDA PICKARD

INTRODUCTION: THE INDEPENDENT SECTORS IN THE MIXED ECONOMY

Policy Trends

Informal care by family, friends, and neighbours is the largest sector of social care for older people in the UK. Informal carers outnumber their paid counterparts in formally organized public and non-public agencies by a factor of more than three to one. However, in the UK, the formal voluntary sector has long been central to the delivery of social care, with and without state support. More recently, the availability of public funds—via social security payments to support residential and nursing home residents—stimulated the rapid growth of the private sector. From the start of the 1990s, these 'independent sector' providers became a central and explicit concern of the designers of social care systems in the UK. Indeed, one of the core objectives of the Conservative government's community care White Paper of 1989 was 'to promote the development of a flourishing independent sector alongside good-quality public services' (Secretary of State, 1989). The White Paper and the 1990 NHS and Community Care Act that followed it proved to be pivotal for the structure and context of social care delivery, and for the routeing of public funding.

The 1990 social care reforms continue to be influential today. The 1997 Labour government's proposals for the support of older people included a long-overdue look at how long-term care is funded, particularly to overcome the anomalies caused by free health care available alongside means-tested social care, and also to address the questions of personal asset depletion and inheritance. However, although the Labour government has taken a close look at performance and quality, and how they are to be assessed and promoted, it has expressly stated that it does not favour any particular provider sector.

The first Labour minister responsible for social services in eighteen years made this clear within days of the 1997 General Election: 'What we are concerned about is quality, value for money, what the user, what the citizen gets out of it, and I don't mind if it is in the public sector or the private sector. The important thing is that we deliver to the service user and the wider community' (Boateng, in Downey, 1997).

In the course of two decades, therefore, Britain has moved from a social care system for older people dominated by public sector provision, to one which gave formally organized independent providers an inside track, and now to a situation of (more) equal opportunity. At the same time, the picture is incomplete in not adequately registering the contribution of family, friends, and neighbours. This informal care has continued to be the largest 'sector' of care for older people, although policy attention has been focused only rather belatedly on this set of providers. In this unfolding context, the purposes of this chapter are to describe independent sector providers of care for older people in the UK, to describe the policy environments in which they operate, how the two have been linked in the past, and what might be achieved in the future. We will discuss how Conservative and Labour government policies have shaped the provider side of social care markets, and what policy and practice challenges there might be for the years ahead. First we highlight some of the implications for the family of the growth of independent sector provision.

The Independent Sectors and the Family

There is some evidence that the growth of the independent sectors has had a profound impact on the care of older people by the family and indeed the relationship is two-way: changes in families' willingness and ability to provide care, of course, has major ramifications for the scale of demands on formal providers.

The growth of residential provision for older people during the 1980s, much of which was in the independent sectors, may have promoted what Grundy has described as the 'substitution of institutional for family care' (Grundy, 1996). Using the ONS Longitudinal Study, Grundy and Glaser (1997) found that, between 1981 and 1991, the rate of transitions to institutions increased substantially among people aged 75 or more. The transition to institutions became more usual than the transition to households in which older people lived with their relatives or friends, which declined. There is some evidence that the impact of these changes has continued into the 1990s. Preliminary work on the British Household Panel Survey suggests that, over the seven-year period between 1991 and 1998, it was rare for older people to move into another private household (Scott et al., 2000). In addition, preliminary analysis comparing the 1995 with the 1985 General Household Survey data on the provision of informal care suggests that, during this period, there was a decline in informal care by children of their elderly parents living in the same household

(Pickard, 2000). It remains to be seen whether these trends in the family care of older people will continue, given the more recent reversal of the rise in residential care for older people. The extent of family care for older people will also be influenced by the growth of intensive domiciliary services which we will describe in this chapter.

Mixed Economy Roles

What, then, are the independent sectors and what roles do they play in modern Britain? We can best answer these questions by charting the mixed economy of funding (purchasing), provision and the governance arrangements which bring them together. Cross-classification of purchaser and provider types produces a simple and familiar representation of the principal interconnections characterizing pluralist welfare systems and their constituent transactions (Table 8.1). We now explain these provider and purchaser classifications and the governance connections.

Providers

It is conventional to distinguish four main provider sectors in discussions of social and health care, each with a distinct legal form (or set of forms), but each in fact comprising a number of organizational types driven by a mix of motivational forces. The 1990 Act brought about a number of changes to the provider side of the mixed economy, not just in the balance *between* the sectors but also *within* these categories. Policy and practice discussions should therefore avoid oversimplified characterisations of providers, their motivations or their likely reactions to changes in funding or governance environments.

The *informal sector* is principally composed of individual carers (family members and others). There are now approximately 5.7 million carers in Great Britain, three-quarters of whom provide care to an older person aged 65 and over (Rowlands, 1998). Much informal help to older people is provided at a low level of intensity, often on a reciprocal basis. However, a small proportion of carers provide highly intensive care to dependent older people, with nearly one million carers providing co-residential care to an older person (Pickard, 2000). Some carers are involved in mutual support groups, and thus shade into the 'self help' limb of the voluntary sector to the extent they organize formally (although many remain essentially ad hoc). The 1990 Act sought to provide more support for family and other carers, and encouraged local authorities to involve them more fully in decision making, and this policy theme has been taken up by the Labour government.

The *public sector* includes local authorities, hospital and community health services, primary care services, the social security system, and criminal justice agencies. Social services authorities—dominant providers for so long—became the key players in the community care system after 1993, with co-ordinating

Table 8.1. *Purchaser–provider connections and examples of governance arrangements*

Purchasing or funding mode	Public providers	Voluntary providers	Private providers	Informal providers
Coerced collective funding	Hierarchical structures; 'internal' quasi-markets	Public contracting-out, i.e. 'external' quasi-markets		Public support for carers; direct payments to users
Uncoerced/voluntary collective funding		Foundation support for voluntary efforts		
Corporate funding		Support/subsidies to professionally orientated providers	Trust funding to 'top up' care home fees	Employers giving paid leave or other support to carers
Individual consumption	User charges for public services	Fee-for-service delivery by charities	Textbook market	
Individual transfers and non-monetized support	Voluntary contributions used within NHS	Formally organized volunteering in day care settings		Family, friends, and neighbourhood contributions

responsibilities across the public sector and enabling responsibilities outside it. The last two decades have seen the waning of local authorities' direct service provision roles (despite the development of various quasi-public, not-for-profit agencies out of former in-house services) and the waxing of their commissioning functions. Locally, they play strategic roles in shaping social care markets.

The *voluntary sector* comprises formal organizations independent of government which, although they may earn surpluses, are bound by a 'non-distribution constraint', which means they cannot distribute these surpluses to any owners or shareholders. Historically, the voluntary sector has played a variety of roles in health and social care, including provider of specialist services, supporter of marginalized population groups, innovator and advocate for change, and direct substitute for public provision (Kendall and Knapp, 1996). Most voluntary organizations in the social and healthcare fields in Britain have charitable status, conferring certain tax and reputation advantages.

Like the voluntary sector, the *private sector* is constitutionally separate from government, but is not bound by any non-distribution constraint: profits may be earned and distributed to owners. Private sector care provision for older people in the UK has long been dominated by small family businesses, many of them running single residential or nursing homes, but recently the corporate sector has begun to acquire a bigger slice of this particular market. In this chapter, we are defining the 'independent sector' to be the set of all (formal) voluntary and private provider sectors.

Purchasing Routes

At least five main routes of purchasing, funding, or demand should be distinguished in Britain's developing mixed economy of care, although again some analyses of policy and practice undoubtedly need a finer-grained approach.

The first purchasing route can be described as *coerced collective funding*, where the public sector acts as purchaser on behalf of citizens, mandated by democratic processes, funded predominantly from taxation. This has been quantitatively the most important source of funding for most formal social care services in England since the late 1940s. Tax-based funding may be routed directly to providers through central government (for example, by the Social Security ministry to independent care homes under the pre-1993 arrangements for supporting lower-income residents); or through local government as the in-house service provider or the purchaser under contract of private and voluntary sector services; or through quasi-independent public sector agencies such as Primary Care Groups which might commission a range of social care services. Of the £9 bn. of public expenditure on social services in England in 1996/97, some £4.6 bn. was spent on services for older people. The lion's share went to residential care (£2.7 bn.), with non-residential care services receiving £1.5 bn. Field social work expenditure was £44 m., whilst expenditure on care management and assessment amounted to £284 m.

A second type of funding in the modern day mixed economy, and one that has been prominent historically, is *uncoerced* or *voluntary collective support*, where voluntary organizations (and occasionally other bodies) use voluntarily donated funds to finance their own or other agencies' services. The choice as to what goods or services to purchase, and for whom, is controlled by the funding organization and not (usually or directly) by individual donors. In recent years voluntary organizations in health and social care have come to depend less on this source, and more on public (coerced collective) funding (Kendall and Almond, 1999).

Corporate funding is demand or purchasing by private-sector corporations or other businesses. Since the late 1940s Britain has had tax-based, universal health and social care systems, generally quite well resourced, so that the need for employer-funded private or social insurance payments has been quite limited. There are nevertheless corporately supported services (such as workplace nurseries for children and occupational health provision for employees), payments of private health insurance premiums and some flexible leave arrangements for carers. Employer-funded long-term care insurance is extremely rare.

The other two main purchasing routes are via individuals. *Individual consumption* is payment for goods or services consumed by the payer, with or without subsidies from social security or other transfer payments. *Individual transfers* are payments for goods and services to be used by someone else. Payments are made directly to suppliers and not to intermediary voluntary organizations (the latter being uncoerced collective support in this schema). This final 'purchasing' or resourcing category also includes formal volunteering, which is a significant if under-recognized input to social care in the UK, as well as informal volunteering and family support (Davis Smith, 1998; Knapp et al., 1996; Pickard et al., 2000).

Governance

Whilst purchasing and providing are the most readily identified and regularly discussed dimensions of a mixed economy, the governance dimension which interconnects them—fashioning the transactions or interrelationships represented in the matrix—is obviously going to be central to any attempt at understanding how health and social care systems function. By *governance* we mean institutions, rules, regulations, and protocols that govern stakeholders in undertaking transactions. Governance structures set the way in which stakeholders plan, exchange, and pay for goods and services. The concept therefore covers an array of associations, from the bureaucratic or hierarchical management structures found in public sector organizations that directly fund their own in-house services, to voluntary market-based exchange mechanisms, such as contracting-out between public authorities and independent providers, individual private exchange arrangements, charitable foundations' support for local voluntary efforts, and state support for informal carers. Each of these governance types can be located in the mixed economy matrix (Table 8.1); some are discussed in more detail later in the chapter.

The nature of governance of social care transactions is affected by legally or politically authorized public sector influence. Examples are the tax treatment of corporations and charities, provider self-regulation through publicly sanctioned codes of practice, judicial review by the courts, and hegemonic influence through the power to set training curricula and professional standards. Regulatory influences stem more directly from law-making and other central government policy prescriptions, including powers under the 1990 Act to call for reports and issue directives to social services departments. Central government's regulatory function is also exercised through the Social Services Inspectorate, responsible for monitoring care standards, and the quasi-independent Audit Commission, responsible *inter alia* for 'best value auditing'. At a local level, 'arm's-length' inspection units were introduced by the 1990 Act, located within the local authority and charged with responsibility for inspecting all provider sectors, whether private, voluntary, or public.

The Labour government's first major policy announcement on social care, the White Paper *Modernising Social Services* (Secretary of State, 1998), identified a number of problems with the regulatory system it inherited. Existing arrangements were argued to have three main deficiencies, lacking *independence* because inspection units were part of the local or health authority, *coherence* because of the rather arbitrary distinction between health and social care and their respective inspection units, and *consistency* because of the large number of local units operating independently of one another. To address these problems, the White Paper expounded the use of eight regional Commissions for Care Standards operating regionally to structure local regulation. This three-dimensional representation of social care arrangements for older people—provision, purchasing, and governance—is used to structure the discussion that follows. We will draw liberally on the ongoing programme of work conducted by the Personal Social Services Research Unit (London School of Economics and Political Science) and the Nuffield Institute for Health (University of Leeds).

LEGISLATIVE AND POLICY FRAMEWORKS

The 1990 Legislation

The enduring impact of the 1990 NHS and Community Care Act has already been commented upon. A great many of the organizational and practice features of social care to be found today were prompted or encouraged by the Act and its subsequent implementation guidance. The broad aims of the legislation were to promote independent living, user choice, innovation, and cost-effectiveness. In pursuit of these aims, the Conservative government sought to alter a number of balances: between central and local government funding responsibilities; between institutional and community-based care; between supply-led, provider-dominated services and needs-led, purchaser-dominated services; between public sector and independent sector provision; and between National Health Service and local government responsibilities for strategic decision making and funding. A key objective was to ensure that service providers made practical support for carers a high priority. Some changes were mandatory (such as the transfer of funding) and others left largely to local agencies (and contexts) to determine the extent, speed, and priority. Here we are primarily interested in the balances of provision: between and within different provider sectors, and between and within service types. However, no one policy dimension can be understood in isolation from the others.

Labour Government Proposals

Although significant developments are in train, in the broader scheme of things neither the Labour government's 1998 White Paper nor subsequent guidance or other announcements suggest strategic policy changes that will greatly alter the broad thrust of the 1990 legislation insofar as it relates to the provider balance. In particular, there is no longer explicit ministerial preference for 'a flourishing independent sector'. The main intentions are to give greater priority to prevention and rehabilitation, and to strengthen and expand the shape of statutory regulation of services in the pursuit of better quality care. Some of the details—particularly on regulation and how quality standards are to be attained—have been developed since the White Paper, including wide consultation on draft standards for residential and nursing home care set out in *Fit for the Future* (Department of Health, 1999a). There is also a draft performance management framework (Department of Health, 1999c). There is a continued emphasis on support for carers, with the development of a National Strategy for Carers (1999).

A potentially considerable influence on the structure of social care provision from outside the field has been the introduction, across the *whole* of local government, of the Best Value requirement. Non-commercial as well as commercial considerations can play a part in deciding from whom to purchase services. It seems likely that this will accelerate the rate at which local authorities run down their in-house provision in favour of independent sector services, Blackmore (2000). Although the Labour government has stressed partnership arrangements between purchasers and providers, it has not done anything to arrest market development, although it is urging the maturation of commissioning arrangements.

FORMAL SECTORAL BALANCES

'Externalization'

One of the most prominent features of social care in the last decade of the last century was the so-called 'externalization' of many services: local authorities transferred much of their in-house residential and (more recently) domiciliary care provision to the independent sectors. A representative cross-sectional survey of residential care in 1996 found that 12.5 per cent of independent residential care homes were purchased or transferred from the local authority (Netten et al., 1998).

This externalization of public provision partly explains the rapid expansion of independent sector domiciliary and residential care, shown graphically in Figure 8.1, but there have been other encouragements for private and voluntary sector providers. The changing sectoral balance of residential care has been a feature for more than two decades, and it was the (unintentionally) liberal social security environment of the 1980s which did so much to stoke private sector growth. The voluntary sector response to the means-tested social security-funded opportunities was much more modest. The 1990 Act brought a halt to such funding, although when this part of the Act was implemented in April 1993, current residential and nursing homes residents supported in this way were given 'preserved rights'. The funding for any new resident who qualified for (means-tested) public support would be administered by their local social services department. Government funding that before would have been administered by the Department of Social Security was transferred to local authorities (in successively increasing proportions).

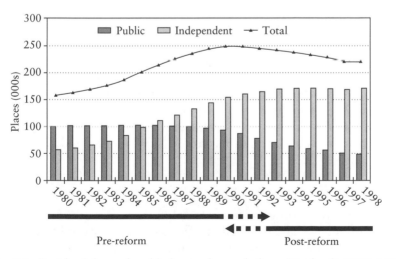

Fig. 8.1. Residential care for elderly people, total places (England), 1980–1998

One of the provisions of this special transitional grant was that 85 per cent of the money was to be spent on the independent sector. Funding therefore shifted to local authority-managed contracting-out arrangements. The 85 per cent rule continued to encourage independent sector growth at the expense (in both senses) of public provision, but especially in the domiciliary care market where the independent sector share was much more modest before 1993 (Walsh, 1997). The rule was less of a factor with respect to residential care private market growth, which was fuelled in particular by poor capitalization prospects for public sector homes and also by another social security benefit, the residential care allowance. This allowance covered some of the housing costs of residential care in the independent sector only, and could exceed a third of the total costs of the placement.

Market Shares

The share of the residential care market taken by the independent sectors reached 78 per cent by 1998 (for the UK as a whole), compared to 61 per cent in 1990 and 37 per cent in 1970. Total residential care places rose steadily until 1993 (when the 1990 Act was fully implemented) and fell back subsequently. Widening the aperture slightly to look at the full range of care accommodation for older and physically disabled people in the UK, including long-stay hospital provision, 81 per cent of residents in 1998 were in independent facilities compared to 61 per cent in 1990. Within this total, long-stay hospital provision fell absolutely (from 68,000 to 35,000 people) and relatively in terms of market share (from 14 to 7 per cent).

Residential care providers, including those from the private sector, do not conform well to the textbook stereotype of the profit-maximizing provider. A recent in-depth study found that less than 10 per cent of all providers stated that profit or income was an important motivating factor (Kendall, 2000). Other motivational factors were pertinent: 'meeting the needs of elderly people' and 'professional accomplishment' were rated as important over 75 per cent of the time, and 'independence and autonomy' as important by 40 per cent of respondents. This subjective evaluation of motivations was also supported by analysis of 'revealed motivations' from actual behaviour. An analysis of actual pricing suggested that on average providers were setting prices below those levels that would maximize profit. Indeed, actual mark-up rates were averaging less than two-thirds of the profit-maximizing level (Forder and Netten, 2000).

DOMICILIARY CARE GROWTH

The last few years have clearly shown the beginnings of the achievement of the 1990 Act's aim of substituting home-based (domiciliary) care for (some) institutional provision. The reversal of fifty years of growth of residential, nursing home and long-stay hospital provision has been made possible by, and has itself required, increases in community-based support. The most notable change has been the rapid growth of domiciliary care. Local authority-funded domiciliary care has grown, as has the proportion contracted out to independent sector providers. Overall there was a 52 per cent increase between 1992 and 1998 in home care hours.

There have been important changes in domiciliary care service range, including increases in the number of weekend and 'out-of-hours' services. Local authority purchasers have increasingly concentrated their resources on more intensive packages of care, with average utilization per household rising from 3.2 to 5.8 hours per week between 1992 and 1998, and the number of people receiving domiciliary care falling by 17 per cent. It is hard to chart sectoral patterns for domiciliary services because of limited national data collections, but recent statistics show that the independent sector's share of that part of the market funded by local authorities has grown rapidly, from 2 per cent of home care hours in 1992 to 46 per cent in 1998, most of it provided by the private sector. As Laing and Saper comment, the 1990 'community care reforms can be credited with kick-starting independent sector supply of home care services for state-funded clients' (1999: 97).

A 20 per cent random sample of independent domiciliary care providers in contract with their local authority was included in a PSSRU/Nuffield Institute survey in 1999. These providers were sampled from a representative sample of local authorities in England. Just over two-thirds of providers were in the private sector. Most were relatively new organizations, with 64 per cent having been established after 1993. The majority were also small organizations operating in a small part of their local authority, and over half provided less than 500 hours of service per week. Providers were asked about changes since 1993 (where applicable). Some 70 per cent of providers said that the number of clients served had increased; over a half described this increase in demand as considerable. Only 30 per cent said that demand was unchanged or had decreased. With regard to the level of dependency of new clients, providers reported that 54 per cent of clients showed higher need compared to the situation in 1993. Almost none said that average dependency had fallen (Matosevic et al., 2000).

COMPARATIVE PERFORMANCE

Voluntary Sector Position

Although most attention has rightly focused on the rapidly expanding private sector, the voluntary sector remains the 'provider of preference' for many local authority purchasers and for many service users, both older people and their families. After providing an almost unchanging absolute number of places in the rapidly expanding residential care market prior to 1990, the voluntary sector's market share has shown signs of recovery, mainly as a result of the creation of hybrid 'not-for-profit' trusts whose place in 'the voluntary sector' is contested (Kendall and Knapp, 1994). Like their counterparts in the much larger private sector, voluntary sector providers are increasingly reliant on local authority funding: the proportion of older residents thus supported grew from 20 per cent in 1994 to 29 per cent in 1996. It is less clear how voluntary sector domiciliary services have been affected by the 1990 Act: many are low-intensity, low-visibility, volunteer-led activities, and the considerable increases in local authority funding have been absorbed almost entirely by the private sector. It is in day care where the voluntary sector is better established, having consolidated its position in recent years, whilst the private sector has only just begun to gain something of a foothold (Laing and Saper, 1999).

The voluntary and private sectors are operating distinctively in a number of ways: offering different service configurations, as we have just seen; employing different resource combinations; supporting slightly different groups of users, historically, but less so currently; and operating under different business conditions (Kendall and Knapp, 2000). The voluntary sector has diversified to a greater extent, with more multi-field organizations, including long-established generalist organizations and newer 'social entrepreneur led' housing associations. The voluntary sector also has a longer tradition of care provision, and often closer and longer-standing links with the public sector. Overlapping management structures with local and health authorities are more common.

Quality of Care

The two independent sectors deliver different combinations of activities which could generate quality of care differences. A large-scale PSSRU study of residential and nursing home care found some relationships between quality of care indicators and provider type (Netten et al., 1998). Seven indicators derived from the Social Care Environment Scale (SCES) were used (Moos and Lemke, 1992). The first, *organization*, measures the importance of order and organization in the home, the extent to which residents know what to expect in their daily routine, and the clarity of rules and procedures. Organization was found to be higher in private homes compared to voluntary homes. Also smaller homes were more organized. The second indicator is *physical comfort* and measures the extent to which comfort, privacy, pleasant décor, and sensory satisfaction are provided in the physical environment. Again, private homes were reported as having higher physical comfort, as were smaller homes. *Resident influence* reflects the extent to which residents can influence the rules and policies of the home and are free from restrictive regulations; no differences were found by home sector or size.

Turning to relationship dimensions, the fourth indicator, *cohesion*, assesses the helpfulness and support of staff towards residents and how involved and supportive residents are of each other. Private sector homes demonstrated more cohesion, but this measure was unrelated to home size directly. *Conflict* measures the extent to which residents express anger and are critical of each other and of the home. Sector did not appear to have any bearing on this indicator, although conflict was higher in large homes. The two final indicators are *independence*, gauging the degree to which residents are encouraged to be self-sufficient regarding their personal affairs and how much responsibility and self-direction they exercise, and *self-disclosure*, measuring how much residents express their feelings and personal concerns. Independence was not related to home sector or home size. However, self-disclosure was greater for private homes, but was not affected by home size.

Overall, homes in the private sector appeared to have greater organization, physical comfort, cohesion, and self-disclosure than those in the voluntary sector. In the other dimensions the sectors were not different statistically.

Staffing and Salaries

Staff turnover was slightly lower in the voluntary sector in 1996 (15 per cent of current staff started or left in the previous year, compared to 22 per cent of private sector staff), but qualification levels were similar: 30 per cent of private and 27 per cent of voluntary sector staff had an RON or NVQ qualification, and 13 and 15 per cent, respectively, of residential care staff had, or were currently studying, for social work qualifications (Local Government Management Board (LGMB), 1997). Voluntary homes were less likely than their private sector counterparts to provide day sitting, night sitting, or live-in services.

Residential care staff salaries in the two-year period 1995–7 were significantly higher in the voluntary sector (mean of £5.61 per hour) than in the private sector (£3.98). There were also salary differences in non-residential social care (£6.02 and £4.32 respectively) (Almond and Kendall, 1999). Volunteer inputs are more heavily concentrated in the voluntary sector (Ware, 1997; Curtice et al., 1997; LGMB, 1997).

Fees and Mark-ups

Residential care prices tend to be lower in the voluntary than the private sector (Forder et al., 1999; Forder and Netten 2000*a*). When account was taken of differences in social environment (the SCES scores), the price difference increased slightly. Turning to domiciliary care, when account is taken of other relevant factors, such as client characteristics, prices are lower in the private sector. However, the same study also suggests that mark-up rates are lower in the non-profit sector (Forder et al., 2000*b*).

Such differences are interesting given the higher wages in the voluntary sector. The voluntary sector is more likely than the private to 'top up' local authority residential care fees by cross-subsidizing from other sources (Forder et al., 2000*a*). Some evidence of motivational differences have also been found: voluntary sector managers place slightly less emphasis on financial reward for themselves and the pursuit of autonomy in running homes than their private sector owner-manager counterparts. However, but the relationship between sector and manager motivation is complex and far from deterministic: each sector contains managers expressing a mix of empathetic, professional, autonomy-oriented, and financial motivations (Kendall, 2001).

Dependency

Resident dependency levels have been significantly lower in voluntary than private care homes for some time (Townsend, 1962), but 'pronounced increases' in dependency across all sectors over the last decade, and particularly in the voluntary (Darton, 1998), have caused average dependency levels more or less to converge (Forder and Netten, 2000*b*). As noted above, significant increases in dependency levels have also been evident in the domiciliary care sector.

MULTIPLE INDEPENDENT SECTORS

We have seen that the independent sector is not a singular entity: it is a mix of organizational forms, legal contexts, and operating interests. At the very least, distinctions need to be made between: (*a*) small, often husband-and-wife run businesses, which are the traditional mainstay of private sector provision; (*b*) rapidly emerging corporate (including publicly-quoted) providers; (*c*) traditional charities, many with long track records pre-dating state involvement; (*d*) housing associations, many of them with growing social and health care responsibilities; (*e*) new voluntary organizations, often involving 'social entrepreneurs' creatively mixing different forms of public finance to generate resources for new types of care package; and (*f*) not-for-profit trusts, including 'floated off' residential homes and domiciliary services formerly run directly by local authorities. Different fields (or markets) are dominated by very different provider types, and the patterns also vary greatly across the country.

Why is it necessary to make these provider distinctions? Obvious considerations are that particular organizational forms have their own histories which affect their *modus operandi*, involve different patterns of resource dependency and styles of governance and management, and operate with contrasting legal rights and responsibilities. Moreover, their executive boards or other strategic decision-makers and their professional staff sometimes appear to operate with different motivations. One consequence has therefore been a different ability and willingness to respond to changes in market opportunities, pricing regimes, and competition. The for-profit sector, for example, led by an explosion of small businesses blending welfare and economic objectives, responded much more rapidly than other sectors to the opportunities in residential and nursing home care for older people in the 1980s and early 1990s created by an open-ended social security regime. In contrast, the voluntary sector has long been, and remains, a major provider of day care, which has to date not proved especially attractive for private sector operators. As we saw above, evidence from the research literature also suggests some differences in resourcing, organization, and levels of performance.

Potentially of considerable future relevance is the observation that different types of organization vary in the routes along which they initiate and cultivate trust and reputation. As launched in the 1998 White Paper *Modern Local Government: In Touch with the People* and described in *A New Approach to Social Services Performance* (Department of Health 1999c), local authorities are now required to seek 'best value' across the full span of their activities, but the social care context is one in which the monitoring of service qualities and user outcomes is recognized to be especially difficult. A well-founded trusting relationship between purchaser and provider removes much of the need for costly monitoring. In this respect, voluntary organizations with their historical 'first-mover advantage' and shared culture and values with social services personnel, have been able to establish good reputations with purchasers and use it to maintain their market niche (Kendall, 2000; Forder, 2000).

Thus, whilst it is necessary to recognize these potential and actual inter-sectoral differences, they should not blind us to the fact that rigid demarcations between the sectors are not always clear or sensible. There are lots of commonalities of perspective and motivation which cut across the sectors and provider types as they are currently defined, both legally and organizationally. For example, career paths of staff and managers often take them from one sector or type of organization to another, and attitudes and behaviours are in part conditioned by previous experiences. Moreover, in as much as most independent sector organizations are sharing to some degree a common environment as contractors with local authorities, they can face similar pressures and opportunities.

ANXIETIES AND CONCERNS

Many providers in the independent sectors and many local authority purchasers express concerns about these recent changes and about the arrangements which currently operate in their localities. Similar concerns have been expressed by families as guardians of older relatives' interests wherever they receive care and as carers themselves too. What are the sources of their concern? We consider each in turn.

Family Concerns

Users and carers express both positive and negative views about the recent changes and about the arrangements which currently operate in their localities. What are the sources of their concerns (see Box 8.1)?

A major source of concern by older people and their families is the increase in means-tested care associated with the recent changes. As described earlier in this chapter, the rising share of the residential care market taken by the

---

Box 8.1. *Family concerns*

- Reduced access to long-term hospital care
- Increase in means-tested residential care
- Difficulties in finding short-term respite care places
- Limited choice of short-term placements
- Limited choice in practice of domiciliary providers
- Reduced access to low intensity domiciliary care
- Carers still feel excluded from mainstream services

---

independent sectors has partly been at the expense of NHS long-stay hospital provision. The growth of the independent sector has therefore been associated with an increase in the numbers who enter means-tested residential care rather than free-at-the-point-of-use hospital care (Joseph Rowntree Foundation Inquiry, 1996). This has contributed to changes in the balance between public funding and private resources which was one of the key issues underlying the establishment of the Royal Commission on Long Term Care. The Royal Commission found that the current system of charging for care had provoked a widespread perception of unfairness, uncertainty, and bitterness among older people and their families (Royal Commission on Long Term Care, 1999). The Royal Commission's recommendations implied a redistribution of funding from private to public expenditure. The Government's subsequent response also implies a measure of redistribution between private and public funding, though less than recommended by the Commission (Department of Health, 2000). How far this issue remains a source of concern for older people and their families has yet to be assessed.

Other family concerns arise from care arrangements for older people living at home. Informal carers looking after older people in the community have found that access to respite care has been affected by the recent changes. The Age Concern Institute of Gerontology (ACIOG) reported to the Royal Commission that 'In the past, many short-term placements have been made in local authority care homes and in the geriatric and psycho-geriatric wards of NHS hospitals. The closure or transfer to the voluntary sector of many local authority residential homes and the sharp decline in NHS hospital beds has had an impact. Although independent sector residential and nursing homes will provide short-term placements there has been a reluctance to designate beds permanently as short term because continuity of income is not guaranteed' (Tinker et al., 1999: 58). ACIOG's own research indicated that carers were experiencing difficulties in finding short-term places in residential care homes, a situation that was perceived to have worsened as local authority care homes, which had been reliable providers in the past, were closing (Tinker et al., 1999: 58). Other research has indicated a shortage of short-term placements and limited carer choice (Moriarty and Levin, 1998; Social Services Inspectorate, 1998). Access to respite care may, however, now be improving as a result of the commitment to short-term breaks in the National Carers' Strategy (1999).

Older people and their carers have also been concerned about other changes in domiciliary care arrangements. Although at a strategic level the number of providers has expanded, this has not necessarily been reflected in improved choice at an operational level. A study of users, carers, and care managers in four local authorities in England found that none of those receiving domiciliary care had been offered a choice between local authority and independent sector services or between individual providers (Hardy et al., 1999*b*). For those considering a permanent move to a residential home, choice is also in practice limited (Office of Fair Trading, 1998). Choice in domiciliary care has been increased in some respects, such as the introduction of a wider range of services by independent sector providers, and should in principle be increased by the recent extension of direct payments to older people. However, in other respects, choice has been restricted. The concentration of resources on more intensive packages of care by local authority purchasers has led to the exclusion of lower intensity provision (such as cleaning and other types of practical support) for the many (Hardy et al., 1999*b*).

Informal carers often still feel excluded from mainstream services. Support for carers is often included at the lowest category of need, so that it effectively falls off the end of provision (Twigg, 1998), although intensive packages of care for older users are now more likely to benefit informal carers than they were before the community care changes were introduced (Davies, 1997). Nevertheless, inspite of some important changes resulting from the community care reforms, community social services are still directed primarily at unsupported older people living alone rather than at those with informal carers (Pickard, 1999). The Royal Commission recommended that better services should be offered to older people with carers, recommending specifically that services should become increasingly 'carer blind' (Royal Commission on Long Term Care, 1999). The NHS Plan, however, did not pursue this policy direction, instead focusing on providing support, such as respite, aimed at the carer rather than the 'cared-for' person (Department of Health, 2000).

Providers' Concerns

Independent sector providers comment both negatively and positively about their relationships with purchasers (see Box 8.2); overall satisfaction ratings appear to be neutral or if anything slightly positive (Hardy et al., 1999*a*, and Matosevic et al., 2000; see Box 8.1). One common anxiety is that occupancy rates in many residential homes are uncomfortably low (from a business perspective), and in many cases this is combined with a perennial 'prices squeeze' from local authorities. With increasingly dependent new residents and consequent increases in running costs, profits or operating surpluses can be very

---

Box 8.2. *Independent sector concerns*

- Low occupancy rates
- Low fees relative to costs (low profit margins)
- Rising dependency and costs
- Labour market regulation and rising costs
- Late payment
- Infrequent reviews of users
- Prices inflexible in the face of changes in user dependency
- Lack of trust
- Insufficient confidence to invest in better quality

---

low or even negative, and cross-subsidizing to cover the revenue gap may not be sustainable beyond the short-term. Between 1985 and 1996 the price of a residential care bed increased, in real terms, by only 3 per cent, and the price of a nursing home bed actually fell (Forder and Netten, 2000*b*). Changes in labour market regulations such as the minimum wage and the EU working time directive are adding further pressures. Many smaller residential care or nursing homes in the private sector have already gone to the wall, and others are close to it (Forder et al., 2000). Even voluntary sector providers well enough resourced to draw on reserves or other funds may potentially face difficulties if by doing so they inappropriately shoulder public financial responsibilities in contravention of charity law.

Second, many providers are finding the current regime of contracting out and regulatory requirements oppressive and obtrusive. Having moved from the public to the independent sector to avoid bureaucracy and seek autonomy, particularly under the liberal arrangements prevailing in the 1980s, some feel frustrated and demotivated by what they see as the 'dead hand' of state control (Kendall, 2001). A number certainly feel they are poorly treated by monopsony purchasers, who can be late with their payments, dilatory with their reviews of users, absent when it comes to follow-up appointments, and biased in favour of in-house providers.

A third source of independent sector concern relates to pricing, not just in terms of its average level, but also its (lack of) flexibility and adjustability. Today's contracts rarely embody reimbursements to respond to contingencies such as changes in user needs (Forder, 1997). All of the risk, many providers argue, is loaded onto them rather than shared with purchasers. Because the dependency levels of most older users are more likely to go up than down, and because fixed prices are generally renegotiated no more frequently than annually, and then often only by the same amount for all providers in the local authority, the present arrangements may leave providers under-resourced, further threatening their viability as business concerns or as solvent charities.

In toto, the current contractual climate—more generally, the current govern-ance structure—may not be conducive to trust, and consequently there is a potentially vicious circle of transaction costs. Intrusive or distracting monitor-ing by purchasers is not only resource-costly for providers, but breeds mistrust and can undermine the latter's disposition to act as co-operatively and con-structively as 'relational contracts'—the government's desired end point—would require. Put differently, providers can feel less willing, on balance, to give purchasers the benefit of the doubt, responding in less positive or imagin-ative ways to changed circumstances without the explicit approval—better still, the confirmed funding—of purchasers. One consequence is that trust is neither established nor reinforced. Facing low profits, and feeling unable to rely on supportive actions by their local purchasers in the future, investment in quality is likely to be limited. Many independent providers recognize that their staff are 'under-skilled' but worry that the future environment is not suf-ficiently stable or attractive for them to direct revenues into training.

Local Authority Concerns

The above litany of independent sector concerns will be familiar and needs to be taken seriously, although, of course, frequent repetition does not of itself con-stitute evidence of purchasers' errors of omission and commission. Local author-ity purchasers might recognize some of these provider concerns as valid, but might feel that others are exaggerated or are misinterpreting what are, in fact, well-intentioned commissioning strategies. Local authorities also have their own concerns (Wistow et al., 1996; see Box 8.3). Many are still worried about a per-ceived loss of control as a result of past and prospective service 'externaliza-tions', and a regret that more cannot be kept in-house. Despite the many changes within the mixed economy of care over the last ten years, there is still a strong ethos of public service running through social services departments.

Authorities express concerns about quality of care, fearing that the low prices which they themselves are driving down (in pursuit of best value) can only be maintained by independent providers if they employ low-paid, low-skilled staff or cut corners on quality. (The PSSRU's 1996 survey of residential care providers found that basic pay rates of care assistants were below £4 per hour for 90 per cent of private sector providers; Netten et al., 1998. See also Almond and Kendall, 2000.) A related anxiety is that it is hard for authorities to know just what the quality effects *are*. They face tremendous difficulty in measuring user outcomes to their complete satisfaction, they have only poor indicators of care quality, but they may not have built the kind of trusting rela-tionship with their providers which gives them the confidence to operate with-out close monitoring.

A potential loss of local authority control also comes from their closer relationships with powerful healthcare purchasers. The roles of the new Primary Care Groups are not yet fully clear or fully matured, but already they

---

Box 8.3. *Purchaser concerns*

- Loss of control
- Relations with healthcare purchasers
- Low quality of care
- Difficulties in monitoring outcomes
- Lack of variety and reduced choice
- Capability gap
- Resource levels

---

are having significant influence on services for elderly people. Of course, closer working with health colleagues also provides positive opportunities, for example to improve co-ordination between geriatric discharge and nursing and residential care provision.

A further source of anxiety may be that standard contractual arrangements and standard service specifications can lead to over-standardized services. That is, experiencing the same environmental pressures and responding defensively to a chronic atmosphere of uncertainty, providers might become more and more similar both to each other and to in-house services (what DiMaggio and Powell, 1983, have called 'coercive isomorphism'). The result could be reductions in variety, the ability to meet user needs, and the facility to offer user choice.

Two other concerns are sometimes expressed. One is about authorities' own 'capability gaps'. This involves a recognition that they have moved an enormous way up the learning curve in terms of market management, and are no longer so under-resourced or under-skilled when it comes to commissioning negotiations with providers. Yet they are generally not sufficiently engaged in the longer-term strategic shaping of markets as to secure the best services for their populations at an affordable price (Wistow et al., 1996). Another issue has been rumbling for a long time, concerning the overall resourcing of social care. Available funding levels, local authorities claim, make it impossible for them to provide the kinds of preventive care services that could save the Exchequer money in the longer-term, or to be able to afford prices which encourage providers to make long-term investments in quality.

SERVING WITH DISTINCTION

Quantitatively, the independent sectors are clearly substantial social care providers. They provide skilled support to large numbers of older people, and they employ some 1 million paid employees (Secretary of State for Health, 1998). These staff are now mainly to be found in the private sector, but just under one-fifth work for voluntary organizations, which also mobilize a quarter of a million full-time equivalent unpaid volunteers. Today there is little public sector provision left in some markets and localities, and local authorities are rapidly externalizing in others (especially home care and day care). This may confer certain advantages. For example, some authorities are finding that some of their independent sector providers offer good value: costs appear to be lower, care quality is satisfactory and sometimes superior, and user outcomes at least as good or perhaps better.

Qualitatively, too, the independent sectors are proving their importance. The independent sectors offer variety and—to a degree—they also offer independence from the state. Consequently, they *potentially* extend the range of choice for families (users and carers), care managers, and purchasers, although as we have seen in practice these benefits may have been limited to date. The independent sectors can be 'niche' providers: for example, voluntary sector residential homes often deliver care with a distinctive religious or other identity-based ethos; private sector nursing homes specialize in terms of scale and scope of their operations; and voluntary sector day care can be distinctive in involving volunteers in valued capacities. The independent sectors have shown an ability to respond flexibly to changing circumstances, and to be innovators in service orientation, arrangement, or quality. For example, private providers pioneered evening and weekend home care services in many localities, and voluntary providers and consortia have been particularly active in pioneering new forms of care and support at the interface between housing, healthcare, and social care.

As we have indicated, there is evidence that the growth of the independent sectors has had a profound impact on the care of older people by families. Family care for older people is being influenced by the expectations of older people and their families, the changes in residential care, and the growth of intensive domiciliary services described in this chapter.

9

Inheritance and Intergenerational Relationships in English Families

JANET FINCH

INTRODUCTION

Inheritance counts as an 'emerging issue' in intergenerational relationships principally because of the spread of home ownership. Between the mid-1960s and the late 1980s the proportion of people within Britain who owned their own homes rose from one-third to two-thirds of the population. The particular relevance of this for inheritance is that many more people than in the past have something of value to bequeath, and many more families therefore are affected by this. It turns the management of inheritance from something which previously concerned only a small minority of wealthy families into a commonplace experience. In principle, the effects could be quite profound, creating new bonds between generations around a shared interest in assets and wealth. John Major recognized this when he talked about the Conservative vision for Britain as being one where large numbers of citizens were able to see wealth 'trickling down the generations'.

A considerable amount of interesting research has been undertaken on the impact of inheritance of house property on the structure of wealth and its distribution over time (Munro, 1987; Forrest and Murie, 1989; Hamnett, Harmer, and Williams, 1991; Hamnett, 1996). Potentially the ownership and transmission of house property alters the nature of relationships across the generations as well as the structure of wealth and property holding. This is apparent from, for example, the work done by Hamnett (1996), which demonstrates that wealth invested in housing represents a major component of estates bequeathed at death, except for the very smallest and the very largest estates. To put the point a different way: most of us have little to bequeath unless we own a house, but those of us who do potentially have something of value to transmit to the next generation. This raises the possibility that relationships across the generations may themselves be altered as property enters the equation.

More recently the issue of inheritance has 'emerged' in a sharp form in relation to paying for long-term care. For many people, the opportunity to pass on assets to their children and grandchildren, probably acquired for the first time in their own generation, may be rapidly removed by the expectation that assets will be used up in old age in order that none of us is a drain on the taxpayer unless absolutely necessary. Important though this is—and we shall return to the issue of paying for care at the end of the chapter—to think about it as the only issue of interest raised by inheritance is to risk missing some import-ant trends. The possibility of transmitting wealth down the generations—the John Major vision—potentially alters the nature of family relationships them-selves, perhaps binding people more closely because they have a common stake in property, perhaps pulling them apart as expectations about what will be inherited are not fulfilled.

Even if we want to fully understand the specific issue of paying for care in old age we need to stand back a little and to take a longer view of how expecta-tions are likely to develop in the future: the specific issue of using assets to fund care in old age is rather new to social policy. The experience of owning assets is also rather new to the majority of the population. The whole issue is there-fore somewhat fluid and we cannot assume that attitudes at this point in time are well formed or fixed. This chapter considers the likely impact of inheritance on cross-generational relationships in the light of what we already know about the nature of family and kin relationships in this country. This has two aspects. First, the impact of kinship on inheritance: how the handling of inheritance within families for whom this is a new experience is shaped by existing practices in cross-generational relationships. Second, the impact of inheritance on kinship: how far, over time, this new experience might stimu-late changes in those relationships. In considering these questions the chapter draws on the ESRC-funded study *The Inheritance Project*[1] to address the impact of English kinship[2] on inheritance. Namely, how does the pre-existing nature of, and expectations about, cross-generational relationships get used to manage the 'new' experience of inheritance?

INDIVIDUALISM IN ENGLISH KINSHIP AND THE MANAGEMENT OF INHERITANCE

The central theme here is the individualistic character of English kinship. This is the key to understanding the interplay between inheritance and cross-generational relationships as they develop. What is meant by the claim that English kinship is fundamentally individualistic? Obviously that term can be used in a variety of ways, but here draws on a usage found in anthropological, sociological, and historical research in kinship. There are a number of different

[1] I am grateful to ESRC for funding the Inheritance Project (Grant Number 000232035).
[2] The references from here onwards to 'English' kinship are deliberate. The available empirical data, including my own, does not include the rest of the British Isles. I believe that it should be left as an open question whether kinship in Scotland, Wales, and Ireland has similar features.

strands to this individualism, of which I think the most important can be summed up in three descriptors: *ego-focused, flexible, affective.*

The idea that kinship is *ego-focused* concerns the ways in which any individual's place in a kinship universe is constructed. In anthropological terms, English kinship is bilateral, that is, descent is reckoned through both mother and father (if the identity of both is known). But more importantly there is no sense of a 'common ancestor', not even a weak one, though aristocratic families may be a partial exception to this. The importance of this feature cannot be overstated. Its significance was demonstrated powerfully and influentially by Macfarlane in his historical work on *The Origins of English Individualism* (1978). Here he contrasts 'ancestor centred' kinship systems, where an individual's place in a kinship universe is reckoned by tracing lineage back to a common ancestor, with 'ego-centred' kinship in which each individual is the centre of his or her own kinship universe, working outwards and delineating a set of relationships which is unique to him or herself. He contrasts this with much of continental Europe, where the ancestor focus was much stronger, underpinning a peasant economy in which rights to land passed from one generation to the next. English individualism, he argues, can be traced to at least the thirteenth century:

Within the recorded period covered by our documents, it is not possible to find a time when the Englishman did not stand alone. Symbolised and shaped by his ego-centred kinship system, he stood at the centre of his own social world.   (1978: 196)

This is complemented by the second feature, namely *flexibility*. All of the best research on kinship in the last half-century has noted that there is a highly variable dimension to English kinship meaning, for example, that people who occupy the same genealogical positions may be treated differently: one brother or sister may be regarded as 'closer' than another, seen more frequently, more likely to be party to exchanges of mutual assistance, and so on. There is a clear choice about which kin to acknowledge actively, who will be included in one's own kinship network, and clearly people do exercise that choice. Strathern (1992), approaching it from the perspective of a distinguished anthropologist, also argues that contemporary English kinship is distinctively individualistic— a system in which individuals relate to each other on the basis of 'persons not positions'. She calls this 'the first fact of English kinship' (1992: 14).

This focus on 'persons not positions' means that the English tend not to relate to each other as 'mother', 'sister', or 'son' in the sense of playing out a role whose normative characteristics are pre-defined. If I have more than one sister or son, then my relationship with each will probably be different. It is *personal*—not *positional*. Of course it is possible to overdraw this distinction. In reality, the balance between the personal and positional elements may vary within any given relationship. Moreover, the degree of optionality in any relationship does vary to an extent with genealogical position, with clear evidence that there is least flexibility about relationships between parents and children (Finch and Mason, 1993).

The third characteristic of English kinship is the importance of the *affective* dimension. This is possibly a rather clumsy word to express the simple fact that personal chemistry does matter in family life. In this kinship universe which I have to construct for myself, and where there is a great deal of choice and flexibility, the dynamics of interpersonal relationships play an important part in defining people in or out, into the core or on the margins. This perhaps makes the process sound rather more fickle than it actually is. To understand fully how the kin universe of any adult has been constructed, we need to introduce the perspective of time. In our own work on family obligations and responsibilities (Finch and Mason, 1993), it became very clear that relationships between specific individuals are built up, and develop their particular character, over long periods of time. In that sense each of us has our own ego-focused kin network which is a lifetime's accomplishment, a project which is reviewed and revised on a regular basis, and indeed is often built up—like geological strata—out of the material of our key life events.

These three features—ego-focused, flexible, affective—define the character of English kinship and have important implications for government action in regulating family relationships. The core of the problem is that it is very difficult to regulate relationships which depend on persons, not positions. To legislate for 'positions' is much easier, since one can attach legal obligations to the role of 'father', 'brother', and so on. The relative absence of legal regulation of family relationships in the UK is itself a reflection of the distinctive character of English kinship.

Inheritance law is a key case here. The regulation of inheritance under English law is a very light touch, by comparison with most Continental jurisdictions. The latter, operating on the basis of the civil code, specify proportions of the estate which must pass to named 'positions' within the kinship universe, with the major emphasis being on children rather than the surviving spouse. Indeed in most Continental legal systems it is not possible to disinherit one's children, and often bequests must be given to each of them in pre-specified proportions. Under English—and indeed Scottish—law the situation is very much more open. This principle of testamentary freedom in both English and Scottish inheritance law could be seen as symbolizing the individualistic character of the kinship system. Whilst one can debate whether the law shapes or follows social life, at the very least it is self-evidently the case that this aspect of the law is *tolerated* in England, and in Scotland.

Having emphasized that English kinship is distinctive in its room for variation, it is plainly also true that there are some limits to the flexibility of family relationships. I have already mentioned the stronger normative expectations attached to parent–child relationships throughout life, though even here much variety is tolerated (Finch and Mason, 1993). There are also some limits as to who can 'count' unproblematically as close family, as people whose family life is based on gay or lesbian relationships would attest. It is within the context of this special approach to kinship—individualistic but not infinitely flexible— that the English people are bound to manage new challenges. When faced with how to handle inheritance for the first time within a family, we should expect that existing practices will be adapted, rather than completely new ones invented. This means that we should expect to find that people feel free to make their own decisions about what happens to their property rather than follow fixed rules, since there are very few fixed rules of kinship obligation in the English context. Of course the right to do precisely that is enshrined in our laws on inheritance. On the other hand, we should not expect the situation to be totally open and unpredictable, especially since the issue of inheritance touches centrally on relationships between parents and children, which is where we find the closest approximation to fixed obligations in the English kinship system.

THE INHERITANCE PROJECT

The following discussion draws on a range of research findings but most particularly on data collected in collaboration with colleagues on an ESRC-funded project on inheritance and family relationships. The project had several different elements, of which two shall be drawn upon, the first of which is the analysis of a randomly selected sample of 800 probated wills, from people who died in the years 1959, 1969, 1979, and 1989. Our reason for selecting these four sample years was to enable us to see whether there have been any changes in the pattern of bequeathing over that period of time when the rate of home ownership has been rising. Secondly, we draw on a set of eighty-eight in-depth interviews about how inheritance issues are handled within families in practice. The interviewees were selected on the basis that they came from 'ordinary' as opposed to wealthy families, but otherwise they covered a reasonable spread of socio-economic circumstances, included housing tenure. Their ages ranged from 18 to 89. They all lived in England, most but not all in the north of England, at the time of the interview, but their places of origin were quite widely varied and included some from the Indian subcontinent. Thirty-two interviewees were in the study as individuals and the rest had one or more members of their own family who also were interviewed. Our largest family group in the study included eight interviewees.

Patterns of Bequeathing in Practice

The starting point for understanding these issues is to look at patterns of bequeathing, to see how far people exercise their right to testamentary freedom by bequeathing their assets to a wide range of individuals, possibly completely outside their families. In essence the evidence about bequeathing over the thirty years since more people started owning their own homes suggests that there is much less variation than the law would actually permit. In broad terms it seems that transmission to members of one's family is the norm. In our own study, we found that 92 per cent of testators included at least one relative in their will and that 83 per cent bequeathed to kin exclusively. There was little change over our four sample years in these percentages.

Within that overall picture of keeping assets in the family, which kin are favoured? Are assets passing from parent to child, and on further down the direct line of descent, or are they spread more widely? In general, passing down the direct line of descent does seem to be the norm, provided there is no surviving spouse. Leaving aside bequests to spouses, the testator's children are much more likely than any other group to figure as beneficiaries. For example, in a study based in Scotland in the 1980s, Munro (1987) found that 43 per cent of the wealth was passing to spouses and 23 per cent to children, including stepchildren. Other relatives figured at a much lower level.

Rather than attempting to estimate the comparative value of bequests, the Inheritance Project looked at the likelihood of different beneficiaries appearing in the will. The data showed that spouses were mentioned in 37 per cent of wills and children in 36 per cent. Other categories of relative appeared much less frequently. The most common pattern where there was a surviving spouse was that she or he inherited the main portion of the estate undivided, though children might receive specific bequests of personal items. In the sample, spouses typically received the total or the residuary estate.[3] Children were the only other beneficiaries who commonly received a share in these 'major' bequests of total or residuary estate.

There was a general tendency therefore to concentrate on the nuclear family in inheritance matters and, in the absence of a surviving spouse, this means that children generally were treated as having the major claim. Beyond that, the picture becomes much more variable. There was little evidence of testators thinking deliberately about their 'wealth trickling down the generations' in the sense that only 12 per cent of wills contained bequests to grandchildren and the typical grandchild bequest was a small cash gift. In less than 2 per cent of cases did a grandchild receive a share of the total or residuary estate. On the other hand 15 per cent of wills contained a bequest to a relative who was genealogically quite distant: step-relatives, in-laws, great-nieces and nephews, cousins. The variations which we see in practice are an indication

---

[3] A 'total estate' bequest is one where the testator simply adds all his or her assets together and bequeaths them without differentiation. This could go to a single beneficiary, or to more than one beneficiary in specified proportions. In other wills, there are specific gifts to named individuals (for example, sums of money, personal possessions) and then what is left is rolled together and bequeathed as the 'residuary estate'. In most cases it appears as if the value of the residuary estate is much greater than the specific bequests taken out first, though this cannot be determined precisely from wills. In my analysis I am referring to both total and residuary estates as 'major' bequests, irrespective of their actual value, to distinguish them from other specific bequests like cash gifts or jewellery.

that some testators—though a minority—do indeed use the mechanism of inheritance to construct and define who constitutes 'my own' family, the people who are important enough *to me* to acknowledge them by naming them in a will.

What do the patterns observed in wills tell us about relationships across generations in the English context, especially in the light of the individualistic character of English kinship? At first sight there exists a real paradox: in England we have the freedom to bequeath to whomsoever we wish, in practice the majority of us leave our property in ways which echo the patterns prescribed in civil code jurisdictions. This had led some legal commentators to argue that the only reason why testamentary freedom has survived in England is that people do in fact bequeath their property to their families in predictable ways. If they did not, there would need to be legislation, it is argued, on the grounds that the stability of any society requires that property passes in an orderly fashion from one generation to the next (Finch et al., 1996).

However, if one looks a little more closely at patterns of bequeathing in England, the situation is not in fact so straightforward. Essentially, the ability to exercise testamentary freedom in this country means that the English management of inheritance is infinitely more flexible and capable of adapting to social changes than is the case under the civil law codes. That point comes out clearly if one considers the treatment of a surviving spouse. Under the Napoleonic Civil Code spouses had practically no rights to inherit, a logical if harsh consequence of seeing property as passing down the blood line. Spouses of course are linked by contract, not by blood ties. Gradually spouses have acquired some rights to inherit under these legal codes but their position remains a live issue, even for example in a country so apparently progressive as the Netherlands, where there remains a very lively debate about whether children's rights should essentially continue to take precedence over those of the surviving parent or step-parent. In England by contrast, our legal system has allowed for inheritance practices to adapt to changing expectations associated with marriage. Over a period of a century we have moved from a situation where married women were not allowed to own property at all, to one where it is presumed that spouses' interest in property is so common and inseparable that it all passes to the survivor more or less automatically when one dies. Indeed it is regarded as so automatic that the Inheritance Project found that people scarcely thought of transmission of property to the surviving spouse as 'inheritance' at all. It was treated as something which just happens when a married person dies. Similarly, inheritance practices are being adapted to divorce, remarriage, and the creation of stepfamilies (Finch, 1997; Burgoyne and Morison, 1997: 391–3).

Inheritance: A New Tie that Binds?

It is clear therefore that the flexibility, adaptability, and individuality of English kinship has made it possible for a significant social change—the spread of property owning—to be incorporated into family life without creating major disruptions. Because both English legal and cultural expectations about inheritance are open-ended, they allow for each individual and each family to make their own decisions. Even though the majority do take decisions that are straightforward and predicable, the *opportunity* to adapt one's own practices to suit circumstances allows room for manoeuvre which some people will wish to exercise. The social change now under way in respect of inheritance is running rather smoothly therefore. However, in the longer term it may have more significant consequences. Once it becomes the common experience of the average family that each generation can expect a fairly substantial bequest from the previous one, over time this could produce changes in intergenerational relationships. Essentially, inheritance could become a new tie which binds generations together through a common interest in property (in all its senses).

Is there evidence that the experience of inheritance is beginning to create these new ties? Though two-thirds of the population were homeowners by the mid-1980s, the biggest changes have occurred as younger generations have purchased property. It will clearly be into the middle years of the next century before these younger homeowners will die. Putting together the age structure of property-owning with changing mortality rates, Hamnett (1996) has calculated that it will be 2025 before the major growth in house purchase percolates through to inheritance, and of course only then if most of today's homeowners preserve their assets until they die rather than using them to finance their own old age.

The 1990s therefore saw only the beginnings of any changes which may be occurring in cross-generational relationships as a consequence of a newly acquired common interest in property, and this was reflected in the Inheritance Project findings. The interview data suggest that there is little evidence, at least as yet, that intergenerational relationships are changing as a result of more people having acquired significant assets to bequeath. There is no evidence that children are seen as having 'rights' over their parents' property, either by older or younger generations. This may seem a curious claim, given that children are predictable beneficiaries of their parents' estates, according to the data. However there is a clear distinction between *being given* something and *having a right* to it.

This distinction is fundamental to understanding how families handle inheritance in the English context. In particular it means that there is rather little emphasis on the need to preserve property in order to pass it on to your children. If there is property left when one dies, then most people will see their children as their natural heirs. But parents are under no obligation to ensure that they do have something to bequeath. These are strong messages and they help to explain, for example, why many people seem relatively uninterested in planning for the transmission of their property, for example, by writing a will, which is still done only by a minority of the population. Material assets are treated essentially as the property of one generation rather than as the foundation of wealth in future generations. It may become that, but there is no common expectation that this is an automatic occurrence. Property belongs to an individual, not to a family.

Most of our interviewees in the Inheritance Project talked about this issue obliquely rather than directly. It is one of the unspoken and unquestioned assumptions upon which families operate. The importance of this assumption comes out in a number of ways, however. Children get roundly condemned when they act as if they had a right to their parents' property, as for example in this quotation from Sheila Brent, a married woman in her early forties and a homeowner:

I read in the paper the other day about this actor who left millions...He left three million to each of his children and twenty-six million to his wife. Now you can't get more—but his children are fighting it. They don't think that they've got enough...They should be grateful for what they've got. I don't think that people deserve to be left everything, what someone else has worked bloody hard for all their life.

Younger generations, not surprisingly, are keen to distance themselves from such censure. Typically children are quoted as telling their parents to spend all their money on a comfortable old age, and not to worry if they have nothing left to pass on. A typical quotation comes from our interview with Sandra Thompson and Paul Watson, a cohabiting couple in their mid-fifties, each having children from previous marriages. They told us how they would have to plan the division of their assets if they were to be fair to all the children. However, their children were not at all concerned about this. Their reaction was:

They said, 'For goodness sake get out and enjoy your life. Spend what you've got.'

Reinforcing that this is a general point of principle, Sandra expressed similar sentiments later in the interview when talking about her own father, who is still alive:

He can go out and enjoy himself and spend every penny he's got. I'm not bothered.

Whilst such sentiments might be regarded as socially acceptable expressions rather than what children really think, their veracity is borne out by the fact that we had no one in our interview study who expressed disappointment that a parent had failed to retain sufficient assets to pass on after death. Disappointment, indeed resentment, was expressed in some other cases where there had been assets but they were deemed to have been acquired by someone who didn't deserve them; but these examples raise different issues. Where there is nothing to pass on because parents have used up all their assets, children apparently accept this and do not feel cheated.

I have interpreted this as evidence that there is no sense of different generations having a common stake in property; as a consequence, children have no right to expect their parents to preserve their property in order to transmit it. Our interviewees also offer two specific reasons why parents should not feel obliged to do his. First, as already indicated in the quote above, some interviewees say that it is more important for older people to have a comfortable end to their lives, than to deny themselves for the sake of having something to pass to their children. My father can 'go out and enjoy himself and spend every penny he's got', as Sandra Thompson put it in the quote above.

The second reason which people offer is rather different and is more of a minority view in our interview data. This is the belief that it is positively good for children to make their own way in the world. Whilst many of our interviewees might rather like to be able to leave something to their children, there are some who think that it is positively a mistake to do so. This point of view is articulated particularly clearly by another couple, Greg and Sarah Henderson, who were in their forties when we interviewed them. Both of them had gone to University as mature students in their thirties and, after graduating, had successfully set up a business together whilst Sarah also undertook professional work on a part-time basis. Both were from manual working-class families who, according to them, never owned anything of value and never had anything to pass on to the next generation. However, Greg and Sarah had acquired property and a successful business and were thinking of buying a second home in France. Yet both were clear that they did not feel it right to plan to preserve assets for their children. It is worth giving fairly full quotes from each of them:

We've discussed this a bit recently. Because we are at the stage where we are thinking of buying a second home in France—selling our present house, buying a smaller one and using the capital to buy a second home in France. So we realise that in twenty or thirty years, there is going to be a lot more to pass on, to argue about, than we ever had...I still think that it would be good for my children to make their own way. They shouldn't be helped too much, shouldn't expect too much...It sounds a bit reactionary, this. But it does build your character. I think that they shouldn't have things too easily. (Greg Henderson)

I haven't given either of my children the impression that there will be a house, you know, that there will be half each. I don't really want to do that. My feelings are that, if we do accumulate money as we get older, I'd like Greg and I to enjoy that together before we go—rather than hand it on to someone. I would like to be able to leave them something. But I wouldn't like to think that they were going to rely on us leaving them vast amounts of money. Plus—I think we have worked for it all our lives, really, that's not what it should be for. I feel that we should benefit from it ourselves while we are still able to enjoy it.   (Sarah Henderson)

One could argue of course that people whose experience of property owning is *very* new—like Greg and Sarah—may take some time to adjust to the idea of assisting their children through inheritance. It must be said, however, that not everyone who expresses these views is a first generation homeowner—for example, the parents of both Sandra Thompson and Paul Watson (quoted above) had been homeowners. Nonetheless, the values articulated by the Hendersons, especially the importance of each generation making its own way in the world, are the characteristic values associated historically with the respectable working classes—hard work, thrift, self-reliance.

These values are deployed alongside others when people are working out how to manage their own family relationships, in circumstances which are much more complex now than in the past, in many ways. It is not necessarily that one sector of the population is trapped within a certain moral order, whilst another holds to a different one. Rather, there are different sets of values which are potentially relevant to handling relatively new situations, like inheritance. As Smart and Neale (1997) have recently pointed out in their work on divorce and post modernity, people who are facing new and trying circumstances:

do not abandon moral values but go through a process of 'balancing' different needs and obligations, negotiating a route through competing value judgements.   (Smart and Neale, 1997: 24)

Whether or not this will change over a longer period of time can only be a matter of speculation. But those moral and cultural values are deeply embedded. There is just as much reason to suppose that they will continue to influence the way inheritance is handled, as there is to speculate that the John Major vision (of wealth trickling down the generations) will take root. Indeed it is most predictable that such values will coexist in the future as they do in the present, with families and individuals free to deploy them as they wish. That indeed is entirely consistent with the individualistic character of English kinship.

POSTSCRIPT: INHERITANCE AND PAYING FOR CARE IN OLD AGE

The main implication of this analysis is that there is no sign of universal resistance to the idea of older people using their assets to ensure a comfortable old age. On the contrary, there is a widely held view that this is perfectly proper and, conversely, that there is no obligation on one generation to preserve wealth simply to pass it on to the next. Of course there will be individuals who are distressed at having nothing to bequeath, but this is not a general expectation. Does this then mean that people generally will find it acceptable to use up their assets in paying for care, especially as it becomes more commonplace to do so? Not necessarily. Whilst it may be acceptable to spend up before you die, it does not necessarily follow that it is acceptable to spend one's money *in this particular way*. The Inheritance Project did not attempt to address this issue directly. However, the indications from those interviewees who spoke about this are that spending money on paying for residential care or home nursing may be much less acceptable than spending money on enjoying oneself, travelling the world, or indulging one's passion for football or opera. We should be cautious therefore about predicting widespread resistance to paying for care out of one's assets on the grounds that people want to be able to preserve wealth to pass to their children. There may, however, be strong resistance, but for a quite different reason; namely, that older people feel that they have contributed to the society through taxation and in other ways all their lives, and are entitled to expect support from current taxpayers when old age and infirmity require it.

10

The American Family as a Context for Healthy Ageing

MARY ELIZABETH HUGHES AND LINDA J. WAITE

INTRODUCTION

As Achenbaum eloquently describes in Chapter 3, the American family looks quite different than it did half a century ago. In fact, fewer people live in *families* as traditionally defined and more live in non-family households. In 1998, 15 per cent of all people lived in non-family households (US Bureau of the Census, 1998), compared with 6 per cent in non-family households in 1950 (US Bureau of the Census, 1955). Meanwhile, life within family households changed as well. In 1994, 78 per cent of family households were headed by a married couple, compared with 88 per cent in 1950 (US Bureau of the Census, 1995). Family change extends beyond the household; for example, family generations are now smaller, although it is likely that more generations are alive at once (Bengtson, Rosenthal, and Burton, 1990).

Many public commentators and some scholars of the family interpret these trends to mean that the family is in decline and under siege from legal, economic, and social change (Popenoe, 1993). And the evidence is compelling, as far as it goes. Nevertheless, most adults are married (although it is a second marriage for many), most have children, and most rate their marriage as very happy and place a high value on family life. Moreover, the American family retains responsibility for reproduction, socialization, and transmission of property across generations. It is the main unit of consumption and often also produces considerable amounts of goods and services. The family provides care and support for its members, especially children and the disabled elderly. Most people's social networks centre on their families. This evidence suggests that the family remains a key social institution in the United States, even in its altered state.

However, the transformation of the American family does mean that people are living their lives in family constellations that may differ from those common in the past. Since the hallmark of family change is increased diversity, Americans are also likely to have families that differ from the families of at least some of their contemporaries. The key issue, then, is not the salience of the family as an institution, but the implications of these new and diverse family forms for family functioning and individual well-being.

The transformation of the American family has overlapped with a second significant social change: population ageing. The Census Bureau estimates that nearly 13 per cent of the US population will be over 65 in the year 2000, compared with 8 per cent in 1950 (US Bureau of the Census, 1996). Demographers expect this trend to continue for the foreseeable future, in part due to the ageing of the large baby-boom cohorts. Over the next fifty years the United States will thus become a mature nation in which one citizen in five is 65 or older. As part of the same process, the older population itself will age, with huge increases in the number of people who are 85 and older (US Bureau of the Census, 1996).

The confluence of family change and population ageing has led to increased interest in family roles and relationships in later life (Cohler and Altergott, 1995; Treas and Lawton, 1999). The bulk of this work has focused on the provision of care for frail elders. For example, researchers have identified the family members most likely to provide care and have considered the implications of such care for caregivers' lives (e.g. Dwyer and Coward, 1991; Moen, Robinson, and Fields, 1994). Family caregiving is clearly a critical issue for an ageing society experiencing family change—especially since the division of responsibility for elder care among family, market, and state is already ambiguous in the US (Soldo and Freedman, 1994).

With some notable exceptions, less attention has been devoted to family experiences among non-disabled older persons—which form the majority of experiences (exceptions include Bengtson and Harootyan, 1994; Cooney and Uhlenberg, 1992; Eggebeen and Hogan, 1990; Logan and Spitze, 1996). Disabled elders and their families need and consume a disproportionate share of resources, which to some extent justifies the attention they have received. On the other hand, a narrow focus on family caregiving reifies an image of a dependent older generation (Logan and Spitze, 1996). Even more important, such a view misses a great deal of the relationship between older persons and their families. For example, exchanges between adult children and their parents are generally more evenly balanced than the literature on caregiving suggests. In fact, parents are much more likely to help their adult children than the reverse until quite late in the parent's life (Bengtson et al., 1990; Logan and Spitze, 1996).

In this chapter we therefore take a different perspective. Rather than considering the impact of ageing on the family, as in the caregiving literature, the reverse is examined: the impact of the family on ageing (Blieszner and Bedford, 1995). We consider the implications of contemporary American family structure for the ageing process itself. In our view, family roles and relationships form a context in which the later lifecourse unfolds. Thus the characteristics of the modern American family may have important consequences for the well-being of future cohorts of mature persons long before they experience any need for care.

The chapter begins by reviewing recent changes in the processes by which families form, persist, and dissolve, and their implications for family and household structure. A conceptual framework for understanding the family as a context for ageing is then sketched, followed by a brief review of what is known about family context and later life well-being. The focus is on the ways in which families influence the health of individuals in the second half of life. Health is arguably the most critical component of 'successful' ageing (Rowe and Kahn, 1997). Moreover, understanding why some older persons remain healthy and others do not is a major research challenge. We contend that family may play an important role in shaping health trajectories in the second half of life. Finally, the implications of contemporary family structure for healthy ageing within future cohorts are assessed, who will mature with family histories that differ markedly from those of previous generations.

FAMILY STRUCTURE IN THE CONTEMPORARY UNITED STATES

In the United States, as in most developed countries, families are social networks formed by ties of blood or marriage. As Achenbaum describes in Chapter 3, changes in the structure of US families can be traced to changes in the processes by which families are produced, maintained, and dissolved: union formation and dissolution, living arrangements, and childbearing. Each of these processes underwent considerable change in the latter half of the Twentieth Century. In each case, the change led to greater heterogeneity in family structure. Currently, American family structure is more diverse than at any point in US history. Let us examine some of the broad national US trends identified in both Chapters 1 and 3 in more detail, in particular highlighting ethnic and racial differences.

Union Formation and Dissolution

As Harper describes in Chapter 1, like the rest of the developed world, American men and women are delaying marriage into their mid-to-late twenties, often entering a cohabitation first. Divorce rates are high and stable, but rates of remarriage have fallen, so that a larger proportion of adults are unmarried now than in the past. In 1970, unmarried people made up 28 per cent of the adult population. In 1996, 40 per cent of all adults were unmarried. Seventy-one per cent of women born in the early 1950s had married by age 25, compared with 54 per cent of those born in the late 1960s (Raley, 2000). In fact, the shift away from marriage has been so dramatic for blacks that now a *majority* of black men and women are not married, compared to about a third of white men and women (Waite, 1995).

Declines in marriage are closely linked to increases in cohabitation, although it is difficult to untangle the nature of the association. Cohabitation has become an increasingly common step in the courtship process; only 7 per cent of the women born in the late 1940s cohabited before age 25 compared with 55 per cent among those born in the late 1960s (Raley, 2000). Most couples begin their intimate life together by cohabiting rather than by marrying, so that the form of the union has changed more than its existence. However, even when we consider both marriage and cohabitation, young adults are less likely to have formed a union now than in the past. Among young women born in the early 1950s, about a quarter had not formed a union by age 25, compared with a third of those born in the late 1960s (Raley, 2000).

A substantial proportion of all marriages end in divorce or separation due to marital discord. The divorce rate, which reflects the number of divorces in a year relative to the number of married people, rose continuously for more than a century, then levelled off at a fairly high level in about 1980 (Goldstein, 1999). The best estimates suggest that around half of all American marriages will be disrupted (Cherlin, 1992). The marriages most likely to end include those with no children, with children from a previous union or older children (Waite and Lillard, 1991), marriages begun at a young age, and marriages between partners with relatively low levels of education (Martin and Bumpass, 1989).

Although high divorce rates make marriages seem unstable, other types of unions are much more likely to dissolve. Cohabitational unions show quite high chances of disruption, with a quarter ending in separation within three to four years compared with only 5 per cent of marriages, according to one study (Wu and Balakrishnan, 1995). Many cohabitations become marriages, but these show lower stability than marriages not preceded by cohabitation (Lillard et al., 1995).

Living Arrangements

Paralleling these trends in union formation and dissolution are increases in the proportion of persons who live alone. Unmarried persons are far more likely to maintain independent households than in the past (Santi, 1990). As discussed above, some of these persons choose to cohabit with a partner. However, others are choosing to form a one-person household. In 1990, 12 per cent of persons lived alone, compared with 7 per cent in 1970 (US Bureau of the Census, 1995). The shift toward living alone is particularly noticeable among unmarried young adults and the elderly, who in the past typically lived with relatives (Goldscheider and Goldscheider, 1993; Schocni, 1998). There are substantial racial and ethnic differences in this regard. Unmarried African-Americans, Hispanics, and Asians are more likely to co-reside with relatives than are whites (Goldscheider and Goldscheider, 1993; Himes, Hogan, and Eggebeen, 1996).

Childbearing

Despite dramatic changes in other family processes over the past three decades, US fertility levels have been relatively stable. The total fertility rate, which expresses fertility rates in terms of the lifetime number of births they imply for a woman, rose from a low point in the mid 1970s and has remained around two births per woman in the 1990s (Ventura et al., 1999). However, this apparent uniformity conceals several characteristics of contemporary US fertility that have important consequences for family structure. First, fertility levels vary markedly by race and ethnicity. In 1997, the total fertility rate for non-Hispanic Whites was 1.8. The comparable figures for Blacks and Hispanics were 2.2 and 3.0, respectively (Ventura et al., 1999). Second, the ages at which women have their first birth vary substantially. Morgan (1996) describes 'early' childbearing, in the teens, 'on time' childbearing, in the twenties, and 'delayed' childbearing, in the thirties. Moreover, the share of births to women of each age is shifting. This is because over the past two decades birth rates for women in their twenties have been relatively stable, while birth rates for women in their thirties have increased steadily and births to teenagers first increased then decreased (Ventura et al., 1999). These patterns are in turn linked to the characteristics and life circumstances of women. Another variation in family structure is introduced by the substantial fraction of women who remain childless. These patterns also differ by race: Blacks and Hispanics show younger ages at first birth than do Whites and others (Morgan, 1996). Finally, as elsewhere in the developed world, unmarried childbearing has reached historically unprecedented levels (Bachrach, 1998). In 1996, 32 per cent of all births and 44 per cent of all first births in the US occurred to women who were not married (Ventura, Martin, Curtin, and Mathews, 1998). However, over a quarter of unmarried mothers are cohabiting with the child's father at the time of the birth so their children are living in 'intact' if unmarried families (Bumpass, Raley, and Sweet, 1995). The proportion of births to unmarried women depends on the share of all women who are unmarried, the fertility of married women, and the fertility of unmarried women. Marital fertility is relatively low in the US, which accounts in part for the high fraction of births to unmarried women.

Unmarried childbearing also varies substantially among racial and ethnic groups in the US. The percentage of births to unmarried women is highest for Black women (69 per cent), and lowest for Chinese Americans (7 per cent), with Whites intermediate between these two extremes at 26 per cent. Rates of unmarried childbearing also vary a good deal within Hispanic origin groups, with rates for Puerto Rican women, approaching rates for Blacks (59 per cent), whereas rates for Cuban-origin women (24 per cent) approximate those of non-Hispanic Whites (Ventura et al., 1999).

Family Diversity

The married, two-parent family has been the most common family form in the US for some centuries. And it still is. However, increases in divorce, the likelihood of remarriage, the rise of cohabitation, and high levels of non-marital childbearing mean that single-parent families and unmarried-couple families are now common alternative family forms. At the same time, the greater like-lihood that an unmarried person will live in his or her own household has increased the fraction of persons living alone—without family. Differentials in family processes by race and ethnicity lead to corresponding racial and ethnic differentials in family structure. For example, single-parent families are much more common among Blacks than among other groups. In 1997, a single woman headed 33 per cent of Black households, compared with 20 per cent of Hispanic households and 10 per cent of White households (US Bureau of the Census, 1998).

Although these shifts in family structure are striking, they should not be over-dramatized. As described by Dimmock and colleagues for the UK in Chapter 5, even at the height of the married-couple family, many people lived in other family types, most often due to the death of one member of the couple before all the children were grown (Watkins et al., 1987). When death ended many marriages relatively early in life, remarriages and stepfamilies were common, as were single-parent families caused by widowhood. The unique aspects of today's patterns are the increases in unmarried-couple families, never-married mother families, and persons living outside families.

Thus far, we have emphasized changes in the co-residential family. However, contemporary family processes have at least three important implications for family structure beyond the bounds of the household. First, parental divorce typically removes one parent from the household, as does the break-up of a cohabiting relationship with children. In the United States as elsewhere, this parent is most often the father (Hogan and Lichter, 1995). Second, variability in age at first birth in successive generations leads to substantial heterogeneity in the age patterning of generations within families (Bengtson, Rosenthal, and Burton, 1990). Similarly, differences in fertility levels—including being childless—change the relative sizes of generations. Third, divorce, cohabitation, and non-marital childbearing produce new family roles—partners, stepchildren, ex-spouses, former in-laws, step-grandchildren, and so on (Riley and Riley, 1993).

The Family as a Context for Healthy Ageing

Both scholars and the public have passionately debated the strengths and weaknesses of contemporary American family structure. If nothing else, the intensity of this debate should testify to the enduring significance of the family in American society. Until recently, most research and dialogue concentrated on the family of the first half of life. The focus on family experiences at relatively young ages reflected the primary interests of family scholars—family formation and the family as a social incubator for the next generation. As a result, vast literatures examine topics such as contemporary union formation and the implications of divorce for children.

Recently, family researchers began adopting a life course approach to the family (Treas and Lawton, 1999). This perspective acknowledges that although the principal *events* that form one's families of origin and procreation occur in the first half of life, family *roles* endure for a lifetime. The family of origin brings lifelong membership. Moreover, lengthening life expectancy and fewer years spent within marriage increase the salience of adult intergenerational relationships and interactions with adult siblings (Treas and Lawton, 1999). Similarly, for most persons, parenthood brings a lifelong role that mirrors the role of the adult child (Logan and Spitze, 1996). For some persons, marriage may still bring a lifelong relationship. Yet even divorced persons may experience significant long-term relationships with former spouses and in-laws, especially if the presence of children brings continuing contact.

Family experiences in the second half of life are thus receiving an increasing amount of research attention (Treas and Lawton, 1999). As noted above, this research extends beyond the narrow focus of caregiving for disabled elderly to consider a broad spectrum of family relationships. For example, recent work has examined the structure and content of relationships between parents and adult children (Cooney and Uhlenberg, 1992; Logan and Spitze, 1996), between adult siblings (Bedford, 1995), and between grandparents and grandchildren (Robertson, 1995). This literature suggests that family members are key members of individuals' 'convoys' of social relations across the lifecourse (Antonucci and Akiyama, 1995). Family members, especially parents and adult children, are involved in reciprocal exchanges of both instrumental and emotional support.

Health in Family Context

A lifecourse perspective on the family suggests that families will be critical to individual well-being at all ages. Thus adult family relationships are of interest not just in and of themselves, but for what they imply for the welfare of family members. Building on broader frameworks of the life course and human development (Setterson, 1999), we here conceptualize the family as a context for healthy ageing. In our view, the family forms a social world that systematically influences individual identity, perceptions, and action. These in turn shape the more proximate determinants of health, such as health behaviours, perceived loneliness, and stress or allostatic load.

The family context is built on sets of social roles—child, sibling, spouse, parent. Entry, incumbency, and exit from these roles structure the lives of individual family members. Each role carries normative expectations and obligations for behaviour and helps to define individual identity. These norms shift with age of the role incumbent; for example the expectations and obligations for a parent of a teenager differ from those the same parent will experience when the child is in his or her thirties. Similarly, normative prescriptions vary in strength; greater consensus surrounds parent–child obligations than obligations between siblings (Rossi and Rossi, 1990).

However, family context is not a simple reflection of family structure. The structural framework of family roles is elaborated by the qualities of family relationships. Family relationships emerge from the day-to-day patterning of social interactions between and among family members. They are based on actual behaviour of family members—which may be measured against internalized norms. These behaviours, and the ways they are interpreted, are rooted in powerful emotions, especially love and guilt (Bengtson and Murray (1993) quoted in Logan and Spitze, 1996). Family relationships may be positive or negative—or perhaps a combination of both (Bengtson, Rosenthal, and Burton, 1996).

Thus the family is characterized by normatively guided roles manifested in relationships based in part on emotionally motivated exchanges. Three features further distinguish the family context from other types of social relationships. First, families have long histories. Family roles and relationships begin in early life. Unlike friendships, family relationships are ascribed and difficult to dissolve, even if they are a source of continued distress (Antonucci and Akiyama, 1995). An event that took place years before may thus mar or cement a relationship (Antonucci and Akiyama, 1995). However, this is not to imply that family relationships are static. Instead, they evolve over time, continuously renegotiated and reconfigured. Second, the lives of individual family members are interdependent (Treas and Lawton, 1999). Events in one person's life may reverberate in the life of other family members. For instance, a child's divorce may lead a parent to give extra help and support to the child, which may include offering co-residence or taking custody of a grandchild. Geographic mobility may alter the relationship between siblings. Third, the family is a critical link between individuals and other social institutions and structures (Bronfenbrenner, 1986). For example, in the United States one's economic well-being is closely tied to one's family structure. Both access to resources and consumption are channelled through the household. Family members benefit from the resources of other family members. Families provide economies of scale in consumption of goods and services, allowing their members to live better than they could alone (Burch and Matthews, 1987). Similarly, the effects of gender stratification, the workplace, and racial and ethnic stratification are also channelled through the family.

We suggest that family context affects individual health via individuals' experiences of family *demands* and *resources*. The tasks and interactions embodied in family roles make physical, cognitive, and emotional *demands* on role incumbents. However, these same roles offer rewards and supports which individuals can use as *resources* to meet these expectations as well as their own needs. In addition, others in the family may constitute a resource, by sharing task demands, by providing positive interactions, or by simply fulfilling the expectations of their own roles. Demands and resources are conceptual tools for specifying the mechanisms by which families influence the health and well-being of their members.

Overall, the greater imbalance in expectations and obligations in a dyadic relationship, the greater the potential for imbalance in experienced demands and resources. Thus the spousal relationship is typically characterized by a greater degree of reciprocity than the relationship between parent and child or between grandparent and grandchild. All else equal however, a dyadic relationship in which one member needs extra instrumental or emotional support will increase demands and reduce the resources available to the other person. A disabled spouse in need of care provides a very different configuration of demands and resources than a healthy spouse. Young co-resident grandchildren bring very different demands and resources than older grandchildren living with their own parents.

The balance of family demands and resources is a link in the causal chain between family structure and relations and individual health. This balance is ultimately subjective—the individual's internal evaluation of his or her situation. We expect that the balance of family demands and resources will in turn shape individuals' health behaviours and their perceptions of stress and loneliness. For example, a demanding family role such as caring for a grandchild may lead to stress. To the extent that bonds with others in the family are absent or unsatisfying, individuals may feel lonely. In turn, health behaviours, loneliness, and stress act on the more proximate biological determinants of health, such as endocrine function and immune response (Cacioppo et al., forthcoming).

In this manner, variation in ageing persons' families may partly explain individual differences in the onset, timing, and severity of health problems (Waite and Hughes, 1999). Chronic conditions are responsible for the bulk of health problems in later life. These conditions develop over long periods and display great variability in age at onset. For both reasons, family structure and relations in late mid-life to early old age may be quite important to health trajectories in the second half of life. Family obligations and expectations clearly transcend the boundaries of the household. However, the immediacy, intimacy, and intensity of household-based family roles will lead to particularly powerful effects on individual well-being. Various family households make very different demands on the adults in them and offer very different levels and types of resources. For example, being married brings the demands of the spousal role, but a member of a married couple may rely on a spouse as a resource. The particular closeness of marital relationships suggests that these reciprocal bonds may be especially well developed. In contrast, although those living alone have no demands placed on them by others within the household, they have no one living with them who may act as a resource. The person living alone must fulfil all of the requirements of independent living and lacks instrumental and emotional support from co-resident others.

Multigenerational households present a more complex case. Co-residence with children, grandchildren, or others may be a response to economic hardship or may reflect cultural traditions that emphasize kin solidarity and intergenerational ties (Himes et al., 1996). Although co-residence between older parents and their children is often assumed to provide for the care of the parent, research suggests that intergenerational households are usually based on the needs of the younger generation (Aquilino, 1990; Ward et al., 1992). Thus, although such households are often expected to be uniquely supportive, they may actually present special stresses and challenges to senior members.

Evidence Linking Family Context and Health

The chapter has outlined a framework for understanding the processes by which family context influences the health of family members. We next turn to a brief review of the evidence regarding the relationship between family context and health. The bulk of this literature concerns the relationship between overall social relations and health and marital status and health. Relatively little research has examined the relationship between other family structures and health. This gap is an important area for future research.

Social support (the emotionally sustaining content of relationships) and social integration (the existence of certain key relationships) are both positively linked with emotional well-being in dozens of studies (George, 1996; Thoits, 1995). Social support reflects the positive quality of relationships, which may also have negative or demanding aspects, called relationship strain. Relationship strain has independent negative effects on well-being. Thoits (1995) argues that although mental health researchers often presume that their findings on social support can be generalized to physical health very little research on this link has been done. This literature has been more concerned with the influence of overall social relations on health, rather than the influence of the family on health (but see Antonucci and Akiyama, 1995). However, family members are prominent members of individuals networks of social support.

A great deal of evidence also attests to the importance of marital status to health and well-being. Being married has consistently positive effects on physical health that do not appear to reflect only selection into marriage (Lilliard and Waite, 1995; Goldman et al., 1995; Umberson, 1992; Ross et al., 1990). For example, married cancer patients are less likely than unmarried patients to die over the five years following diagnosis, even taking into account stage at diagnosis and treatment. Ross et al. (1990) conclude that unmarried women face risks of dying that are 50 per cent higher and unmarried men face risks that are 250 per cent higher than those faced by their married counterparts. Married men and married women rate their health more positively than unmarried men and women. Married men and women are also less likely than singles to suffer from long-term chronic illnesses or disabilities (Waite and Hughes, 1999).

Umberson et al. (1996) conclude the evidence on the emotional benefits of marriage is inconclusive, at least when the married are compared with the never-married, although the divorced and widowed seem substantially worse off than the married. However, a recent paper by Marks and Lambert (1998) finds large and significant advantages for the married across a range of measures of psychological well-being for both men and women, compared with those who either become or remain unmarried. Only those who marry for the first time during the period of observation do better than the stably-married. And Horwitz, White, and Howell-White (1996) find that after controlling for premarital rates of disorder, marriage enhances mental health for both young men and young women.

Whether and how other family households affect health is less clear. Most analyses group non-marital household structures together in comparisons to marriage. Marital households are rarely distinguished by presence of others such as dependent or adult children or others. However, Rogers, Hummer, and Nam (2000) argue that *family composition* captures the complex relationship between family arrangements and mortality much better than marital status alone. They argue that large and important differences exist between married couples living with dependent or adult children, with other relatives, or alone. They find substantial effects of family composition on mortality, which they speculate are due to differences across household types in economic resources, social support, and stress.

In our own work, we have found that the relationship between household structure and health does not follow a simple married–not married distinction (Waite and Hughes, 1999; Hughes and Waite, 1999). In one study, older adults living in married-couple households (with or without own children) show higher levels of functioning across physical, emotional, and cognitive dimensions compared with adults in married-couple households that also include other persons. Adults in any type of married-couple household tend to show higher levels of functioning across dimensions than single adults living alone, single adults living with their own children, or single adults living with others. In fact, household types tend to array themselves by average levels of functioning across physical, emotional, and cognitive measures so that older adults in married-couple households (with or without own children) show the highest levels of functioning, followed by married-couple households with others, then by single adults alone, then by single adults with their own children, with single adults living with others consistently showing the lowest levels of functioning (Waite and Hughes, 1999). We find that these patterns for the most part persist when we examine change in health, rather than health at a point in time (Hughes and Waite, 1999).

CONTEMPORARY FAMILY STRUCTURE AND THE FUTURE OF HEALTHY AGEING

Mature Americans are embedded in family contexts that differ substantially from those of the past. However, the experience of current elderly does not capture the full implications of contemporary family patterns for healthy ageing. The family behaviours described above evolved over several decades. In general terms, successive cohorts of older persons will thus have spent successively more of their life courses experiencing these patterns. For example, persons who are currently aged 65 and over were born into families of origin and formed families of procreation before the main shifts in family behaviour. Their children and grandchildren did participate in these shifts, which in part shapes the older generation's experience of ageing. In contrast, the baby-boom cohorts will reach age 65 having experienced families of procreation that follow contemporary patterns. Members of Generation X will presumably have both grown up in new-style families and formed new-style families.

Let us conclude by considering the consequences of contemporary family structure for the ageing of future generations. In particular, we have in mind the baby-boom cohorts. These cohorts were in the vanguard of family change and are now beginning to reach their fiftieth birthdays. Their numerical strength will accelerate the long-term ageing of the US population, raising critical questions regarding their well-being in maturity and the subsequent consequences for society. Based on their experience thus far, it is likely that members of the baby-boom cohorts will reach maturity with a more diverse set of family structures relative to members of preceding generations. They will be less likely to be currently married, more likely to be living alone, and perhaps more likely to be living in a complex household. Their family histories will certainly be more variable. The incidence of cohabitation, multiple marriages, non-marital childbearing and childlessness will all be greater in these cohorts. Baby boomers will have spent less of their life in married-couple households and more living alone, in single-parent or in complex households.

At first glance, it seems that these differences in family structure would place these cohorts at a health disadvantage relative to earlier cohorts, all else equal. The distribution of family types is shifting toward types that previous research has shown to be linked to poorer health outcomes. The shift in marital status is particularly important in this regard. Recall that it is not just an individual's family status when he or she enters later life that is critical—it is equally his or her family history. Thus by this line of reasoning, baby boomers' relatively diverse families should correspond to both greater diversity in health outcomes and an overall lower level of health. However, while this rather pessimistic scenario may be accurate at a high level of generality, it offers limited insight into the heterogeneous processes that will underlie this gross pattern. Understanding these processes is likely to be critical for both research and policy in the coming years. Furthermore, the actual implications of the contemporary family for health will depend heavily on how family roles and relationships continue to evolve. Thus a more useful way of assessing the future is to pose questions about some unresolved issues relating to family context and health in the second half of life.

What Expectations and Obligations Will Family Roles Entail?

Social roles are the foundation of the family. However, these roles are changing quickly. This change takes two forms: the redefinition of traditional roles and the creation of new roles. For example, the role of mother has been redefined by increases in women's work outside the home and increases in non-marital childbearing. The role of father is bifurcating—the 'good' dads who are fully involved with their children and are equal partners in maintaining the household and the 'bad' dads who are absent and essentially divorced from their children (Furstenberg, 1988). New family roles include never-married mother, step-parent, ex-spouse, partner, and stepchild. The roles are currently ill-defined; families negotiate their expectations and obligations as they arise.

Because the expectations embedded in family roles are a central determinant of family demands and resources, the way these roles evolve should have important implications for individual health. For example, will shifts in the gendered division of household labour mean that co-resident adult children will demand less of mothers' time? As formerly unusual family roles become more common, will greater normative consensus emerge regarding what is owed to and expected from family members? If so, the stress that family members experience from 'ad hoc' family norms will be reduced.

On Balance, What Will Be the Qualities of Family Relationships?

Contemporary families bring opportunities for both increased family solidarity and increased family conflict (Bengtson et al., 1996). For example, the easy availability of divorce suggests that any marriages that persist into maturity will be especially strong. Stepfamilies and other new family forms introduce others who may provide fulfilling relationships of all types. As Riley and Riley (1993) argue, these new relationships are 'latent' and as such are likely to be activated based on compatibility and mutual gain. On the other hand, divorce and remarriage bring the potential for greater conflict—not only between spouses, but between parent and child and among siblings. The balance of these potential solidarities and conflicts as individuals age is critical to how individuals experience family relationships and in turn to their health.

A related issue is how other types of relationships will substitute for absent or difficult family relationships. For example, childlessness may leave people more time to develop friendships and other voluntary associations, which, unlike families, are unambiguously beneficial to health (Antonucci and Akiyama, 1995). Although the sibling relationship is unique in its degree of shared experience, only children can compensate by investing in friendships or in relationships with senior family members. The possibility of adaptation to family 'losses', especially since these adaptations may be beneficial for health, is an important corrective to the view that lack of family is inevitably harmful.

What are the Long-Term Implications of Contemporary Family Structure for Family Relations?

We argued earlier that family relationships both endure and evolve over time. Because the baby-boom cohorts are only now reaching later mid-life, we know relatively little about the long-term effects of contemporary family patterns. For example, how will the relationship of single mothers to their children develop as the children reach adulthood? How will parental divorce and remarriage affect relationships among siblings and stepsiblings in adulthood? The ways in which these and other long-term family relationships unfold will have implications for the well-being of mature baby boomers.

What Will Other Family Members Need?

Because the lives of family members are intertwined, mature baby boomers' family configurations will depend in part on the needs of their children and grandchildren. For example, co-residence with adult children is usually due to circumstances in the younger adults' life. To the extent that young persons in the future experience difficulties such as divorce or job loss, their parents may be called upon to provide co-residence or other support. Adult children in the home increase the demands placed on parents, especially mothers and especially single mothers (Logan and Spitze, 1996). As another example, difficulties in the lives of adult children are leading to dramatic increases in the prevalence of custodial grandparents. Here again, the senior generation is devoting time and resources to problems encountered in the younger generation. To the extent to which some baby-boomer parents will be involved in these demanding exchanges, their health may suffer.

How Will Other Aspects of Social Structure Intersect with Family Configurations?

We have already referred to several ways in which changes in gender roles intersect with family change. Because family patterns differ dramatically by race and ethnicity, heterogeneity in the family will be cross-cut by race and ethnicity. Similarly, economic well-being will be reciprocally related to family status. To the extent that persons with more demanding family situations are also disadvantaged by minority status or low socioeconomic status they will be at even greater risk of health problems in maturity (Waite and Hughes, 1999).

The chapter began by noting the confluence of two key social trends: changes in the structure of the American family and the ageing of the American population. Although the implications are unclear, it is quite clear that mature Americans will have increasingly heterogeneous family histories and statuses. Thus the family is likely to become ever more important in differentiating the ageing experience. For researchers, this offers many exciting opportunities to clarify the mechanisms by which American families shape healthy ageing. Policy makers will face the challenge of designing flexible strategies to meet the needs of various kinds of ageing families.

References

Achenbaum, W. Andrew (1986). *Social Security: Visions and Revisions*. New York: Cambridge University Press.

—— (forthcoming). 'Social Scientists, Policy Makers, and Population Aging'. In David L. Featherman and Maris A.Vinovskis (eds.), *Doing Social Science and Making Public Policy*. Ann Arbor: University of Michigan Press.

Allan, G. A., Crow, G. P., and Hawker, S. (1999). 'Grandparents in Step-Family Network'. Draft working paper, University of Southampton Department of Sociology and Social Policy.

Allen, I., and Perkins, E. (1995). *The Future of Family Care for Older People*. London: HMSO.

Almond, S., and Kendall, J. (2000). 'Low Pay in the UK: The Case for a Three Sector Comparative Approach (2001)'. *Annals of Public and Cooperative Economics*, 72(1): 47–76.

Amato, P. R. (1994). 'The Implications of Research Findings on Children in Stepfamilies'. In A. Booth and J. Dunn (eds.), *Stepfamilies: Who Benefits? Who Does Not?* Hillsdale, New Jersey: Lawrence Erlbaum.

Anderson, M. (1982). Paper presented to *Family History*.

Anderson, R. N. (1999). *United States Life Tables, 1997*. National Vital Statistics Reports 47(28). Hyattsville, Md.: National Center for Health Statistics.

Antonucci, T. C., and Akiyama, H. (1995). 'Convoys of Social Relations: Family and Friendships within a Life Span Context'. In R. Blieszner and V. H. Bedford (eds.), *Handbook of Aging and the Family*. Westport, Conn.: Greenwood Press, 355–71.

Aquilino, W. S. (1990). 'The Likelihood of Parent–Adult Child Coresidence: Effects of Family Structure and Parental Characteristics'. *Journal of Marriage and the Family*, 52: 405–19.

Arber, S., and Ginn, J. (1992). *Gender and Later Life*. London: Sage.

Armitage, R., and Babb, P. (1996). 'Population Review (4): Trends in Fertility'. *Population Trends*, 84: 7–13.

Askam, J. (1998). 'Kinship Models'. Paper presented to Nuffield Conference, Oxford.

Australia Bureau of Statistics (1995). *How Many Marriages End in Divorce*. Canberra: Australia.

Babchuck, N. (1965). 'Primary Friends and Kin: A Study of the Associations of Middle-Class Couples'. *Social Forces*, 43: 483–93.

Bachrach, Christine (1998). 'The Changing Circumstances of Marriage and Fertility in the United States'. In R. A. Moffitt (ed.), *Welfare, the Family and Reproductive Behavior*. Washington, DC: National Academy Press.

Baltes, P. B., and Mayer, K. U. (1999) (eds.), *The Berlin Aging Study*. Cambridge: Cambridge University Press.

Batchelor, J., Dimmock, B., and Smith, D. (1994). *Understanding Stepfamilies*. London: Stepfamily Books.

Bedford, V. H. (1995). 'Sibling Relationships in Middle and Old Age'. In R. Blieszner and V. H. Bedford (eds.), *Handbook of Aging and the Family*. Westport, Conn.: Greenwood, 201–22.

Bengtson, V., and Kuypers, J. A. (1971). 'Generational Difference and the "Developmental Stake"'. *Ageing and Human Development*, 2: 249–60.

——Rosenthal, C., and Burton, L. (1990). 'Families and Aging: Diversity and Heterogenity'. In R. H. Binstock and L. K. George (eds.), *Handbook of Aging and the Social Sciences*, 3rd edn., San Diego, Calif.: Academic Press, 263–87.

——and Murray, T. M. (1993). '"Justice" across Generations (and Cohorts): Sociological Perspectives on the Life Course and Reciprocities over Time'. In L. Cohen (ed.), *Justice across Generations: What Does It Mean?* Washington: American Association of Retired Persons, 111–38.

——and Hayrootyan, R. (1994) (eds.). *Intergenerational Linkages: Hidden Connections in American Society*. New York: Springer.

——Rosenthal, C., and Burton, L. (1996). 'Paradoxes of Families and Aging'. In R. Binstock and L. K. George (eds.) (2001), *Handbook of Aging and the Social Sciences*. 5th edn., San Diego, Calif.: Academic Press, 254–82.

——Schaie, K., and Burton, L. (1995) (eds.) *Adult Intergenerational Relations*. New York: Springer.

Bernardes, J. (1997). *Family Studies: An Introduction*. London: Routledge.

Berry-Lound, D. (1994). *The Help the Aged Seniorcare Survey*. London: Help the Aged.

Bettio, F., and Prechal, S. (1998). *Care in Europe*. Brussels: European Commission.

Bevan, S., Dench, S., Tamkin, P., and Cummings, J. (1999). *Family-Friendly Employment: The Business Case*. London: DfEE, Research Report RR136.

Birnbaum, Norman (1988). *The Radical Renewal: The Politics of Ideas in Modern America*. New York: Pantheon Books.

Blackmore, A. (2000). 'Local Government Reform and the Voluntary Sector'. In *Dimensions 2000: Income from Government Sources*. West Malling: Charities Aid Foundation.

Bliezner, R., and Bedford, V. H. (1995). 'The Family Context of Aging: Trends and Challenges'. In R. Bliezner and V. H. Bedford (eds.), *Handbook of Aging and the Family*, Westport Conn.: Greenwood, 3–12.

Boaz, R. F. (1996). 'Full-Time Employment and Informal Caregiving in the 1980s'. *Medical Care*, 34(6): 524–36.

——Hu, J., and Ye, Y. (1999). 'The Transfer of Resources from Middle-Aged Children to Functionally Limited Elderly Parents: Providing Time, Giving Money, Sharing Space'. *Gerontologist*, 39(6): 648–57.

Bornat, J., Dimmock, B., Jones, D., and Peace, S. (1998*a*). 'Generational Ties in the "New" Family: Changing Contexts for Traditional Obligations'. In E. Da Silva and C. Smart (eds.), *The 'New' Family?* New York: Sage.

————————(1998*b*). 'Finding People to Interview: Issues in Sampling in a Study of the Impact of Family Change on Older People'. Paper given at IV International Conference on Social Science Methodology, University of Essex.

————————(1999). 'Stepfamilies and Older People: Evaluating the Implications of Family Change for an Ageing Population'. *Ageing and Society*, 19: 239–61.

Borsch-Supan, A., Gokhale, J., Kotlikoff, L. J., and Morris, J. N. (1992). 'The Provision of Time to the Elderly by their Children'. In David A. Wise (ed.), *Topics in the Economics of Aging*. Chicago: University of Chicago Press, 109–34.

Brehm, S. (1992). *Intimate Relationships*. New York: McGraw-Hill.

Brody, E. M., and Schoonover, C. B. (1986). 'Patterns of Parent-Care when Adult Daughters Work and When They Do Not'. *Gerontologist*, 26(4): 372–81.

Bronfenbrenner, U. (1986). 'Ecology of the Family as a Context for Human Development'. *Developmental Psychology*, 22(6): 723–42.

Buck, N., and Scott, J. (1994). 'Household and Family Change'. In N. Buck et al. (eds.), *Changing Households: The British Household Panel Survey 1990–2*. University of Essex: ESRC Centre on Micro-Social Change.

Bumpass, L. L., Raley, R. K., and Sweet, J. A. (1995). 'The Changing Character of Stepfamilies: Implications of Cohabitation and Nonmarital Childbearing'. *Demography*, 32: 425–36.

Burch, T. K., and Matthews, B. J. (1987). 'Household Formation in Developed Societies'. *Population and Development Review*, 13: 495–511.

Burchardt, N. (1990). 'Stepchildren's Memories: Myth, Understanding and Forgiveness'. In R. Samuel and P. Thompson (eds.), *The Myths We Live By*. London: Routledge.

Burgoyne, C., and Morison, V. (1997). 'Money in Remarriage: Keeping Things Simple—and Separate'. *Sociological Review*, 45(3): 363–95.

Cacioppo, J., Ernst, J. M., Burleson, M. H., McClintock, M. K., Malarkey, W. B., Hawkley, L. C., Kowalewski, R. B., Paulsen, A., Hobson, J. A., Hugdahl, K., Spiegel, D., and Berntson, G. G. (2000). 'Lonely Traits and Concomitant Physiological Processes: The MacArthur Social Neuroscience Studies'. *International Journal of Psychophysiology*. 35(2–3), Cambridge: Cambridge University Press.

Cantor, M. H. (1979). 'Neighbors and Friends: An Overlooked Resource in the Informal Support System'. *Research on Aging*, 1: 434–63.

Carers in Employment Group (1995). *Carers in Employment: A Report on the Development of Policies to Support Carers at Work*. London: The Princess Royal Trust for Carers.

Chatters, L. M., Taylor, R. J., and Jackson, J. S. (1986). 'Aged Blacks' Choices for an Informal Helper Network'. *Journal of Gerontology*, 41: 94–100.

Cherlin, A. J. (1992). *Marriage, Divorce, Remarriage*. Rev. ed., Cambridge, Mass.: Harvard University Press.

Chudacoff, H. P. (1989). *How Old Are You?: Age Consciousness in American Culture*. Princeton: Princeton University Press.

Cicirelli, V. G. (1983). 'A Comparison of Helping Behavior to Elderly Parents of Adult Children with Intact and Disrupted Marriages'. *Gerontologist*, 23(6): 619–25.

Cohler, B. J., and Altergott, K. (1995). 'The Family of the Second Half of Life: Connecting Theories and Findings'. In R. Bliezner and V. H. Bedford (eds.), *Handbook of Aging and the Family*. Westport, Conn.: Greenwood, 59–94.

Coke, Marguerite M. (1991). *Correlates of Life Satisfaction among the African-American Elderly*. New York: Garland Publishing.

Cooney, T., and Uhlenberg, P. (1992). 'Support from Parents over the Life Course: The Adult Child's Perspective'. *Social Forces*, 71: 63–84.

Corti, L., and Dex, S. (1995). 'Informal Carers and Employment'. *Employment Gazette* (March): 101–7.

Couch, K. A., Daly, M. C., and Wolf, D. A. (1999). 'Time? Money? Both? The Allocation of Resources to Older Parents'. *Demography*, 36(2): 219–32.

Crimmins, E. (1986). 'The Social Impact of Recent and Prospective Mortality Decline among Older Americans'. *Sociology and Social Research*, 70: 192–9.

Crohan, S. E., and Antonucci, T. C. (1989). 'Friends as a Source of Social Support in Old Age'. In R. G. Adams and R. Blieszner (eds.), *Older Adult Friendship*. Newbury Park, CA: Sage, 129–46.

Cumming, E., and Henry, W. E. (1961). *Growing Old: The Process of Disengagement*. New York: Basic Books.

Curtice, L., Fraser, F., and Leca, T. (1997). *The Range and Availability of Domiciliary Care Services in Scotland*. Edinburgh: Scottish Office Home Department Central Research Unit.

Daniels, L., and McCarraher, L. (2000). *The Work-Life Manual*. London: The Industrial Society.

Darton, R. A. (1998). 'PSSRU Survey of Residential and Nursing Home Care'. *Mental Health Research Review*, 5: 26–30.

David, M. (1998). 'Editor's Introduction'. In M. David (ed.). *The Fragmenting Family: Does it Matter?* London: Institute of Economic Affairs.

Davies, B. (1997). 'Equity and Efficiency in Community Care: From Muddle to Model and Model to . . .?' *Policy and Politics*, 25: 337–59.

Davis, S. J. (1998). *The 1997 National Survey of Volunteering*. London: National Centre for Volunteering.

de Regt (1997). 'Inheritance and Relationships between Family Members'. In M.Gullestad and M. Segalen (eds.), *Family and Kinship in Europe*. London: Pinter.

De Tocqueville, A. (1835–40). *Democracy in America*, 2 vols., trans. Phillip Bradley (1945). New York: Vintage.

DeMaris, A., and MacDonald, W. (1992). 'Pre-marital Cohabitation and Subsequent Marital Stability in the United States: A Reassessment'. *Journal of Marriage and the Family*, 55(2): 399–407.

Dench, G. (1996). *The Place of Men in Changing Family Cultures*. London: Institute of Community Studies.

——(1997). 'Nearing Full Circle in the Sexual Revolution'. In G. Dench (ed.), *Rewriting the Sexual Contract: Collected Views on Changing Relationships and Sexual Divisions of Labour*. London: Institute of Community Studies.

——Ogg, J., and Thompson, K. (1999). 'The Role of Grandparents'. In R. Jowell, J. Curtice, I. Park, and K. Thompson (eds.), *British Social Attitudes Survey: The 16th Report*. Aldershot: Ashgate, ch. 7.

Dentinger, Emma, and Clarkberg, Marin (1999). 'Informal Caregiving Effects on Retirement Timing: A Life Course Approach'. BLCC Working Paper No. 99–14. Ithaca, NY: Cornell University.

Department for Education and Employment (2000). *Work-Life Balance: Changing Patterns in a Changing World: A Discussion Document*. London: DfEE.

Department of Health (1999a). *Fit for the Future: National Required Standards for Residential and Nursing Homes for Older People*. London: DoH.

——(1999b). *Caring about Carers: A National Strategy for Carers*. London: DoH.

——(1999c). *A New Approach to Social Services Performance*, London: DoH.

——(2000). *The NHS Plan. The Government's Response to the Royal Commission on Long Term Care*, Cm 4818-II, London: HMSO.

DiMaggio, P., and Powell, W. W. (1983). 'Institutional Isomorphism'. *American Sociological Review*, 48: 147–60.

Doty, P., Jackson, M. E., and Crown, W. (1998). 'The Impact of Female Caregivers' Employment Status on Patterns of Formal and Informal Eldercare'. *Gerontologist*, 38(3): 331–41.

Downey, R. (1997). 'Minister's Counsel for Care'. *Community Care*, 12–18 June: 21–2.

Drew, L. M., and Smith, P. K. (1998). 'The Impact of Parental Separation/Divorce on Grandparent–Grandchild Relationships'. *International Journal of Ageing and Human Development*.

Duran, M. A. (2000). 'The Future of Work in Europe: Gendered Patterns of Time Use'. In European Commission, *Gender Use of Time: Three European Studies*. Luxembourg: Office for Official Publications of the European Communities, 77–138.

Dwyer, J. W., and Coward, R. (1991). 'A Multivariate Comparison of the Involvement of Adult Sons versus Daughters in the Care of Impaired Parents'. *Journal of Gerontology: Social Sciences*, 46: S259–69.

Dykstra, P. A. (1993). 'The Differential Availability of Relationships and the Provision and Effectiveness of Support to Older Adults'. *Journal of Social and Personal Relationships*, 10: 355–70.

Eggebeen, D. J., and Hogan, D. P. (1990). 'Giving between Generations in American Families'. *Human Nature*, 1: 211–32.

Ermisch, J., and Franceseconi, M. (1996). *Partnership Formation and Dissolution in Great Britain*. ESRC Research Centre on Micro-Social Change, WP 96–10.

——(1998). *Cohabitation in Great Britain: Not for Long but here to Stay*. ESRC Research Centre, Essex, WP 98–1.

Ettner, S. L. (1995). 'The Impact of "Parent Care" on Female Labor Supply Decisions'. *Demography*, 32(1): 63–79.

——(1996). 'The Opportunity Costs of Elder Care'. *Journal of Human Resources*, 31(1): 189–205.

European Commission (1993). *Growth Competitiveness Employment. The Challenges and Ways forward into the 21st Century*. White Paper.

——(1994). *European Social Policy – a Way Forward for the Union*. White Paper COM (94) 333 final.

——(1995). *Annual Report on Social Protection*. Luxembourg: Office for Official Publications of the European Communities.

——(1998). *Reconciliation between Work and Family Life in Europe: Report to the Belfast Informal Council of Equality Ministers*. Brussels: European Commission (ref. CE-V/2-98-008-EN-C).

——(1999a). *Social Protection for Dependency in Old Age in the 15 EU Member States and Norway*. Luxembourg: Office for Official Publications of the European Communities.

——(1999b). *Equal Opportunities for Women and Men in the European Union: Annual Report 1998*. Luxembourg: Office for Official Publications of the European Communities.

——(1999c). *Living Conditions in Europe. Statistical Pocketbook, 1999 Edition*. Luxembourg: Office for Official Publications of the European Communities.

——(1999e). *The Future European Labour Supply*. Luxembourg: Office for Official Publications of the European Communities.

——(2000*a*). *Equal Opportunities for Women and Men in the European Union: Annual Report, 1999*. Luxembourg: Office for Official Publications of the European Communities.

——(2000*b*). *Report on Social Protection in Europe 1999*. Luxembourg: Office for Official Publications of the European Communities.

——(2000*c*). *Communication from the Commission. Social Trends: Prospects and Challenges*. Brussels: Commission of the European Communities.

——(2000*d*). *The Social Situation in the European Union 2000*. Luxembourg: Office for Official Publications of the European Communities.

——(2000*e*). (Directorate General for Employment and Social Affairs). *Missoc Info: Long Term Care*. Luxembourg: Office for Official Publications of the European Communities.

European Foundation for the Improvement of Living and Working Conditions (1999). *Strengthening and Mainstreaming Equal Opportunities through Collective Bargaining*. Luxembourg: Office for Official Publications of the European Communities.

Fagan, C., Rubery, J., and McAllister, I. (2002). *Gender and Employment Preferences in Europe*. Luxembourg: European Foundation for the Improvement of Living and Working Conditions. (http://www.eurofound.eu.int/publications/files/EF0249EN.pdf)

Farkas, J., and Hogan, D. (1995). 'The Demography of Changing Intergenerational Relationships'. In V. Bengtson, K. Schaie, and L. Burton (eds.), *Adult Intergenerational Relations*. New York: Springer, 1–18.

Farley, R. (1996). *The New American Reality*. New York: Russell Sage Foundation.

Fass, P. (1977). *The Damned and the Beautiful: American Youth in the 1920s*. New York: Oxford University Press.

Felton, B. J., and Berry, C. A. (1992). 'Do the Sources of the Urban Elderly Social Support Determine its Psychological Consequences?' *Psychology and Aging*, 7: 89–97.

Finch, J. (1989*a*). *Family Obligations and Social Change*. Cambridge: Polity.

——(1996). 'Inheritance and Financial Transfer in Families'. In A. Walker (ed.), *The New Generational Contract: Intergenerational Relations, Old Age and Welfare*. London: UCL Press.

——(1997). 'Individuality and Adaptability in English Kinship'. In M.Gullestad and M. Segalen (eds.), *Family and Kinship in Europe*. London: Pinter.

——and Mason, J. (1993). *Negotiating Family Responsibilities*. London: Routledge.

————Masson, J., Wallis, L., and Hayes, L. (1996). *Wills, Inheritance, and Families*. Oxford: Oxford University Press.

Forder, J. E. (1997). 'Contracts and Purchaser–Provider Relationships in Community Care'. *Journal of Health Economics*, 16: 517–42.

——(2000). 'Mental Health: Market Power and Governance'. *Journal of Health Economics*, 19(6): 829–1144.

——and Netten, A. (2000*a*). 'The Effects of Population Dependency Changes on Costs, Prices and Total Expenditure'. PSSRU Discussion Paper 1581, Personal Social Services Research Unit, London School of Economics and University of Kent.

————(2000*b*). 'The Price of Placement in Residential and Nursing Home Care: The Effects of Contracts and Competition'. *Health Economics*. (Journal not online, so cannot check this also PSSRU DP 1263/2).

Forder, J. E., Hardy, B., Kendall, J., Knapp, M. R. J., and Wistow, G. (1999). 'Residential Care Providers in the Independent Sector: Motivations, Pricing and Links with Purchasers'. Report to the Department of Health.

——————(2000a). 'Prices, Contracts and Competition'. PSSRU (not on PSSRU list/search) Discussion Paper 1580, Personal Social Services Research Unit, London School of Economics and University of Kent.

——Kendall, J., Knapp, M. R. J., Hardy, B., Matosevic, T., and Ware, P. (2000b). 'Prices, Contracts and Domicliary Care'. PSSRU Discussion Paper 1609/2, Personal Social Services Research Unit, London School of Economics.

Forrest, R., and Murie, A. (1989). 'Differential Accumulation: Wealth, Inheritance and Housing Policy'. *Policy and Politics*, 17(2): 25–39.

Fox, G., and Kelly, R. (1995). 'Determinants of Child Custody Arrangements at Divorce'. *Journal of Marriage and the Family*, 57: 693–708.

Freedman, V. A., Wolf, D. A., Soldo, B. J., and Stephen, E. H. (1991). 'Intergenerational Transfers: A Question of Perspective'. *Gerontologist*, 31(5): 640–7.

Furstenberg, F. F. (1988). 'Good Dads/Bad Dads: The Two Faces of Fatherhood'. In A. J. Cherlin (ed.), *The Changing American Family and Public Policy*. Washington: Urban Institute Press, 193–218.

George, L. K. (1996). 'Social Factors and Illness'. In R. Binstock and L. K. George (eds.), *Handbook of Aging and the Social Sciences*. San Diego, Calif.: Academic Press, 229–52.

Giddens, A. (1999). *Runaway World—Family*. London: BBC Reith Lectures.

Goldman, N. (1986). 'Effects of Mortality Levels on Kinship'. In *Consequences of Mortality Trends and Differentials*. New York: UN.

——Korenman, S., and Weinstein, R. (1995). 'Marital Status and Health of the Elderly'. *Social Science and Medicine*, 40(12): 1717–30.

Goldscheider, F. K., and Goldscheider, C. (1993). *Leaving Home before Marriage: Ethnicity, Familism, and Generational Relationships*. Madison: University of Wisconsin Press.

——————(1994). 'Leaving and Returning Home in Twentieth Century America'. *Population Bulletin*, 48: 1–35.

Goldstein, J. R. (1999). 'The Leveling of Divorce in the United States'. *Demography*, 36: 409–14.

Gorell Barnes, G., Thompson, P., Daniel, G., and Burchardt, N. (1998). *Growing up in Stepfamilies*. Oxford: Clarendon Press.

Gouldner, A. W. (1960). 'The Norm of Reciprocity: A Preliminary Statement'. *American Sociological Review*, 25: 161–78.

Greene, W. H. (1997). *Econometric Analysis*. 3rd edn., New York: Macmillan.

Greiner, P. A., Snowdon, D. A., and Greiner, L. H. (1996). 'The Relationship of Self-Rated Function and Self-Rated Health to Concurrent Functional Ability, Functional Decline, and Mortality: Findings from the Nun Study'. *Journals of Gerontology: Social Sciences*, 51B(5): S234–S241.

Grundy, E. (1996). 'The Population Aged 60 and Over', *Population Trends*, 84: 14–20.

——(1999a). 'Intergenerational Perspectives on Family and Household Change in Mid- and Later Life in England and Wales'. In S. McRae (ed.), *Changing Britain: Families and Households in the 1990s*. Oxford: Oxford University Press.

——and Glaser, K. (1997). 'Trends in, and Transitions to, Institutional Residence among Older People in England and Wales, 1971 to 1991'. *Journal of Epidemiology and Community Health*, 51: 531–40.

——and Murphy, M. (1999). 'Looking beyond the Household: Intergenerational Perspectives on Living Kin and Contacts with Kin in Great Britain'. *Population Trends*, 97: 19–27.

Hamnett, C. (1996). 'Housing Inheritance in Britain: Its Size, Scale and Future'. In A.Walker (ed.), *The New Generational Contract: Intergenerational Relations, Old Age and Welfare*. London: UCL Press.

——Harmer, M., and Williams, P. (1991). *Safe as Houses: Housing Inheritance in Britain*. London: Paul Chapman.

Hancock, R., and Jarvis, C. (1994). *Long-Term Effects of Being a Carer: Main Findings from a Research Study*. London: Age Concern Institute of Gerontology.

Hardy, B., Forder, J., Kendall, J., Knapp, M. R. J., and Wistow, G. (1999). 'Provider Relationships with Local Authority Purchasers'. MEOC discussion paper, Nuffield Institute for Health, University of Leeds.

——Young, R., and Wistow, G. (1999). 'Dimensions of Choice in the Assessment and Care Management Process: The Views of Older People, Carers and Care Managers'. *Health and Social Care in the Community*, 7(6): 483–91.

Hareven, T. (1978). 'The Dynamics of Kin in an Industrialised Community'. In J. Demos and S. Boocock (eds.), *Turning Points: Historical and Sociological Essays on the Family*. Chicago: University of Chicago Press.

Harkins, E. (1978). 'Effects of Empty Nest Transition on Self Report of Psychological and Physical Well-Being'. *Journal of Marriage and the Family*, 40: 549–56.

Harper, S. (2003). *Ageing Societies*. London: Edward Arnold.

——and Zeilig, H. (2000). *Locating Grandparents*. OCPA WP0300. In S. Harper (ed.), The Family in an Ageing Society. Oxford: Oxford University Press.

Hashimoto, A. (1996). *The Gift of Generations: Japanese and American Perspectives on Aging and the Social Contract*. New York: Cambridge University Press.

Haskey, J. (1992). 'Pre-marital Cohabitation and the Probability of Subsequent Divorce'. *Population Trends*, 68: 10–19.

——(1998). 'Families: Their Historical Context, and Recent Trends in the Factors Influencing their Formation and Dissolution'. In M. David (ed.), *The Fragmenting Family: Does it Matter?* London: Institute of Economic Affairs.

——(1999). 'Cohabitational and Maritial Histories of Adults in Great Britain'. *Population Trends*, 96:13–24.

Henretta, J. (2001). 'The Availability of Children to Provide Support in Later Life'. In Himes, C. L., Hogan, D. P., and Eggebeen, D. J. (1996). 'Living Arrangements of Minority Elders'. *Journal of Gerontology: Social Sciences*, 51B(1): S42–8.

Hoffmann, M. (1992). *Family Care of the Older Elderly: Company Policies and Initiatives to Support Workers who are Carers*. Report for the European Foundation for the Improvement of Living and Working Conditions, Dublin.

Hogan, D. P., and Lichter, D. T. (1995). 'Children and Youth: Living Arrangements and Welfare'. In R. Farley (ed.), *State of the Union: America in the 1990s*. New York: Russell Sage.

Home Office (1998). *Supporting Families: A Consultation Document*. London: HMSO.

Hornby, N. (1998). *About a Boy*. London: Indigo.

Horwitz, A. V., White, H. R., and Howell-White, S. (1996). 'Becoming Married and Mental Health: A Longitudinal Study of a Cohort of Young Adults'. *Journal of Marriage and the Family*, 58: 895–907.

Hoskins, I. (1993). 'Combining Work and Care for the Elderly: An Overview of the Issues'. *International Labour Review*, 132(3): 347–69.

——(1994). 'Working Women and Eldercare: A Six-Nation Overview'. *Ageing International*, June: 58–62.

Hughes, M. E., and Waite, L. J. (1999). 'Health in Household Context: Living Arrangements and Health Trajectories among Black, White and Hispanic Adults'. Paper presented at the meetings of the Population Association of America, New York.

Hutten, J. B. F., and Kerkstra, A. (1996) (eds.). *Home Care in Europe*. Aldershot: Arena, Ashgate Publishing.

Idler, E. L., Kasl, S. V., and Lemke, J. H. (1990). 'Self-Evaluated Health and Mortality among the Elderly in New Haven, Connecticut and Iowa and Washington Counties, Iowa, 1982–1986'. *American Journal of Epidemiology*, 131(1): 91–103.

Industrial Relations Services (2000). 'Employment Trends: Family-Friendly Employment'. *IRS Employment Review*, No. 697: 2–16.

Jacobzone, S. (2000). 'An Overview of International Perspectives in the Field of Ageing and Care for Frail Elderly Persons'. In *Modernizing and Improving EU Social Protection: Conference on Long-Term Care of Elderly Dependent People in the EU and Norway*. London: Department of Health, 33–85.

Jani-Le Bris, H. (1993). *Family Care for Dependent Older People in the European Community*. Dublin: European Foundation for the Improvement of Working and Living Conditions.

——and Luquet, V. (1993). *Perte d'autonomie et soutien familial. Enquête sur les allocataires de l'AGRIC*. Paris: CLEIRPPA.

Johnson, C. L., and Barer, B. M. (1997). *Life beyond 85 Years: The Aura of Survivorship*. New York: Springer.

Joseph Rowntree Foundation Inquiry (1996). *Meeting the Costs of Continuing Care. Report and Recommendations*. York: Joseph Rowntree Foundation.

Kahn, R. L., and Antonucci, T. C. (1980). 'Convoys over the Life Course. Attachment, Roles and Social Support'. In P. B. Baltes and O. G. Brim (eds.), *Life-Span Development and Behavior*. New York: Academic Press, 254–83.

Kaufmann, F.-X. (1990). *Zukunft der Familie* (Future of the Family). Munich: Beck.

Kendall, J. (2000). 'The Third Sector and Social Care for Older People in England: Towards an Explanation of its Contrasting Contributions in Residential Care'. Centre for Civil Society Working Paper 8, London School of Economics and Political Science.

——(2001). 'Of Knights, Knaves and Merchants: The Case of Residential Care for Older People in England in the Late 1990s'. Discussion Paper 1565, Personal Social Services Research Unit, London School of Economics and Political Science (also Social Policy and Administration, 35(4): 360–75).

——and Almond, S. (1999). 'The United Kingdom'. In L. M. Salamon, H. K. Anheier, R. List, S. Toepler, S. J. Sokolowski, and Associates, *Global Civil Society: Dimensions of the Nonprofit Sector*. Baltimore, Md.: Johns Hopkins' Center for Civil Society Studies.

——and Knapp, M. R. J. (1994). 'A Loose and Baggy Monster: Boundaries, Definitions and Typologies'. In Smith J. Davis, C. Rochester, and R. Hedley (eds.), *An Introduction to the Voluntary Sector*. London: Routledge.

————(1996). *The Voluntary Sector in the UK*. Manchester: Manchester University Press.

——— (2000). 'Voluntary Sector Providers of Care for Older People in Comparative Perspective'. In M. Harris and C. Rochester (eds.), *Voluntary Organisations and Social Policy: Perspectives on Change and Choice*. London: Macmillan.

Kiernan, K. (1992). 'The Impact of Family Disruption in Childhood on Transitions in Young Adult Life'. *Population Studies*, 46: 213–34.

——— (2000). 'European Perspectives on Union Formation'. In L. Waite, C. Bachrach, M. Hindin, E. Thomson, and A. Thorton (eds.), *Ties that Bind: Perspectives on Marriage and Cohabitation*. New York: Aldine de Gruyter.

Killingsworth, Mark R. (1983). *Labor Supply*. Cambridge: Cambridge University Press.

Knapp, M. R. J., Koutsogeorgopoulou, V., and Davis, S. J. (1996). 'Volunteer Participation in Community Care'. *Policy and* Politics, 24(20): 171–92.

Laing, W., and Saper, P. (1999). 'Promoting the Development of a Flourishing Independent Sector alongside Good Quality Public Services'. In *With Respect to Old Age: Long Term Care—Rights and Responsibilities*. Research vol. 3 of the Report of the Royal Commission on Long Term Care, Cm 4192-II/3, London: HMSO.

Lang, F. R. (2000). 'Endings and Continuity of Social Relationships:Maximizing Intrinsic Benefits within Personal Networks when Feeling Near to Death?' *Journal of Social and Personal Relationships*, 17: 157–84.

——— Staudinger, U. M., and Carstensen, L. L. (1998). 'Perspectives on Sociocmotional Selectivity in Late Life: How Personality and Social Context Do (and Do Not) Make A Difference'. *Journals of Gerontology: Psychological Science*, 53B: P21–P30.

Lasch, C. (1977). *Haven in a Heartless World: The Family Besieged*, New York, Basic Books (also, New york, W.W. Norton 1995).

——— (1978). *The Culture of Narcissism: American Life in an Age of Diminishing Expectations*. New York: W. W. Norton.

Lazcko, F., and Noden, S. (1992). 'Combining Paid Work with Eldercare: The Implications for Social Policy'. *Health and Social Care in the Community*, Vol. 1.

Lilja, R., and Hämäläinen, U. (forthcoming). *Age and Employment*. European Foundation for the Improvement of Living and Working Conditions. (Different title – Working time preferences at different phases of life EF0127 2001) (or same title, but different author).

Lilliard, L. A., and Waite, L. J. (1995). ' "Til death do us part": Marital Disruption and Mortality'. *American Journal of Sociology*, 100(5): 1131–56.

——— Brien, M. J., and Waite, L. J. (1995). 'Pre-Marital Cohabitation and Subsequent Marital Dissolution: A Metter of Self Selection?' *Demography*, 32(3): 437–57.

Lindenberger, U., Gilberg, R., Little, T., Nuthmann, R., Pötter, U., and Baltes, P. B. (1999). 'Sample Selectivity and Generalizability of Results of the Berlin Aging Study'. In P. B. Baltes and K. U. Mayer (eds.), *The Berlin Aging Study*. Cambridge: Cambridge University Press.

Litwak, E. (1985). *Helping the Elderly*. New York: Guilford Press.

——— and Kulis, S. (1987). 'Technology, Proximity, and Measures of Kin Support'. *Journal of Marriage and the Family*, 49: 649–61.

——— and Szelenyi, I. (1969). 'Primary Group Structures and their Functions: Kin, Neighbors, and Friends'. *American Sociological Review*, 34: 465–81.

——— Messeri, P., and Silverstein, M. (1991). 'Choice of Optimal Social Support among the Elderly: A Meta-Analysis of Competing Theoretical Perspectives'. Paper presented at the annual meeting of the American Sociological Association. August, Cincinnati, Ohio.

Liu, K., Manton, K. G., and Aragon, C. (2000). 'Changes in Home Care Use by Older People with Disabilities: 1982–1994'. AARP Public Policy Institute Report No. 2000–02. Washington: AARP.

Local Government Management Board (1997). *Independent Sector Workforce Survey 1996: Residential and Nursing Homes in Great Britain*. London: Local Government Management Board.

Logan, J. R., and Spitze, G. D. (1996). *Family Ties: Enduring Relations between Parents and their Grown Children*. Philadelphia, Penn: Temple University Press.

Lüschen, G. (1989). 'Verwandtschaft, Freundschaft, Nachbarschaft (Kinship, Friendship, and Neighbors)'. In R. Nave-Herz and M. Markefka (eds.), *Handbuch der Familien- und Jugendforschung. Band 1: Familienforschung*. Darmstadt: Lucherhand, 435–52.

Maas, I., Borchelt, M., and Mayer, K. U. (1999). 'Generational Experiences of Old People in Berlin'. In P. B. Baltes and K. U. Mayer (eds.), *The Berlin Aging Study*. Cambridge: Cambridge University Press, 83–110.

McGarry, Kathleen (1998). 'Caring for the Elderly: The Role of Adult Children'. In David A. Wise (ed.), *Frontiers in the Economics of Aging*. Chicago: University of Chicago Press, 133–63.

——and Schoeni, Robert F. (1995). 'Transfer Behavior in the Health and Retirement Study: Measurement and the Redistribution of Resources within the Family'. *Journal of Human Resources*, 30 (Supp): S184–S226.

McRea, S. (1993). *Cohabiting Mothers: Changing Marriage and Motherhood*. London: Policy Studies Institute.

——(1999). *Changing Britain: Families and Households in the 1990s*. Oxford: Oxford University Press.

Manton, K. G., Corder, L., and Stallard, E. (1997). 'Chronic Disability Trends in Elderly United States Populations: 1982–1994'. *Proceedings of the National Academy of Sciences*, 94(6): 2593–8.

Marks, N. F. (1996). 'Caregiving across the Lifespan: National Prevalence and Predictors'. *Family Relations*, 45: 27–36.

——and Lambert, J. D. (1998). 'Marital Status Continuity and Change among Young and Midlife Adults: Longitudinal Effects on Psychological Well-Being'. *Journal of Family Issues*, 19: 652–86.

Martin, T. C., and Bumpass, L. L. (1989). 'Recent Trends in Marital Disruption'. *Demography*, 26: 37–51.

Martin-Matthews, A. (1999). 'Die Vereinbarkeit von Ewerbstätigkeit und Pflege in Kanada'. In Reichert and Naegele (1999), 297–326.

Mathers, C., and Robine, J. (1997). 'International Trends in Health Expectancies: A Review'. Paper presented at World Congress of Gerontology, Adelaide.

Matosevic, T., Ware, P., Forder, J. E., Kendall, J., Knapp, M. R. J., and Wistow, G. (2000). 'Independent Sector Domiciliary Care Providers in 1999'. Discussion Paper 1605, PSSRU, London School of Economics.

May, Elaine Tyler (1988). *Homeward Bound: American Families in the Cold War Era*. New York: Basic Books.

Medical Research Council (1999). 'Profile of Disability in Elderly People: Estimates from a Longitudinal Population Study'. *British Medical Journal*, 318: 1108–11.

Metlife Mature Market Institute (1999). *The Metlife Juggling Act Study*. New York: Metropolitan Life Insurance Company.

Moen, P., Robinson, J., and Fields, V. (1994). 'Women's Work and Caregiving Roles: A Life Course Approach'. *Journals of Gerontology: Social Sciences*, 49: S176–86.

Moos, R., and Lemke, S. (1992). *Sheltered Care Environment Scale Manual*. Palo Alto, Calif.: Department of Veterans Affairs.

Morgan, D. L. (1989). 'Adjusting to Widowhood: Do Social Networks Really Make it Easier?' *Gerontologist*, 29: 101–7.

Morgan, S. P. (1996). 'Characteristic Features of Modern American Fertility'. In J. Casterline, R. Lee, and K. Foote (eds.), *Fertility in the United States: New Patterns, New Theories*. New York: Population Council, 19–67.

Moriarty, J., and Levin, E. (1998). 'Respite Care in Homes and Hospitals'. In R. Jack (ed.), *Residential versus Community Care*. London: Macmillan.

Mui, A. C. (1995). 'Caring for Frail Elderly Parents: A Comparison of Sons and Daughters'. *Gerontologist*, 35(1): 86–93.

Munro, M. (1987). 'Housing, Health and Inheritance'. *Journal of Social Policy*, 17(4): 417–36.

Murphy, M. and Grundy, E. (1996). 'Changes in Intergenerational Support Transfers in the 20th Century'. In EAPS and IUSSP (eds.), *European Population Conference Proceeding: Evolution or Revolution V. 2*. Franco Angeli, 249–64.

Muurinen, Jaana-Marja (1986). 'The Economics of Informal Care: Labor Market Effects in the National Hospice Study'. *Medical Care*, 24(11): 1007–17.

National Center for Health Statistics (1963). *Vital Statistics of the United States: 1960*. vol. 2: *Mortality*. Washington: National Center for Health Statistics.

——(1998). *Health, United States, 1998*. DHHS Publication No. (PHS) 98–1232. Hyattsville, Md.: US Department of Health and Human Services.

National Strategy for Carers (1999). *Caring about Carers*. London: HMSO.

Netten, A., Bebbington, A., Darton, R., Forder, J., and Miles, K. (1998). '1996 Survey of Care Homes for Elderly People (Final Report)'. Discussion Paper 1423/2, Personal Social Services Research Unit. London School of Economics.

Nock, S. (1995). 'A Comparison of Marriages and Cohabiting Relationships'. *Journal of Family Issues*, 8: 373–93.

Nocon, A., and Pearson, M. (2000). 'The Role of Friends and Neighbours in Providing Support for Older People'. *Ageing and Society*, 20: 341–67.

O'Connor, J., and Ruddle, H. (1988). *Caring for the Elderly, Part II, The Caring Process: A Study of Carers in the Home*. Dublin: National Council for the Aged, Report No. 19.

Office of Fair Trading (1998). *Older People as Consumers in Care Homes*. London: Office of Fair Trading.

Pavalko, E. K., and Artis, J. E. (1997). 'Women's Caregiving and Paid Work: Causal Relationships in Late Midlife'. *Journal of Gerontology: Social Sciences*, 52B(4): S170–S179.

Pearson, M. (1996). *Experience, Skill and Competitiveness: The Implications of an Ageing Population for the Workplace. Conference Report*. European Foundation for the Improvement of Living and Working Conditions. Luxembourg: Office for Official Publications of the European Communities.

Peterson, P. (1999). *Gray Dawn: How the Coming Age Wave will Transform America—and the World*. New York: Times Books.

Pezzin, L. E., and Schone, B. S. (1999). 'Intergenerational Household Formation, Female Labor Supply and Informal Caregiving: A Bargaining Approach'. *Journal of Human Resources*, 34(3): 475–503.

Phillips, J. (1994). 'The Employment Consequences of Caring for Older People'. *Health and Social Care in the Community*, 2(3): 143–52.

——(1996). *Working and Caring: Developments at the Workplace for Family Carers of Disabled and Older People*. Dublin: European Foundation for the Improvement of Living and Working Conditions.

——(1999). 'Vereinbarkeit von Ewerbstätigkeit und Pflege in Grossbritannien—Zum Stand der Forschung'. In Reichert and Naegele (1999), 119–45.

Pickard, L. (1999). 'Policy Options for Informal Carers of Elderly People, Royal Commission on Long Term Care'. *With Respect to Old Age: Long Term Care— Rights and Responsibilities*. Research Vol. 3, Cm 4192-II/3, London: HMSO.

——(2000). 'The Decline of Intensive Intergenerational Care in Great Britain? The Contribution of Children towards Informal Care of Elderly Parents, 1985–1995'. In A. Dickinson, H. Bartlett, and S. Wade (eds.), *Old Age in a New Age*. Proceedings of the British Society of Gerontology 29th Annual Conference, Oxford, 8–10 September 2000, 113–17. Oxford Brookes University.

——Wittenberg, R., Comas, A., Davies, B., and Darton, R. (2000). 'Relying on Informal Care in the New Century? Informal Care for Elderly People in England to 2031'. *Ageing and Society*.

Popenoe, D. (1993). 'American Family Decline, 1960–1990: A Review and Appraisal'. *Journal of Marriage and the Family*, 55: 527–55.

Qureshi, H., and Walker, A. (1989). *The Caring Relationship*. London: Philadelphia: Temple University Press.

Raley, K. (2000). 'Recent Trends in Marriage and Cohabitation'. In L. Waite, C. Bachrach, M. Hindin, E. Thomson, and A. Thorton (eds.), *Ties that Bind: Perspectives on Marriage and Cohabitation*. New York: Aldine de Gruyter.

Reher, D. (1998). 'Family Ties in Western Europe: Persistent Contrasts.' *Population and Development Review*, 24: 203–34.

Reichert, M., and Naegele, G. (1999) (eds.). *Vereinbarkeit von Erwerbstätigkeit und Pflege: Nationale und Internationale Perspektiven II*. Hanover: Vincentz Verlag.

Riley, M. (1983). 'The Family in an Aging Society: A Matrix of Latent Relationships'. *Journal of Family Issues*, 4: 439–54.

——and Riley, J. W. (1993). 'Connections: Kin and Cohort'. In V. L. Bengtson and W. A. Achenbaum (eds.), *The Changing Contract across Generations*. New York: Aldine de Gruyter, 169–90.

Robertson, J. F. (1995). 'Grandparenting in an Era of Rapid Change'. In R. Bliezner and V. H. Bedford (eds.), *Handbook of Aging and the Family*. Westport, Conn.: Greenwood, 243–60.

Robinson, M., and Smith, D. (1993). *Step by Step: Focus on Stepfamilies*. Hemel Hempstead: Harvester Wheatsheaf.

Rogers, B., and Pryor, J. (1998). *Divorce and Separation: The Outcomes for Children*. York: Joseph Rowntree Foundation.

Rogers, R. G., Hummer, R. A., and Nam, C. B. (2000). *Living and Dying in the USA: Behavioral, Health and Social Differentials of Adult Mortality*. San Diego, Calif.: Academic Press.

Rook, K. S., and Schuster, T. L. (1996). 'Compensatory Processes in the Social Networks of Older Adults'. In G. Pierce, B. R. Sarason, and I. G. Sarason (eds.), *The Handbook of Social Support and Family Relationships*. New York: Plenum Press, 219–48.

Ross, C. E., Mirowsky, J., and Goldsteen K. (1990). 'The Impact of the Family on Health: Decade in Review'. *Journal of Marriage and the Family*, 52: 1059–78.

Rossi, A. (1986). 'Gender'. In Alan Pifer and Lydia Bronte (eds.), *Our Aging Society: Paradox and Promise*. New York: W. W. Norton, 96–111.

——(1987). 'Parenthood in Transition: From Lineage to Child to Self-Orientation'. In J. Lancaster, J. Altman, A. Rossi, and L. Sherrod (eds.), *Parenting across the Lifespan: Biosocial Dimensions*. New York: Aldine.

——and Rossi, P. H. (1990). *Of Human Bonding: Parent–Child Relations across the Life Course*. New York: Aldine de Gruyter.

Rowe, J. W., and Kahn, R. L. (1997). 'Successful Aging'. Gerontologist, 37(4): 443–40.

Rowlands, O. (1998). *Informal Carers*. An independent study carried out by the Office for National Statistics on behalf of the Department of Health as part of the 1995 General Household Survey, London: HMSO.

Royal Commission on Long Term Care (1999). *With Respect to Old Age: Long Term Care—Rights and Responsibilities*. Cm 4192-I, London: HMSO.

Safe on the Streets Research Team (1999). *Still Running: Children on the Streets in the UK*. London: The Children's Society.

Salvage, A. (1995). *Who Will Care? Future Prospects for Family Care of Older People in the European Union*. Dublin: European Foundation for the Improvement of Living and Working Conditions.

Santi, L. L. (1990). 'Household Headship among Unmarried Persons in the United States, 1970–1985'. *Demography*, 27: 219–323.

Schneekloth, U., and Potthoff, P. (1993). *Hilfe und Pflegebedürftige in privaten Haushalten*. Schriftenreihe des Bundesministeriums für Familie und Senioren. Bd 20.2, Stuttgart: Kohlhammer.

Schoeni, R. F. (1998). 'Reassessing the Decline in Parent–Child Old-Age Co-residence during the Twentieth Century'. *Demography*, 35: 307–13.

Scott, A., Evandrou, M., Falkingham, J., and Rake, K. (2000). 'The Dynamics of Living Arrangements in Later Life'. In A. Dickinson, H. Bartlett, and S. Wade (eds.), *Old Age in a New Age*. Proceedings of the British Society of Gerontology 29th Annual Conference, Oxford, 8–10 September 2000, 203–6.

Secretary of State (1989). *Caring for People*. Cm 849, London: HMSO.

——(1998). *Modernising Social Services: Promoting Independence, Improving Protection, Raising Standards*. Cm 4169, London: HMSO.

Segalen, M. (1997). 'Introduction'. In M. Gullestad and M. Segalen (eds.), *Family and Kinship in Europe*. London: Pinter.

Setterson, R. A. (1999). *Lives in Time and Place: The Problems and Prospects of Developmental Science*. Amityville, N.Y.: Baywood Publishing Company.

Shanas, E. (1979). 'The Family as a Support System in Old Age'. *Gerontologist*, 19: 169–74.

——and Sussman, M. B. (1977) (eds.). *Family, Bureaucracy, and the Elderly*. Durham, N. Carolina: Duke University Press.

Silverstein, M., and Waite, L. J. (1993). 'Are Blacks More Likely than Whites to Receive and Provide Social Support in Middle and Old Age? Yes, No, Maybe So'. *Journal of Gerontology: Social Sciences*, 48(4): S212–S222.

Simons, R. L. (1984). 'Specificity and Substitution in the Social Networks of the Elderly'. *International Journal of Aging and Human Development*, 18: 121–39.

Skocpol, T. (1992). *Protecting Soldiers and Mothers: The Political Origins of Social Policy in the United States*. Cambridge, Mass.: Harvard University Press.

Sloan, F. J., Picone, G., and Hoerger, T. J. (1997). 'The Supply of Children's Time to Disabled Elderly Parents'. *Economic Inquiry*, 35: 295–308.

Smart, C. (1998). 'The New Parenthood: Fathers and Mothers after Divorce'. In E. Silva and C. Smart (eds.), *The New Family*. London: Sage.

——and Neale, B. (1997). 'Good Enough Morality? Divorce and Postmodernity'. *Critical Social Policy*, 17(4): 3–27.

——(1999). *Family Fragments?* Cambridge: Polity Press.

Smith, D. (1990). *Stepmothering*. Hemel Hempstead: Harvester Wheatsheaf.

Social Services Inspectorate (1998). *A Matter of Chance for Carers? Inspection of Local Authority Support for Carers*. London: Department of Health.

Soldo, B. J., and Freedman, V. A. (1994). 'Care of the Elderly: Division of Labor among the Family, the Market, and the State'. In S. Preston and L. Martin (eds.), *Demography of Aging*. Washington: National Academy Press, 195–216.

——and Hill, Martha S. (1995). 'Family Structure and Transfer Measures in the Health and Retirement Study'. *Journal of Human Resources*, 30 (supp): S108–S137.

Spitze, G., and Logan, J. (1989). 'Gender Differences in Family Support: Is There a Payoff?' *Gerontologist*, 29(1): 108–13.

——(1990). 'Sons, Daughters, and Intergenerational Social Support'. *Journal of Marriage and the Family*, 52: 420–30.

——(1992). 'Helping as a Component of Parent–Adult Child Relations'. *Research on Aging*, 14(3): 291–312.

Stacey, J. (1998). *Brave New Families: Stories of Domestic Upheaval in Late Twentieth-Century America*. Berkeley and Los Angeles: University of California Press.

Stern, S. (1995). 'Estimating Family Long-Term Care Decisions in the Presence of Endogenous Child Characteristics'. *Journal of Human Resources*, 30(3): 551–80.

Stokes, P. J. (1985). 'The Relation of Social Network and Individual Difference Variables to Loneliness'. *Journal of Personality and Social Psychology*, 48: 981–90.

Stoller, E. P., and Earl, L. E. (1983). 'Help with Activities of Everyday Life: Sources of Support for the Noninstitutionalized Elderly'. *Gerontologist*, 23: 64–70.

Stone, R. I., and Short, P. F. (1990). 'The Competing Demands of Employment and Informal Caregiving to Disabled Elders'. *Medical Care*, 28(6): 513–26.

Strathern, M. (1992). *After Nature: English Kinship in the Late Twentieth Century*. Cambridge: Cambridge University Press.

Sussman, M. B. (1985). 'The Family life of Old People'. In R. H. Binstock and E. Shanas (eds.), *Handbook of Aging and the Social Sciences*. 2nd edn., New York: Van Nostrand Reinhold, 415–49.

Sweet, J. A., and Bumpass, L. L. (1987). *American Families and Households*. New York: Russell Sage.

Taylor, S. E., Repetti, R. L., and Seeman, T. (1997). 'Health Psychology: What is an Unhealthy Environment and How Does It Get under the Skin? *Annual Review of Psychology*, 48: 411–47.

Thoits, P. A. (1995). 'Stress, Coping, and Social Support Processes: Where Are We? What Next?' *Journal of Health and Social Behavior*. Extra Issue, 53–79.

Thompson, P. (1999). 'The Role of Grandparents when Parents Part or Die: Some Reflections on the Mythical Decline of the Extended Family'. *Ageing and Society*, 19: 471–503.

Tinker, A., Wright, F., McCreadie, C., Askham, J., Hancock, R., and Holmans, A. (1999). 'Alternative Models of Care for Older People'. In Royal Commission on Long Term Care, *With Respect to Old Age: Long Term Care—Rights and Responsibilities*, Research vol. 2, Cm 4192-II/2, London: HMSO.

Townsend, P. (1962). *The Last Refuge*. London: Routledge and Kegan Paul.

Treas, J., and Lawton, L. (1999). 'Family Relations in Adulthood'. In M. B. Sussman, S. K. Steinmetz, and G. W. Peterson (eds.), *Handbook of Marriage and the Family*. New York: Plenum Press, 425–38.

Twigg, J. (1998). 'Informal Care of Older People'. In M. Bernard and J. Phillips (eds.), *The Social Policy of Old Age*. London: Centre for Policy on Ageing, 128–41.

Uhlenberg, P. (1995). 'Demographic Influences on Intergenerational Relationships'. In

Umberson, D. (1992). 'Gender, Marital Status and the Social Control of Health Behavior'. *Social Science and Medicine*, 34(8): 907–17.

——Chen, M. D., House, J. S., Hopkins, K., and Slaten, E. (1996). 'The Effect of Social Relationships on Psychological Well-Being: Are Men and Women Really so Different?' *American Sociological Review*, 61: 837–7.

United States Bureau of the Census (1955). 'Household and Family Characteristics: March 1954'. In *Current Population Report, P20-55*. Washington: US Government Printing Office.

——(1995*a*). 'Household and Family Characteristics: March 1994'. In *Current Population Report, P20-483*. Washington: US Government Printing Office.

——(1995*b*). 'Marital Status and Living Arrangements: March 1994'. In *Current Population Report, P20-484*. Washington: US Government Printing Office.

——(1996). *65+ in the United States*. Current Population Reports, P23-190. Washington, DC: US Government Printing Office.

——(1998). 'Household and Family Characteristics: March 1998 (Update)'. In *Current Population Report, P20-515*. Washington, DC: US Government Printing Office.

United States Census Bureau (1998). *Statistical Abstract of the United States 1998*. 118th edn., Washington: US Department of Commerce.

Van Solinge, H., et al. (1998). *Population, Labour and Social Protection in the European Union: Dilemmas and Prospects*. Netherlands Interdisciplinary Demographic Institute. Report No. 52. The Hague: NIDI.

Ventura, S. J., Martin, J. A., Curtin, S. C., and Mathews, T. J. (1998). 'Report of Final Natality Statistics, 1996'. *Monthly Vital Statistics Report*, 46(11) Supplement. Hyattsville, Md.: National Center for Health Statistics.

————————(1999). 'Births: Final Data for 1997'. *National Vital Statistics Report* 47(18). Hyattsville, Md.: National Center for Health Statistics.

Visher, E. B., and Visher, J. S. (1996). *Therapy with Stepfamilies*. New York: Brunner/Mazel.

Vowinckel, G. (1995). *Verwandtschaft, Freundschaft und die Gesellschaft der Fremden* (Kinship, Friendship, and the Society of Strangers). Darmstadt: Wissenschaftliche Buchgesellschaft.

Wachter, K. W. (1997). 'Kinship Resources for the Elderly'. *Philosophical Transactions of the Royal Society of London Series B Biological Sciences*, 352(1363):1811–17.

Waite, L. J. (1995). 'Does Marriage Matter?' *Demography*, 32(4): 483–507.

——and Hughes, M. E. (1999). 'At Risk on the Cusp of Old Age: Living Arrangements and Functional Status among Black, White and Hispanic Adults'. *Journal of Gerontology: Social Sciences*, 54B(3): S136–S144.

Waite, L. J., and Lilliard, L. A. (1991). 'Children and Marital Disruption'. *American Journal of Sociology*, 96: 930–53.

Walker, A. (1993). *Age and Attitudes: Main Results from a Eurobarometer Survey.* Brussels: Commission of the European Communities, DG V.

——(1997). *Combating Age Barriers in Employment: European Report.* European Foundation for the Improvement of Living and Working Conditions. Luxembourg: Office for Official Publications of the European Communities.

——(1999). *Attitudes to Population Ageing in Europe: A Comparison of the 1992 and 1999 Eurobarometer Surveys.* Sheffield: University of Sheffield.

Walsh, K., et al. (1997). *Contracting for Change.* Oxford: Oxford University Press.

Ward, R., Logan, J., and Spitze, G. (1992). 'The Influence of Parent and Child Needs on Coresidence in Middle and Later Life'. *Journal of Marriage and the Family*, 54: 209–21.

Ware, P. (1997). 'Independent Domiciliary Services and the Reform of Community Care'. Unpublished Ph.D. thesis, Department of Law, University of Sheffield.

Watkins, S. C., Menken, J. A., and Bongaarts, J. (1987). 'Demographic Foundations of Family Change'. *American Sociological Review*, 52 (June): 346–58.

Wellman, B., and Hall, A. (1986) 'Social Networks and Social Support: Implications for Later Life'. In V. W. Marshall (ed.), *Later Life: The Social Psychology of Aging.* Beverly Hills, Calif.: Sage, 191–231.

Wentowski, G. J. (1981). 'Reciprocity and the Coping Strategies of Older People: Cultural Dimensions of Network Building'. *Gerontologist*, 21: 600–9.

Wertheimer, A., and McRae, S. (1999). *Family and Household Change in Britain: A Summary of Findings from Projects in the ESRC Population and Household Change Programme.* Oxford: Centre for Family and Household Research.

Wistow, G., Knapp, M. R. J., Hardy, B., and Allen, C. (1994). *Social Care in a Mixed Economy.* Buckingham: Open University Press.

——————Forder, J., Kendall, J., and Manning, R. (1996). *Social Care Markets: Progress and Prospects.* Buckingham: Open University Press.

Wolf, D. A., and Soldo, B. J. (1994). 'Married Women's Allocation of Time to Employment and Care of Elderly Parents'. *Journal of Human Resources*, 29(3): 1259–76.

World Health Organization (2000). *Towards an International Consensus on Policy for Long-Term Care of the Ageing.* Geneva: WHO.

Wu, Z., and Balakrishnan, T. R. (1995). 'Dissolution of Premarital Cohabitation in Canada'. *Demography*, 32(4): 521–32.

Author Index

Subject Index